The Psychological
Treatment
of Insomnia

THE WILEY SERIES IN CLINICAL PSYCHOLOGY

Series Editors:

Fraser N. Watts
MRC Applied Psychology Unit
Cambridge

J. Mark G. Williams
Department of Psychology
University College of North Wales, Bangor

Severe Learning Disability
and Psychological Handicap
John Clements

Cognitive Psychology
and Emotional Disorders
J. Mark, G. Williams, Fraser N. Watts,
Colin MacLeod and Andrew Mathews

Community Care in Practice
Services for the Continuing Care Client
Edited by Anthony Lavender and Frank Holloway

Attribution Theory in
Clinical Psychology
Freidrich Försterling

Panic Disorder:
Theory, Research and Therapy
Edited by Roger Baker

Measuring Human Problems
A Practical Guide
Edited by David Peck and C. M. Shapiro

Clinical Psychology for the Child
Development, Social Learning and Behaviour
Martin Herbert

The Challenge of Severe Mental Handicap
A Behaviour Analytic Approach
Bob Remington

The Psychological Treatment of Insomnia
Colin A. Espie

Further titles in preparation

The Psychological Treatment of Insomnia

Colin A. Espie

Ravenspark Hospital, Irvine, Scotland

JOHN WILEY & SONS

Chichester · New York · Brisbane · Toronto · Singapore

Other Wiley Editorial Offices

John Wiley & Sons, Inc., 605 Third Avenue,
New York, NY 10158-0012, USA

Jacaranda Wiley Ltd, G.P.O. Box 859, Brisbane,
Queensland 4001, Australia

John Wiley & Sons (Canada) Ltd, 22 Worcester Road,
Rexdale, Ontario M9W 1L1, Canada

John Wiley & Sons (SEA) Pte Ltd, 37 Jalan Pemimpin #05-04,
Block B, Union Industrial Building, Singapore 2057

Library of Congress Cataloging-in-Publication Data:

Espie, Colin A.
    The psychological treatment of insomnia / Colin A. Espie.
        p.   cm. — (The Wiley series in clinical psychology)
    Includes bibliographical references and index.
    ISBN 0-471-92369-9 (ppc)
    ISBN 0-471-92982-4 (paper)
    1. Insomnia—Treatment.   2. Psychotherapy.   I. Title.
    II. Series.
        [DNLM: 1. Insomnia—psychology.   2. Insomnia—therapy.
    3. Psychotherapy—methods.   WM 188 E77p]
    RC548.E77   1991   616.8'498—dc20
    DNLM/DLC
    for Library of Congress   90–13157
                                                 CIP

British Library Cataloguing in Publication Data:

Espie, Colin A.
    The psychological treatment of insomnia.
    1. Man. Insomnia
    I. Title
    616.8498

    ISBN 0-471-92369-9 (cloth)
    ISBN 0-471-92982-4 (paper)

Typeset in 10/12pt Palatino
Printed and bound in Great Britain by Biddles Ltd, Guildford, Surrey

To
Lynne

Contents

Series Editor's Preface

The Wiley Series in Clinical Psychology includes texts on clinical problems with which significant advances are currently being made. Insomnia represents a very common complaint that presents frequently in the clinic. The question of how best to treat cases of insomnia will be of concern to many clinicians in general psychological practice.

Until recently, the predominant treatment approach was by medication. However, recently, effective psychological alternatives have been developed, including relaxation therapy and "stimulus control" procedures. There is also currently increasing interest in cognitive methods which, despite the importance of thought processes in insomnia, have tended to be neglected.

Colin Espie's approach is refreshingly open-minded. He resists the temptation to "push" one approach, more than is warranted by the evidence, at the expense of others. Readers of this book will obtain a balanced presentation of the full range of available psychological methods. His own research, described here, has made a significant contribution to evaluating the relative effectiveness of alternative approaches.

I believe that this will prove a most valuable book for clinical psychologists working with insomnia. Its basic orientation is practical, and the author's own clinical experience with insomnia shows through. However, the approach is firmly grounded in the relevant scientific evidence and readers will find themselves equipped with the necessary background information to work with cases of insomnia.

Clinical psychology is a field with close links with many other professions and scientific disciplines. I hope that the Series will have a broad appeal to all those concerned with the application of psychological knowledge to clinical problems. The development of effective psychological treatments for insomnia is a matter of general importance in clinical services.

FRASER WATTS
Series Editor

Preface

This book is an attempt to integrate, within a single volume, both theory and practice concerning insomnia. The book is written from the viewpoint of an applied scientist working within the discipline of clinical psychology. The intention is to provide an informative and informed text, with comprehensive review, which nonetheless provides the clinician with guidelines on how to proceed in assessment and treatment. Hopefully, the balance is about right—not too "dry" and academic and not to prescriptively clinical. If the book satisfies some appetite for the subject, stimulates some more and fosters some good clinical practice then I shall be well pleased.

Sleeplessness is a problem which most people experience at some time in their lives. Insomnia, therefore, is a condition with which we all have at least an ephemeral acquaintance. The book begins, therefore, with an explanation of normal sleep processes and sleep experiences which lead into descriptions of the sleep disorders per se and insomnia in particular. In Chapter 2, the chronic insomniac who presents frequently at primary care clinics emerges in more phenomenological form. The reader is provided, therefore, not only with the skeletal structure but also with flesh on the bones.

Chapter 3 then examines the psychological concepts and models which have been proposed to account for the development and maintenance of insomnia. The research evidence is sifted and the way is pointed to derivative assessment and treatment methods. Appraisal of insomnia involves gathering a wide range of data, not only on quantitative and qualitative aspects of sleep but also on the sleeper and the sleep environment. Chapter 4 provides a comprehensive overview of assessment methods and practices. Particular emphasis is placed upon establishment of valid therapeutic goals and how to measure these.

Successful management of insomnia often begins with the provision of information about sleep, its stages and phases, changing patterns with age and so on. Advice on sleep practices (often called "sleep hygiene") also may be helpful. Chapter 5 gathers together these educational components under the heading of non-specific treatments. Chapters 6, 7 and 8 follow on with detailed descriptions of the specific psychological procedures which have been applied to sleep disorders. Each approach is evaluated with reference to the available research evidence. Chapter 6 focuses upon relaxation based interventions, Chapter 7 explores cognitive treatments and Chapter 8 examines stimulus control procedures as applied to insomnia.

It is important for clinicians to be able to discriminate the relative strengths and limitations of alternative treatment approaches. Chapter 9, therefore, provides a detailed comparative analysis of the treatments introduced in Chapters 6 to 8. The available outcome literature is reviewed in depth.

The final Chapter of the book focuses upon the management of the (many) hypnotic-using insomniacs who present for therapy. Here there is the double challenge of withdrawing medication and substituting effective psychological therapy. Chapter 10 provides information on the particular difficulties in management which these insomniacs present and guides the reader through two drug-withdrawal/psychological treatment protocols, which prove adaptable to most presenting circumstances.

There are many people without whose help and encouragement this book would never have been written. In particular, Dr Bill Lindsay (Tayside Health Board), Professor Neil Brooks (University of Glasgow) and Dr Eileen Hood (Lanarkshire Health Board) have been, for many years, valued friends and colleagues whose company has stimulated my interest in research work and whose advice has always been helpful. I am grateful also to present colleagues in Ayrshire and Arran Health Board, particularly the staff in my own department who at times have had to suffer a bear with a sore head! Writing a book is, of course, a major project but one that has been made infinitely easier for me by having a typist who has been able to decipher and reconstruct from a jumble of Dictaphone tapes and drafting paper to produce a finished text. My grateful thanks, therefore, to Janette White for dotting the i's and crossing the t's and never (well . . .seldom) complaining. My thanks also to Dr Fraser Watts, series editor of the Wiley Series in Clinical Psychology, for encouraging me to write this book, and again to him and the staff of the editorial and production departments of John Wiley & Sons for keeping me on the right tracks. Finally, I wish to thank my wife, Lynne and my children, Craig and Carolyn for all their support and for the sacrifices which they have been willing to make.

I hope that the reader finds this text useful both for reference purposes and for day to day practice in treating insomnia. There have been times when the writing of it has involved burning the midnight oil and the (occasional!) sleepless night...but I feel much better now!

Colin A. Espie, PhD
December 1990
Ayr, Scotland

Abbreviations

ASDC	Association of Sleep Disorder Centers
BDI	Beck Depression Inventory
CNS	Central Nervous System
DIMS	disorders of initiating and maintaining sleep
EEG	electroencephalogram
EMG	electromyogram
EOG	electro-oculogram
GABA	gamma-aminobutyric acid
GAD	generalised anxiety disorder
GHQ	General Health Questionnaire
HADS	Hospital Anxiety and Depression Scale
MMPI	Minnesota Multiphasic Personality Inventory
MSLT	Multiple Sleep Latency Test
NEPI	norepinephrine
NREM	non-rapid eye movement
RAS	Reticular Activating System
REM	rapid eye movement
SAD	Sleep Assessment Device ("Somtrak")
SDQ	Sleep Disturbance Questionnaire
SMR	sensorimotor rhythm
SOL	sleep-onset latency
STAI	State–Trait Anxiety Inventory
SWS	slow-wave sleep
TMAS	Taylor Manifest Anxiety Scale
WASO	wake time after sleep-onset
ZAS	Zung Anxiety Scale
ZDS	Zung Depression Scale

Chapter 1

An Introduction to Sleep Processes and Sleep Disorders

It is a generalisation, but nevertheless a reasonable one, to say that insomnia is what a patient goes to the clinic to complain of when she becomes sufficiently dissatisfied with the quantity and/or quality of her nighttime sleep. (Since more women than men report insomnia the convention adopted in this book is to employ female pronouns when characterising the insomniac.) A popular definition of insomnia then might be that it is something to do with "not getting *enough* of a *proper* sleep". The actual experience of sleep may feel unsatisfactory to the insomniac and its restorative powers may be perceived as inadequate for daytime purposes. Clearly there is much emphasis here upon the subjective world of the sleeper. But what is the clinician to make of the patient's subjective complaint? Is insomnia independently and objectively diagnosable in the conventional sense, or is it a self-statement; a self-diagnosis with varying personal meaning? What is insomnia (really)?

These are just some of the key questions which will be discussed in this first and introductory chapter. Chapter 2 then explores further the personal experience of the insomniac and Chapter 3 formulates the theoretical contexts and models within which clinic-presenting sleep complaints may be understood.

Chapter 4 will examine the literature on assessment techniques and outlines how reliable, valid and sensitive data may be derived for clinical purposes. Although clinicians seldom discover insomnia unbeknown to the patient, since subjective experience and complaint usually come first, appraisal and assessment are required to direct and evaluate treatment intervention. Chapters 5 to 9 focus on the different psychological treatments which have been presented in the literature and will guide the clinician in selecting and applying the most appropriate techniques for the individual patient. Finally, Chapter 10 deals with the specific challenges associated with the insomniac who habitually takes sleep medication.

However, before pursuing all these matters it is essential for the clinician to have a good understanding of the background against which sleep complaints may become manifest. This requires knowledge of the functions of sleep, of normal sleep processes, and of normal developmental changes associated with age. The clinician must be able also to distinguish amongst a variety of presenting sleep complaints. A recognized classification system is available to assist in differential diagnosis. The remainder of this chapter is devoted, therefore, to consideration of the above-mentioned background knowledge, to the presentation of a classification of sleep disorders, and to evaluation of insomniacs' self-reports.

THE FUNCTIONS OF SLEEP

Sleep should be regarded as harmonising with waking as part of a normal 24-hour rhythmic cycle which enables the individual to function efficiently and effectively at the physical, cognitive, emotional and interpersonal level. The importance of a harmonised circadian rhythm perhaps becomes most evident where dysharmonies arise and the sleep–wake schedule is put out of phase. Common examples of this phenomenon are the "jet-lag" syndrome and the impact of changing occupational shifts upon workers. Put in its simplest terms people sleep best when biological factors predict sleep, and are most alert when rhythms predict arousal and wakefulness. It seems likely that there will be an optimal period for sleep for each individual.

Consideration of a person's functioning from a 24-hour perspective appears to be important since advancing, delaying, extending or reducing established sleep periods has been found to impoverish waking behaviours significantly. Also, chronically irregular sleepers have been found to have demonstrably lower physiological arousal, poorer psychomotor performance and to report a greater frequency of negative mood states than sleepers who maintain regular sleep–wake cycles (Johnson, 1973; Taub and Berger, 1973, 1976; Taub and Hawkins, 1979; Webb and Agnew, 1974, 1978). The question, therefore, ought not to be simply "why do we sleep?", but rather "what is the function of sleep within the sleep–wake system?". Several hypotheses regarding the function of sleep will be considered briefly.

Probably the most commonly held lay view of sleep is that the body requires sleep in order to recover from physical exertion. From this point of view sleep can be regarded as a recuperative process to rejuvenate tired muscles and limbs, and to replenish reserves of energy for the forthcoming day. It is not uncommon to find people who suffer from insomnia attempting to tire themselves out, through physical exercise, in an attempt to promote a good night's sleep. Research evidence for the physical restorative function of sleep has been available for some time (Oswald, 1980). Sleep facilitates the synthesis of protein (Adam and Oswald, 1977), and the secretion of growth hormone is sleep dependent (Sassin et al, 1969). Since proteins are the building blocks of development it is also thought that tissue restoration progresses at a faster rate during sleep (Adam, 1980a). Certainly, there appears to be strong evidence for this being so for brain tissue, although there is some doubt about the generality of the process for other tissues (Horne, 1983). It seems then that sleep does have various physically restorative functions.

As far as psychological functioning is concerned studies of sleep deprivation have shown that perceptual and thought disorders resembling schizophrenia may be provoked by total deprivation of several days' sleep (Johnson, 1969). Fatigue and decrements in performance tasks (e.g. reaction time) have also been observed during prolonged wakefulness, particularly during those early morning hours when individuals would normally be asleep, i.e. when biological rhythms predict de-arousal and sleep. Selective deprivation of rapid eye movement (REM) sleep has been said to produce a "hyper-response state" with increased irritability and emotional liability (Agnew, Webb and Williams, 1967) and it may be that the recovery of REM sleep is particularly important for mental functioning since REM rebounds considerably beyond its usual proportion during early recovery nights after deprivation (Dement, 1960). This reflects the widely held view that REM sleep plays a critical role in memory and learning (Dewan, 1970). There arises therefore a second theory concerning the function of sleep, that is, its central role in the human capacity to learn, unlearn and remember. Information may be programmed and memory consolidated during sleep, and REM sleep particularly may be responsible for the integration process.

Clearly, the physical restorative function and the cognitive development function are not mutually exclusive and it seems likely from research studies that sleep is important for both physical and psychological processes. A recent textbook by Horne (1988) provides an excellent and detailed analysis of these areas. There appears to be considerable public awareness of the value of a "good night's sleep" for healthy physical, mental and emotional functioning. Not infrequently it becomes a major preoccupation of the insomniac that daytime intellectual and problem-solving performance will be impaired if nighttime sleep is inadequate, and that physical fatigue will reduce efficiency through limited energy reserves.

NORMAL SLEEP PROCESSES

It is too simple by far to imagine that an individual is either awake or asleep, as if to infer that sleep is a relatively inert state. Indeed it is neither inert nor is it a state, but rather an active process which follows complex but quite regular electrophysiological cycles. In discussing the common misconception that sleep is some form of "time out" Dement (1986) draws an interesting analogy with the motor car. He suggests that sleep is more like an automobile with the clutch disengaged and the motor racing than a car which is garaged for the night. This analogy emphasises the activity of the sleep process. It is important therefore to consider polygraphic studies of nighttime sleep which have been available for some time. These have provided evidence of distinctive sleep stages and cycles (Loomis, Harvey and Hobart, 1937; Aserinsky and Kleitman, 1953; Rechtschaffen and Kales, 1968).

The electroencephalogram (EEG) trace of an awake subject reveals low-amplitude but high-frequency electrical activity in the brain. The characteristic wave formation reduces in frequency during quiet wakefulness prior to sleep onset, at which time alpha waves are present (Figure 1). Further slowing of EEG frequency is associated with sleep-onset, and slower theta waves predominate during stages 1 and 2 of orthodox or non-rapid eye movement (NREM) sleep. Stage 2 sleep can be discriminated by the EEG presentation of sleep spindles (brief bursts of high-frequency waves of uniform amplitude) and K-complexes (sharp rise and fall in the wave pattern). It is legitimate to think of sleep as "deepening" further still when larger and even slower delta waves appear within stages 3 and 4 of sleep which together are termed slow-wave sleep (SWS). There is therefore, a characteristic "descent" into deeper sleep, in terms of electrical brain activity, which is also associated with observed physiological changes in other body systems (Kales and Kales, 1984). These latter are generally similar to those accompanying relaxation, e.g. reduced oxygen consumption, cardiac output and muscle activity.

NREM sleep is interrupted intermittently, however, throughout the night by REM sleep. During these REM periods the EEG trace changes noticeably and appears more similar to that associated with a wakeful as opposed to a sleeping brain. Regular saw-toothed waves appear accompanied by evidence from electromyogram (EMG) recordings which indicate considerable reduction in muscle activity. Electro-oculogram (EOG) measures of eye movement indicate considerable activity which is peculiar to this sleep phase, and which gives it its name. NREM and REM sleep alternate cyclically throughout the night four or five times in the normal young adult (Figure 2). REM sleep can be differentiated also by its physiological correlates which include increases in blood pressure, in heart and respiration rate, and in body temperature. Penile erections also occur in conjunction with REM periods (Kales and Kales, 1984). REM sleep is sometimes referred to as "dreaming sleep" since subjects awakened from this phase frequently report vivid and detailed dreams (Dement and Kleitman, 1957).

From a neurological point of view sleep may be regarded as the active inhibition of the brain's central activation system, i.e. the reticular formation of the brainstem associated with the intrinsic thalamic nuclei and the posterior hypothalamus (Moruzzi, 1964; Van Oot, Lane and Borkovec, 1982; Mancio and Mariotti, 1985). Put simply, sleep is the switching "off" of this central arousal system. At the neurochemical level sleep induction and the maintenance of SWS appear to be governed by the neurotransmitter 5HT (serotonin) (Mendelson, Gillin and Wyatt, 1977; Van Oot, Lane and Borkovec, 1982), whereas attention and arousal responses are associated with dopamine and norepinephrine (NEPI) levels and gamma-aminobutyric acid (GABA) appears also to be involved in REM manifestations (Jalfre et al, 1972).

These descriptions indicate the complexity and diversity of the processes, episodes, phases and stages of what we commonly refer to quite simply as "sleep". Somehow the individual associates with or attributes to this sleep, qualitative concepts, and comes to conclusions concerning what was or was not "a good sleep". Since judgements are made, at least in part, based on experience and expectation it is logical next to consider what is known about predictable changes in sleep pattern associated with age.

AGE AND SLEEP PATTERN CHANGES

It is a generally held cultural belief that eight hours sleep is the adult norm. Large scale descriptive studies reveal, in fact, that this is not far from the truth (McGhie and Russell, 1962; Tune, 1969). The data presented in Figure 3 are from the study by McGhie and Russell and suggest that some 62% of the adult population may expect to obtain between seven and eight hours sleep per night. The data conform to a normal distribution with variation around this average figure.

However, there are numerous studies which indicate that sleep pattern changes reliably and substantially with age, and in particular with older age. An age-related reduction in the duration of nighttime sleep, largely accounted for by increased frequency of intermittent wakening during the night, has been observed (Webb and Campbell, 1980; Webb, 1982; Spiegel, 1981; Reynolds et al, 1985) (see Figure 2). These wakenings tend to be more concentrated during the second half of the night, and are relatively more problematic for

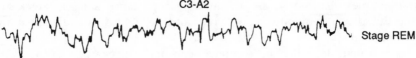

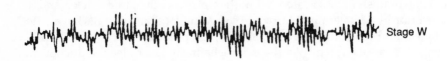

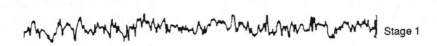

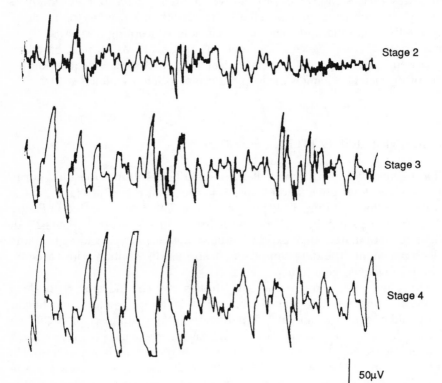

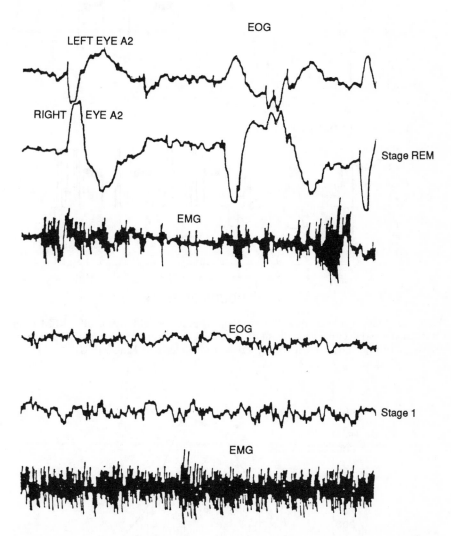

Figure 1   Polygraphic characteristics of normal sleep. Sleep stages are characterised by tracings from electrode placement C3-A2. EOG and EMG tracings permit comparison of REM and NREM sleep. (Reproduced by courtesy of Janssen Research Foundation, Oxon, OX12 0DQ, UK)

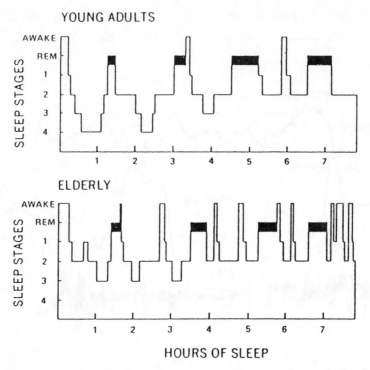

Figure 2   Sleep cycles across the night in young and elderly adults. REM sleep (darkened area) occurs cyclically at approximately 90 minute intervals (Reproduced by permission of Oxford University Press from Kales and Kales, 1984)

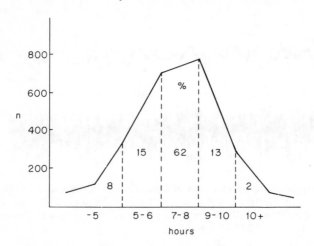

Figure 3   Distribution of hours slept per night across the adult population (Reproduced by permission of the Royal College of Psychiatrists from an extensive survey by McGhie and Russell, 1962)

females of middle age or older (McGhie and Russell, 1962). In one study of non-insomniac elderly people (mean age approximately 70 years) a strong positive correlation was found between the amount of time spent awake after sleep-onset (WASO) and subjective ratings of sleep restlessness, but only amongst female respondents (Hoch et al, 1987). Sleep stage changes have been noted also with an increased proportion of the "lighter" NREM sleep stages 1 and 2 and decreases in "deeper" sleep, that is, slow wave sleep stages 3 and 4 with increasing age (Coates and Thoresen, 1980: Dement, Miles and Carskadon, 1982). These pattern changes are illustrated in Figure 4.

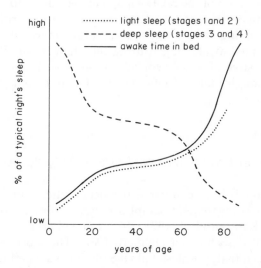

Figure 4 Representation of changes in sleep stages and sleep pattern with increasing age (Reproduced by permission of Plenum Publishing Corp. from Lichstein and Fischer, 1985)

Since SWS was found to correlate significantly with perceived "soundness" of sleep in Hoch et al's (1987) female group it may be suggested that sleep becomes a less enjoyable experience with increasing age. Webb and Schneider-Helmert (1984), however, have reported a tendency towards longer awakenings with age among men, with longer sleep latencies being disproportionately higher in women. Research studies, therefore, do not afford an unequivocal picture concerning differential effects with age between the sexes. It should be noted also that sleep loss in older insomniac adults has not been associated with slower recovery rates than for non-insomniac seniors, which again suggests that ageing effects on sleep are developmental rather than degenerative (Bonnet and Rosa, 1987).

There has arisen nevertheless sufficient consistency in research studies on sleep and the ageing process to regard age-related changes in sleep as constituting a type of "developmental insomnia" which may be best regarded as non-pathological sleep disturbance. There is relatively little evidence to suggest that initial sleep latency is affected by age although latency to returning to sleep during the night may be greater in later years (Kales et al, 1984). These findings need not imply that all intermittent sleep disturbance in the elderly population is non-pathological. Morin and Gramling (1989), for example, have reported that time spent awake during the night was greater amongst elderly insomniacs than in a control sample of similar demographic characteristics.

Further investigation of the relationship between age and perceived sleep quality is now required since the latter may be an important moderating factor of complaining behaviour. The preponderance of more frequent and more prolonged awakenings during the night in middle to older age subjects is suggestive of a need for education of such patients with sleep complaints, although more specific behavioural intervention also may be necessary.

COMPARISONS BETWEEN INSOMNIACS AND NORMAL SLEEPERS

A number of studies have compared the sleep patterns of normal subjects with insomniacs using patient samples ranging from 10 to 18 per group (Monroe, 1967; Karacan et al, 1971, 1973; Frankel et al, 1976; Gillin et al, 1979; Galliard, 1978; Schneider-Helmert, 1987). The most extensive study, however, has been that of Kales et al (1984) who evaluated the sleep of 150 insomniacs (age range 19–90 years) and compared sleep characteristics with 100 normal control subjects. Insomniacs were found to have significantly longer mean sleep-onset latencies (SOL) within each of the age-bands studied, thus confirming the results of the earlier, less extensive reports. This increased sleep latency accounted for the greater "total wake time" also experienced by the insomniac group. No significant differences were found, however, on the amount of wakefulness after sleep-onset, a result that contrasts with most other findings (Monroe, 1967; Galliard, 1978; Schneider-Helmert, 1987; Morin and Gramling, 1989). Kales et al also considered the duration of nightly wakenings, however, and found that more protracted wakenings were typical of the insomniac group. In other words, insomniacs had greater difficulty returning to sleep. In common with the research literature on age-related changes in sleep patterns, wakenings after sleep-onset increased with age in both experimental groups, suggesting that this type of developmental, sleep-maintenance insomnia is, in fact, non-pathological. Kales et al concluded that "the insomniac's primary difficulty is initiating sleep whether at the beginning of the sleep period or following awakenings during the night". Interestingly, Haynes et al (1985) found that SOL related to planned nap sessions in a sleep laboratory also discriminated between insomniac and non-insomniac subjects.

Schneider-Helmert (1987), in a recent polysomnographic study comparing 16 insomniacs with 16 matched control normal sleepers, found that all sleep measures except final waking time differed significantly between groups. Insomniacs' WASO scores were twice those of control subjects and SOL was 54 minutes compared with 21 minutes on average for the respective groups. Insomniacs also spent a significantly lower proportion of the night in stage 4 sleep and rated their sleep as qualitatively poorer than non-insomniacs.

THE PREVALENCE OF INSOMNIA

It has been reported that more than 50% of adults complain of current or past sleep disorder and 38% experience current difficulties with sleep (Bixler et al, 1979). Insomnia was by far the most prevalent problem in this major study, accounting for 32% of the present sleep disorders; a finding which is in broad agreement with other reports where 10–15% of subjects experienced mild insomnia, and a further 10–15% severe or frequent insomnia (Kales et al, 1974a; Montgomery, Perkin and Wise, 1975). In an American national prospective study of over one million men and women, Hammond (1964) reported that 13% of men and 26.4% of women complained of insomnia and, in the United Kingdom, samples have yielded prevalence rates of 18–25% (Shepherd et al, 1966; Dunnell and Cartwright, 1972), and 38% in elderly populations (Morgan et al, 1988). In addition, more than 15% of a Scottish sample were found to suffer from chronic insomnia (McGhie and Russell, 1962). A recent epidemiological survey in San Marino (north-east Italy) revealed that 10% of men and 17% of women rarely or never slept well, with prevalence rates rising to almost 40% amongst women within the age range 50–54 years (Cirignotta et al, 1985). Difficulties in sleeping are not, however, confined to the adult population. In one study, 13% of high school students were found to be sleep-disturbed on four or more nights per week, with a further 33% complaining of occasional sleep difficulty (Price et al, 1978).

Prevalence rates of course reflect the criteria which are used to define inclusion and exclusion. Another recent study conducted in Sweden by Liljenberg et al (1988) applied very stringent criteria to define sleep disorder operationally. These workers reported prevalence rates of only 1.7% for women and 1.4% for men. What is particularly interesting about this study, however, was that when the criterion of "daytime sleepiness" was excluded from the analyses, prevalence rates increased by a factor of three. The necessity or otherwise of including daytime effects within the definition of insomnia is a matter which will be addressed at a later point.

Apart from these prevalence figures, evidence for the widespread problems posed by poor sleep can be drawn from studies which have reported on the prescribing of sleep medication. In the USA, studies have found that as many as 82% of patients presenting at sleep clinics make regular use of nighttime medication (Roth, Kramer and Lutz, 1976). Concern has been expressed at such unacceptably high levels of drug prescribing (Cooper, 1977; Institute of Medicine, 1979). Other reports have suggested that up to 70% of all prescriptions for hypnotics may be written by the receptionist, compared with only 22% for other types of drugs (Freed, 1976). Recent statistics have indicated that benzodiazepine drugs continue to account for around 10% of all prescribed drugs in Scotland, and benzodiazepine hypnotics comprised a greater proportion of these prescriptions than minor tranquillisers (Health Service Statistics, 1989).

CLASSIFICATION OF INSOMNIA

The Association of Sleep Disorders Centers (ASDC) (1979) has published a "diagnostic classification of sleep and arousal disorders" which is also summarised in the American Psychiatric Association's (1987) *Diagnostic and Statistical Manual of Mental Disorders* (DSM III-R). This system separates the insomnias, defined as "disorders of initiating and maintaining sleep" (DIMS), from three other categories of sleep disturbance. These are (a) disorders of excessive somnolence (including narcolepsy and hypersomnolence), (b) disorders of the sleep–wake schedule (exemplified by jet-lag and shift-work effects), and (c) the parasomnias (a heterogeneous group including sleep-walking, sleep terrors and sleep-related enuresis). It is not possible within the constraints of this book to provide further detail on these three other categories of sleep disturbance. What is important, however, is to provide definition of the sub-types within the DIMS classification system.

In Figure 5 the DIMS classification represents the third and most detailed level of analysis in the hierarchy. These disorders have been grouped into sets of "primary", "secondary" and "specific" disorders at the second level, since such terminology is also frequently found in the literature. At the first level of the hierarchy the generic term "insomnia" is applied to describe disorders of initiating and/or maintaining sleep in relation to three commonly used terms (initial, maintenance, terminal) which reflect the portion of the sleep period most affected by wakefulness. The text which follows will work through each level of analysis in turn.

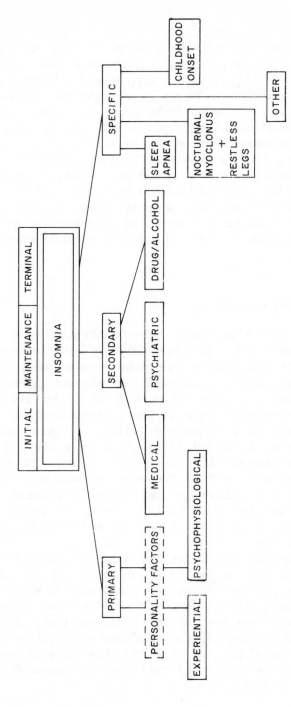

Figure 5 The classification of insomnia. The Disorders of Initiating and Maintaining Sleep (DIMS) classification comprises the most detailed level of the hierarchy

Initial insomnia

As the name suggests, initial insomnia describes a problem in getting to sleep, hence the alternative terms "early insomnia" and "sleep-onset insomnia". In the normal population SOL appears to be in the region of 0-15 minutes and predictably so on a night by night basis (Carskadon et al, 1975; Coates et al, 1982a; Birrell, 1983). Most good sleepers will report being asleep within 30 minutes. Subjects with initial insomnia in research studies by comparison have exhibited self-reported average sleep latencies of 60-90 minutes (e.g. Turner and Ascher, 1979a; Lacks et al, 1983a; Espie et al, 1989). The minimum criterion for classification of sleep-onset insomnia has been, therefore, SOL of 30 minutes occurring on four out of seven nights per week. A more conservative criterion would be 45 minutes, and this may discriminate more reliably between non-complaining normal sleepers with some delay to sleep-onset and the mild end of the initial insomniac range (Espie et al, 1988).

Maintenance insomnia

Not infrequently subjects who have difficulty falling asleep also have problems remaining asleep. The latter complaint does, however, also occur independently. Sleep-maintenance insomnia, sometimes referred to as "middle" or "intermittent" insomnia, refers to sleep disruption during the night occurring after sleep induction. Reference has been made already to the age-related, developmental changes in sleep which comprise an increased frequency and duration of nighttime wakenings occurring particularly during the second half of the night amongst older subjects.

Assessment of maintenance insomnia is likely to involve recording of the frequency of arousals per night, the latency to returning to sleep of each arousal, and some indication of the "efficiency" of nightly sleep. Self-reporting of such data is known to be less reliable than for SOL (Baekeland and Hoy, 1971; Espie et al, 1988) due in part to the subjective imperceptibility of frequent, brief arousals as discrete episodes, although these will be discernible from EEG records. Rather, patients tend to make qualitative complaints of "restless nights" or of "tossing and turning". The most intrusive, lengthy wakenings are not surprisingly recalled more clearly. Sleep efficiency, which is the ratio of total time slept to time spent in bed, expressed as a percentage, may be a particularly useful clinical and research measure since it quantifies the overall intrusiveness of wakefulness while in bed. A cut-off point of 85 to 88% sleep efficiency has been recommended as a criterion for significant sleep disturbance (Frankel et al, 1976; Coates et al, 1982a).

Terminal insomnia

Terminal insomnia is also called "late" insomnia or "early morning wakening". It refers to a final, and sometimes abrupt arousal occurring during the night with a subsequent failure to return to sleep prior to what is considered to be the usual wakening time for the individual. Although early morning wakening has been regarded as a common symptom, especially in the field of adult psychiatry, in fact it presents less frequently than either initial or maintenance insomnia (Roth, Kramer and Lutz, 1976; Bixler et al, 1979).

Terminal insomnia has been regarded as a biological marker for depressive illness. It seems, however, that sleep disturbance of whatever type (initial, maintenance or terminal) may be associated with symptoms consistent with DSM III criteria of major depression (Mellinger, Balter and Uhlenhuth, 1985). It is the *severity* of insomnia which predicts the association more than the nighttime period during which sleep is most disturbed. Furthermore, abnormalities in sleep pattern, of all types, are especially evident in older depressives (aged 50 years and over) (Gillin et al, 1981; Mellinger, Balter and Uhlenhuth, 1985). Early wakening may occur also as a side effect of drug administration or drug (or alcohol) withdrawal, particularly so where very short-acting benzodiazepine hypnotics were prescribed (Kales et al, 1983b).

Primary insomnia

Primary insomnia is a sleep disorder of one of the above types which has no apparent physical or mental illness aetiology. It is presumed that the insomnia stands alone as a disorder. In other words, the patient's problem would be expected to resolve with successful treatment of the sleep disturbance per se. Although most psychological researchers have been careful to exclude from research studies subjects with known physical or mental conditions which may affect the sleep process, the term primary insomnia cannot be taken to exclude from consideration the substantial number of insomniacs who present with trait or state anxiety characteristics (see Chapter 2). These may be sub-clinical in terms of mental health but are, nonetheless, consistently correlated with sleep complaint. For this reason such characteristics have been regarded here as "moderating variables" (Figure 5).

Secondary insomnia

Here insomnia may be viewed as symptomatic of an underlying medical or psychiatric condition. Drugs (whether prescribed or non-prescribed) and alcohol also may cause insomnia, either during administration or upon withdrawal. Effective treatment of a secondary insomnia requires focusing upon the known aetiological process, and direct treatment of that underlying cause, or at least effective management at a symptomatic level (e.g. physical discomfort, pain), is appropriate. Secondary insomnia, therefore, except in the case of chronic illness or disability, is likely to be short-lived and thus readily managed. Even where it is more persistent, the possibility of accurate attribution may alleviate concern over sleep loss and encourage adaptive coping. Since there is greater ambiguity associated with primary insomnia complaints it is these which present the greater therapeutic challenge.

Specific insomnias

The second level of the hierarchy in Figure 5 is completed by a "category" of insomnias which do not fit readily into the primary/secondary dichotomy. Each of these require separate, brief consideration within the DIMS classification system which comprises the third level of the hierarchical analysis to follow.

Experiential insomnia

Experiential or subjective insomnia is the starting point of almost all clinical complaints of sleep disturbance. Personal concern over quantity and/or quality of sleep is *sine qua non* and in clinical practice decisions as to treatment approach and measurement of outcome are based on the self-reported sleep experiences of the insomniac. Consequently, experiential insomnia might be regarded as subsuming all psychophysiological insomnia. It is the fact that the inverse position may not hold true which has led to these two separate DIMS classifications. Experiential insomnia is then a persistent inability to obtain adequate sleep (Williams, Karacan and Hursch, 1974; Bootzin and Nicassio, 1978) which is not substantiated by polygraphic evidence. The validity or otherwise of such subjective complaints of insomnia has been much studied and a separate section on EEG and self-report is devoted below to this debate. It is noteworthy, however, that a recent critical examination of this DIMS classification has suggested that there is insufficient evidence to conclude that there is a separate class of patients with a subjective insomnia without objective sleep deficiencies (Trinder, 1988).

Psychophysiological insomnia

Here EEG evidence is found to corroborate the experiential insomnia, i.e. subjective insomnia becomes objective insomnia. Some workers have postulated that there may be fundamental differences in the aetiology of these two "types" of insomnia. Borkovec (1979) has suggested that psychophysiological insomnia may be related to "central" disturbance of the nervous system, where either an overly active reticular system (governing arousal) fails to switch off and/or a neurotransmitter-dependent sleep system fails to switch on. By way of contrast Borkovec suggests that experiential insomnia without EEG evidence is one effect of overly active cognitive processing of anxiety-laden thoughts. A critical examination of the relationships between self and EEG reported data may be helpful.

EEG and self-report

Over the past 20 years researchers have attempted to validate self-report against EEG criteria, with the assumption that EEG is the criterion measure which identifies "true insomnia". More recently, however, there has been recognition of the possibility that EEG may not be sensitive to some crucial variables which predict clinical reporting.

During the 1970s a number of studies suggested that insomniacs were not accurate in their estimates of sleep parameters. In particular, they overestimated sleep latency and underestimated total sleep time and sleep efficiency (Frankel et al, 1976; Carskadon et al, 1976; Borkovec et al, 1979). Control subjects' reports by comparison were not significantly different from EEG measures but they tended to rate in the opposite direction to the insomniacs' errors (Frankel et al, 1976). Both earlier and later reports, however, were consistent in finding that significant correlation existed between insomniac self-report and EEG measures, indicating that although subjects were not accurate in their estimates, their reports did shift in the same direction as objective measures (Baekeland and Hoy, 1971; Johns, 1975; Carskadon et al, 1976; Haynes et al, 1982, 1985). Nevertheless, the problems in distinguishing normal subjects from insomniacs on the basis of EEG assessment alone (in one study as many as half of the insomniac group could not be discriminated on this basis (Frankel et al, 1976)) contributed towards the view that it was reasonable to regard primary insomniacs as belonging to two distinctive sub-types, i.e. objective and experiential, or as the DIMS classification puts it, psychophysiological and subjective.

The discussion of EEG and self-report in terms of "agreement", however, presupposes that the same question is being asked of both measures. That is, if according to EEG criteria the subject is awake, then she should report that self-perception. Conversely, if objectively asleep she should corroborate this upon being aroused. It is only if these consistencies are found to apply that verbal report can be considered unreliable compared with the EEG "standard". Interestingly, therefore, in one study where 25 insomniacs were awakened out of stage 2 sleep, less than 12% reported having been asleep, and even in a control group of normal sleepers only 30% stated that they had been asleep when "awakened" (Borkovec, Lane and Van Oot, 1981). Similar effects have been found in other studies with between 40 and 80% of subjects reporting having been awake when roused after the onset of stage 2 sleep (Agnew and Webb, 1972; Slama, 1979; Campbell and Webb, 1981). These findings raise the question of what cues the insomniac uses to determine whether or not she is asleep, and how these cues differ from those used by normal sleepers.

A study by Coates et al (1982b) compared the relationship between EEG and subjective reports using different EEG criteria to determine sleep-onset. These workers found that the significant differences between the measures which were evident when using a NREM stage 1 sleep criterion disappeared when comparison was made at the onset of EEG-defined stage 2 sleep. Coates et al concluded that "if the EEG is to be regarded as the criterion of sleep, then self-reports of minutes to sleep-onset are reliable and valid measures for good sleepers. Self-reports of minutes to sleep-onset and minutes awake after sleep-onset provide a reliable and valid relative index for insomniacs." Other workers also have supported the use of stage 2 onset as the EEG equivalent of perceived sleep in insomniacs. Hauri and Olmstead (1983) found that insomniacs were about as accurate in sleep latency estimates using this criterion as were good sleepers using an earlier onset criterion. They concluded that there is no advantage in accepting, as fact, the statement that insomniacs habitually overestimate sleep latency, but rather the issue of importance is the establishment of appropriate criteria, suitable for them. The beginning of the first 15 minutes of uninterrupted sleep, of stage 2 or better, may be such a valid criterion (Hauri and Olmstead, 1983; Birrell, 1983). Schneider-Helmert (1987) in fact, using the criterion of at least five minutes of continuous stage 2, found that SOL was overestimated by *both* insomniacs and controls, with the latter overestimating to a proportionately greater degree.

Ogilvie and Wilkinson (1988) conducted an experimental study to investigate subjects' ability to perceive and respond to faint tones during different EEG stages. The subjects were asked to press a palm-mounted button to switch tones off whenever they heard them. Interestingly, these workers found that in stage 1 "sleep" behavioural response was almost as likely to occur as not to occur, and that even in stage 2, particularly during the first five minutes, responses were still present. Ogilvie and Wilkinson recommend, therefore, the idea of a "sleep-onset period" corresponding to this uncertain period between wakefulness and sleep. They have suggested that an analogy may be drawn between "alpha reduction" (stage 1) and "spindle" (stage 2) EEG definitions of sleep-onset and the experimenter's decision regarding committing Type 1 and Type 2 errors (Ogilvie and Wilkinson, 1984).

Our own research work in this area supports the view that insomniacs do tend to overestimate sleep latencies, but correlation between subjective and objective measures (Kelley and Lichstein's (1980) Sleep Assessment Device) has been uniformly high. Of particular interest is the finding that overestimation was accounted for by those subject-nights where sleep latency was longer (both objectively and subjectively), and therefore, that inaccuracy varied directly with the difficulty of the task (Espie, Lindsay and Espie, 1989) (Table 1). It is simply a harder task to estimate a sleep latency of 60 minutes than it is to estimate one of 10 minutes. The insomniac (like the normal sleeper) is more likely to get an easier task right, but even with a harder task may provide a valid self-report in correlational terms.

Trinder (1988) has completed a detailed reappraisal of the DIMS criteria for subjective insomnia and has highlighted significant methodological flaws in the differential diagnosis procedure. In particular he points to possible sampling deficiencies in some studies. Given that night to night variability in sleep is the norm amongst insomniacs it should be expected that a good proportion of insomniacs will evidence normal or near normal sleep upon EEG investigation over a sample of only one or two nights of sleep laboratory assessment.

Clearly further research is required before definitive statements can be made regarding the precise relationship between the experience of sleep and wakening and its objectively measurable concomitants. Certainly, it is possible that a number of early studies which doubted the accuracy of self-report may have provided less critical results had alternative criteria been used for scoring the EEG traces. At the very least there is the consistent finding of a significant correlation between objective and verbal report, and the strong possibility that concordance may be further strengthened where appropriate EEG indices are finally established.

In conclusion, it should be noted that subjective complaint normally incorporates an element of dissatisfaction with sleep quality variables such as "restedness after sleep". The absence of EEG evidence of sleep pattern disruption cannot invalidate such complaints. Indeed, the lack of sensitivity of polygraphic assessment to such potentially critical variables weakens the role of EEG as a criterion measure.

Insomnia associated with medical and other conditions

The ASDC Classification System recognises a group of secondary insomnias which are "DIMS associated with medical, toxic, and environmental conditions". Kales and Kales (1984) provide useful commentary on a number of medical conditions which may be associated with sleep disruption. Pain and physical discomfort may affect sleep directly, e.g.

Table 1 Comparisons between Sleep Assessment Device (SAD; objective measure) and Daily Sleep Questionnaire (DSQ; self-report) estimates of sleep-onset latency (SOL; min.). Data from 110 subject-nights are allocated either to SOL range ≤40 min. or to SOL range >40 min., according to objective assessment. This permits analysis of comparisons within bands of "shorter" versus "longer" sleep latencies. (Adapted from Espie, Lindsay and Espie, 1989, by permission of Plenum Publishing Corp.)

Variable	Defined range	Measure	n	Mean (SD)	Standard error	T-test T	df prob.	Pearson correlation r prob.
SOL (min.)	≤40	SAD	51	23.6 (13.7)				
		DSQ		23.4 (9.5)	1.43	0.15	50 0.881	0.665 <0.001
SOL (min.)	>40	SAD	59	89.9 (61.7)				
		DSQ		110.2 (64.8)	5.71	-3.56	58 0.001	0.761 <0.001

nocturnal angina, duodenal ulcer. Disease states, however, usually evoke an emotional response and it may not be easy to separate the effects of apprehension, anxiety and depression from the impact of the illness itself. A variety of cardiovascular, pulmonary, gastrointenstinal, renal, endocrine and neurological problems have been known to affect sleep induction and/or continuity and some conditions have fairly stage-specific effects. Migraine headaches, for example, have been associated with REM sleep and hypothyroidism may reduce the amounts of stage 3 and 4 sleep. Surgical aftercare, circulatory disorders and rheumatic disorders were the conditions most frequently associated with hospital physician prescription of hypnotic drugs in one large study (Mellinger, Balter and Uhlenhuth, 1985).

Toxic effects are relatively uncommon as a cause of insomnia, apart from the influence of drugs and alcohol which comprise a separate sub-classification. Specific environmental factors, e.g. extreme noise or overcrowding, may contribute to sleep disturbance. In most cases, however, this is transient and adaptation takes place even where external triggers remain. The relationship between the stimulus environment and sleep will be considered in detail in Chapters 3 and 8.

Insomnia associated with psychiatric disorders

The relationship between mood and sleep has been studied widely and it is recognised that causality is not easy to determine. For practical purposes it is useful to distinguish between diagnosed formal psychiatric illnesses and aspects of personality functioning and state anxiety when it comes to considering effects upon sleep. (The latter will be addressed in Chapter 2 as part of the typical phenomenology of insomnia.) Psychiatric conditions such as schizophrenia, depressive illness and anorexia nervosa may have sleep disturbance as presenting symptoms (DSM III-R). The relationship between sleep and depression was introduced in an earlier section. With mental illnesses, insomnia is again regarded as secondary and effective treatment of the presenting psychiatric condition can be expected to contribute to an improvement in sleep pattern. People suffering from schizophrenia, for example, may experience considerable anxiety at night, have problems with sleep-onset and report vivid, frightening dreams. The clear priority, however, is to address the underlying schizophrenic illness.

Reynolds' (1987) review of sleep and affective disorders is a helpful resource. EEG changes occur most predictably in patients with endogenous depression. Abbreviated REM sleep latency and increased density of rapid eye movements during the first REM period have been consistent findings. Decreased sleep continuity (prolonged SOL and increased awakenings) presents both in depression and schizophrenia and increases with patient age and illness severity (Reynolds, 1987; Ganguli, Reynolds and Kupfer, 1987). Patients with generalised anxiety disorders (GAD) may also present with delayed SOL and sleep maintenance problems but it is suggested that GAD patients can be distinguished from depressives by a reduction in REM percentage and an absence of short REM latency. Gierz, Campbell and Gillin's (1987) article is a useful source of further information.

Insomnia associated with the use of drugs and alcohol

Both Central Nervous System (CNS) stimulants and CNS depressants may interfere with normal sleep pattern during administration, and drug tolerance and withdrawal effects can be marked in some cases. The ingestion of caffeine in coffee, tea and cola and also in certain analgesics and weight-control agents has long been associated with sleep disruption. Racing thoughts (Goodman and Gilman, 1969), increased SOL and reduced sleep time and more frequent and prolonged nighttime wakenings have been noted (Karacan et al, 1976; Levy and Zylber-Katz, 1983). Steroids and bronchodilating drugs may cause acute insomnia and the side effects of anti-hypertensive agents may cause sleep impairment (Kales and Kales, 1984). Other iatrogenic causes of insomnia arise from psychoactive drug prescriptions of anti-depressants (Schoonover, 1983) and benzodiazepines. The latter deserve more thorough examination.

Although benzodiazepines are commonly subdivided on the basis of anxiolytic versus sedative effects, this distinction is somewhat arbitrary since the effects appear to be dose related (Greenblatt et al, 1982) and with regular administration tolerance develops after several weeks with many of these preparations (Kales et al, 1974b, 1975). Carry-over effects may also occur including morning drowsiness and headache (Oswald, 1968; Greenblatt and Koch-Weser, 1975; Dement, Seidel and Carskadon, 1984), particularly with longer acting drugs. Hypnotic drugs are known to distort normal sleep by suppressing REM sleep and NREM stage 4 sleep. Also, paradoxically, sleep medications may be responsible for a specific type of withdrawal sleep disturbance, usually termed "rebound insomnia" (Kales, Scharf and Kales, 1978; Kales et al, 1983b). Rebound effects occur particularly with the short elimination half-life drugs and comprise difficulty in initiating sleep and a fragmentation of sleep pattern associated with marked increase in REM sleep above baseline levels. The clinical problem posed by these phenomena is even more apparent when two other factors are taken into consideration. Firstly, withdrawal effects may endure for up to five weeks after total drug withdrawal (Oswald and Priest, 1965; Nicholson, 1980), and secondly, rebound effects have been associated with increased levels of daytime anxiety (Kales, Scharf and Kales, 1978; Kales et al, 1983b). The reader is referred to Chapter 10 for further discussion on drug effects and management of drug-dependent patients.

Alcohol is also a CNS depressant and a commonly self-prescribed hypnotic agent. There are substantially similar effects between alcohol and prescribed medications and the withdrawal syndrome typically includes nausea, excitation, agitation, insomnia and nightmares (Pokorny, 1978).

Sleep apnea

The classification of sleep-induced respiratory impairment and nocturnal myoclonus amongst "the insomnias" may be misleading. Kales and Kales (1984) have reviewed a series of studies comparing insomniac and normal sleep control subjects which indicates that prevalence rates in the two subject groups are similar. These workers conclude that sleep apnea and nocturnal myoclonus are rarely causative factors in insomnia. Nevertheless, sleep apnea is regarded as a disorder of maintaining sleep and is one specific element in the DIMS classification. Apnea refers to respiratory irregularities during sleep when breathing becomes shallow or ceases entirely. Minimal criteria for diagnosis are 30 such episodes of at least 10 seconds duration per night, or at least five apneic periods within each hour of sleep. In extreme cases respiration may cease for more than one minute and/or episodes may be numbered in hundreds (Guilleminault and Dement, 1978). Apneas usually occur in sleep stages 1 and 2 and during REM sleep, and, particularly with obstructive sleep apnea, deep sleep (SWS) is reduced because of a continuous pattern of arousal and awakening (Van Oot, Lane and Borkovec, 1982).

Some subjects may complain of intermittent arousals during the night but commonly reports of a room-mate are required to establish other clinical signs of sleep apnea, e.g. noisy snoring, apparent shortness of breath (gasping for air), the sudden restoration of normal breathing and heavy nighttime sweating. The sufferer may be unaware of the problem and it seems likely that many cases of sleep apnea go undetected. Excessive daytime sleepiness is another central feature and almost half of such presenting cases may be subsequently diagnosed as sleep apnea (Coleman, Roffwarg and Kennedy, 1982). Other symptoms can include morning headache and obesity. Craske and Barlow (1989) have discussed helpfully the differentiation of nocturnal panic attacks, sleep apnea, night terrors and dream-induced anxiety.

A recent clinical review of obstructive sleep apnea syndrome provides detailed descriptive information on symptoms of apnea during sleep and daytime symptoms and on the frequency of each symptom presentation

(Guilleminault, 1987). Guilleminault notes that sleep apnea is a common syndrome the prevalence of which increases with age, perhaps reaching more than 50% of the over 60 year old male population, with much lower rates of 1–10% in earlier age groups. It is helpful, therefore, that Kapuniai et al (1988) have evaluated a self-report sleep apnea assessment based on questions concerning interruptions to respiration and snoring. These workers found that their apnea score correctly identified 80–88% of sleep apnea cases although high numbers of false positives were also reported.

Nocturnal myoclonus and "restless legs" syndrome

Both of these DIMS are medical conditions and have not been the subject of psychological interventions. Nocturnal myoclonus involves periodic episodes of involuntary leg muscle jerks (partial flexion of ankle, knee and hip) which may disturb the sufferer's sleep or the sleep of the sufferer's bed partner. Movements last for several seconds followed by relaxation prior to the next movement some 30 seconds later. It is this periodicity and stereotypy which distinguishes the condition. There is some evidence that nocturnal myoclonus is an age-related condition, presenting more frequently from middle life on.

Restless legs syndrome is characterised by unpleasant sensory and motor symptoms occurring mainly in the legs, but also in the arms, during relaxation. Creeping, crawling sensations deep within the muscles are commonly reported, relieved only by leg exercise (Frankel, Patten and Gillin, 1974). The sufferer may be unable to remain in bed, feeling the need to walk around, and is likely to find returning to sleep problematic. Again, bed partners may be aware of the restless legs problem and the two conditions, nocturnal myoclonus and restless legs, commonly present together.

Childhood onset insomnia

Childhood onset DIMS is defined by the ASDC classification as a relentless insomnia characterised by a history of unexplained sleep disturbance starting well before puberty. This form of sleep disturbance is likely to be associated with other central arousal difficulties, such as attention-deficit disorder and it is postulated that there is neurological impairment of the basic sleep–wake system.

DIMS associated with other conditions

This final category comprises a number of sleep disturbances diagnosable only by polygraphic monitoring. Examples include repeated REM sleep interruptions where the patient wakens during almost every REM period, and alpha-delta sleep or non-restorative sleep where alpha waves occur during SWS and leave the patient feeling unrefreshed and complaining of poor quality sleep.

Chapter 2

The Presentation of Insomnia
at the Clinic

The previous chapter outlined sleep processes and its functions, and provided definition and classification of insomnia. However, a more complete understanding requires consideration of the sleeper as well as her sleep pattern. Descriptive criteria and categorical labels formed the skeletal structure—it is important now to put flesh on the bones. Chapter 2, therefore, introduces the insomniac—as a person. The chapter attempts to convey the richness and diversity of symptoms, perspectives and traits which may characterise the individual who sits in the consulting room awaiting assessment and treatment. The aim is to identify and illustrate characteristics of the presenting complaint and the complainant, both from the research literature and from clinical experience. In doing so the author recognises the danger of caricature—this is *not* what is intended. Rather the reader is asked to consider the phenomenological world of the insomniac where *n* always equals 1; but there are things in common.

Since it is largely the personal perspective of the insomniac which mediates the severity of the sleep complaint at the consulting room, the practitioner must have an understanding of insomnia from the patient's vantage point. The practitioner must appreciate the personal meaning which the insomniac attributes to sleep (or lack of it), and how that meaning is derived. Just as the assessment of fear involves appraisal of three systems (behavioural, physiological and subjective), and an understanding of the synchrony or desynchrony amongst those systems (Lang, Rice and Sternbach, 1972; Rachman and Hodgson, 1974; Hugdahl, 1981), so the assessment of insomnia comprises both quantitative and qualitative study, in relation to both nighttime and daytime variables. Actual assessment methods are discussed in detail in Chapter 4; the task at this point is to understand how the insomniac attaches meaning to sleep. A number of factors may act as moderating variables and influence the insomniac complaint.

PAST PERSONAL EXPERIENCE

Commonly the insomniac will refer to changes which have taken place over time in sleep pattern. This is particularly so where sleep at some previous point was regarded as satisfactory, and the individual can find no substantive or acceptable reason for why this is no longer the case. The prior sleep pattern may be held up as evidence of what is (still) possible and the discrepancy with present sleep may be regarded as pathological. Thus, perfectly normal age-related changes in sleep requirement, sleep pattern or sleep quality may be misinterpreted and unreasonable concern over one's ability to control the sleep process may be generated. For others, of course, reflection upon the past simply confirms the chronic nature of the insomnia. Such individuals may believe that they have never had a normal or satisfactory sleep pattern as far back as they can remember. They lack the reference point in personal experience which provides the prior "norm" as a therapeutic goal. Short spells of better sleep are sometimes recalled, usually accompanied, however, by the frustration of not knowing how or why sleep was improved at that time, thus making replication elusive.

For many individuals both of the above scenarios are telescoped into the experience of a variable sleep pattern. Good nights come and go with no clear determinants and are interspersed by equally unpredictable bad nights. A common strand of self-evidence available to the insomniac, therefore, is that of personal ineffectiveness in restoring or maintaining a reasonable sleep pattern. The insomniac lacks confidence in dealing with sleep and feels threatened by the problem rather than having mastery and control. Bandura's work on self-efficacy, and his examination of the relationship between thoughts, beliefs and behaviour, are very relevant to an understanding of the insomniac's outlook (Bandura, 1977, 1986). The insomniac usually has a negative mental set concerning sleep. These points will be further developed shortly.

PERCEPTIONS OF HOW OTHERS SLEEP

An alternative reference point for the insomniac is the sleep pattern of others known to her, or of society at large. Not invariably, but nevertheless frequently, the insomniac has a partner who "sleeps like a log", apparently managing to fall asleep quickly and to remain asleep soundly. Night by night observations serve only to convince the individual that (a) her sleep pattern is abnormal by comparison, and (b) it seems to be easy to fall asleep. Conflict and confusion arise once more and self-efficacy is further challenged. Since situational factors are similar for the insomniac and her partner, the source of the problem is likely to be regarded as personal and not environmental. The apparent simplicity of the sleep process for the good sleeper may be hard for the insomniac to accept. Equally, empathic understanding may not be forthcoming towards the insomniac from individuals who sleep with effortless ease. Since a good sleeper does not "do" anything to get to sleep, such advice as may be given to the insomniac may appear trite and critical.

The insomniac may find some comfort in examining a broader sample of the human experience of sleep. She will usually know one or two people who also sleep poorly and may recognise that sleep needs vary considerably amongst people, making it unreasonable to suppose that she should have as much sleep as her peers. Such knowledge does not, however, always lead to acceptance of the sleep pattern as it is, and the actual experience of sleep may continue to be unsatisfying or even aversive. The insomniac is more likely to ruminate on the fact that others in the household or neighbourhood are now asleep than to remember that there are those, like her, who sleep poorly and are probably awake.

SLEEP PATTERN VARIABILITY

Although it may seem reasonable to ask the insomniac to describe a "typical" night's sleep, this may be a harder task than it at first appears. Experience suggests that insomniacs do not have a predictable sleep pattern but rather a mixture of "good nights" and "bad nights". Average values, therefore, do not quantify the sleep problem adequately.

There is research evidence which indicates that insomniacs exhibit greater night to night variability on most sleep parameters compared with good sleepers (Coates et al, 1978, 1982a). Indeed, the within-subject night to night discrepancy in sleep latency for some patients was found to be as great as two hours in one study (Roth, Kramer and Lutz, 1976). It seems possible that the unpredictability of what sleep will be like on a given night may bear some important relationship to subjective concern over sleep. The individual who *habitually* takes 90 minutes to fall asleep experiences no ambiguity and may accommodate this sleep habit without undue anxiety or frustration. There is no uncertainty. However, the individual who *at times* takes this long to fall asleep and at other times falls asleep rapidly does not know what to expect on a particular night. In these circumstances the sleep pattern may be perceived to be out of control. Killen and Coates (1979) have proposed that the uncertainty which arises from a variable sleep pattern might interact with other worries and concerns to inhibit sleep further. In one study which attempted to identify the characteristics of sleep efficiency which are of principal concern to poor sleepers the factor of "voluntary control of sleep" emerged to account for the greatest proportion of variance (Evans, 1977). Self-efficacy perceptions of this type are likely to reduce where variability in sleep pattern is evident.

Insomniacs treated within our own research programme also exhibited considerable night to night variability in sleep. Close examination of a sub-group of 14 patients' sleep latency scores, at baseline, revealed that only four subjects had sleep-onset patterns which could be interpreted as stable. The remaining 10 patients exhibited marked variability, usually presenting three or four rapid onset-of-sleep nights and three or four delayed sleep-onset nights. The *average* range of baseline SOL scores for the total group ($n = 14$) was 125 minutes. For one subject the difference between best and worst nights was 3.5 hours and for another subject the range was 4.5 hours. In order more systematically to examine sources of variability an analysis of variance model was applied. This approach partitioned components of variance due to differences among subjects, differences among nights and differences among nights nested within subjects. The results indicated that 70% of the variance amongst scores was accounted for by within subject variability in SOL. Night to night variability per se, independent of this within subject factor, however, accounted for only 2% of variance (Espie, Lindsay and Hood, 1987). For these reasons we have included a measure of raw score variance (standard deviation) in our investigations of comparative treatment outcome (Espie et al, 1989).

How then may the insomniac presenting at the clinic be characterised? She is likely to be a poor sleeper ... but not always so. There are likely to be good nights, or at least, better nights, where sleep is more acceptable; but these will come and go independent of the individual's efforts to predict or control them. Hence, might it be reasonable to expect to find the insomniac presenting with symptoms of emotional upset associated with sleep dissatisfaction? This possibility forms the focus of the next section.

PERSONALITY VARIABLES

Numerous studies have documented differences between good and poor sleepers on measures of psychopathology and personality. Free-floating anxiety, phobic anxiety, somatic concomitants of anxiety and neurotic depression have all been elevated within the poor sleeper group (Kumar and Vaidya, 1984), and several studies have found that a formal assessment of anxiety level discriminated insomniacs from non-insomniacs (Haynes, Follingstad and McGowan, 1974; Hicks and Pellegrini 1977; Kumar and Vaidya, 1984). The most commonly adopted measure has been the MMPI

(Minnesota Multiphasic Personality Inventory) where research results have been consistent over a wide range of insomniacs in terms of age, chronicity, presence or absence of medication and source of sample. There is some evidence, however, that psychopathology is more prominent in younger insomniac subjects (Roehrs et al, 1982). Perhaps associations for the older age groups are more likely to be with the natural ageing process.

In general, insomniacs have exhibited "neurotic" profiles on the MMPI, with elevations on the depression, hypochondriasis, psychopathic deviance, psychasthenia and hysteria scales (Monroe, 1967; Johns et al, 1971; Coursey Buchsbaum and Frankel, 1975; Frankel et al, 1976; Freedman, 1976; Kales et al, 1976; Monroe and Marks, 1977; Shealy, Lowe and Ritzler, 1980; Kales et al, 1983a; Levin, Bertelson and Lacks, 1984). MMPI reports have been further corroborated by other studies reporting higher rates of dysphoric mood (Beutler, Thornby and Karacan, 1978; Johnson et al, 1979), depression (Coursey, Buchsbaum and Frankel, 1975) and general medical complaint (Monroe, 1967; Roth, Kramer and Lutz, 1976). Thus, the insomniac can be characterised as a person who is mildly depressed, anxious, hypochondriacal and overly worrisome.

Borkovec (1982) has pointed out that there are interpretative problems with personality study data since these psychological features may not be related causatively to disturbed sleep, and few significant correlations have been found between personality variables and objective sleep parameters. He also refers to studies which failed to establish personality differences between insomniacs and good sleepers (Rechtschaffen, 1968; Gering and Mahrer, 1972). Kales et al (1983a), however, suggest that the homogeneity of the MMPI profiles amongst their (and other) chronic insomniacs should be interpreted as strong evidence of psychopathology being primary to sleep disorder. They propose that, during the day, the insomniac typically inhibits, denies and represses conflicts which at night, in the relative absence of external stimulation, re-emerge, resulting in an internalised focusing of attention. This process of internalisation is hypothesised to lead to chronic emotional arousal, in turn also provoking physiological arousal, and rendering the subject unable to sleep.

Edinger, Stout and Hoelscher (1988) recently conducted an investigation to explore further the usefulness of the MMPI for defining homogeneous personality types among insomniacs. One hundred and one out-patient insomniacs completed a sleep history questionnaire and the MMPI in this study. These workers derived two major personality "types" from cluster analyses of MMPI data which together accounted for 88% of their sample. Type 1 insomniacs appeared to be less well defended psychologically and were more aroused than Type 2 patients. Type 1 insomniacs could be characterised as being younger with earlier presentation of sleep problems, often associated with bedtime anxieties and intrusive cognitions. These patients were found to make a relatively poor response to behavioural treatment. Type 2 insomniacs, however, typically presented sleep difficulties for the first time during adulthood. These individuals appeared less upset by their sleep problems (which may have been less severe) and made a much better response to psychological treatment.

The predictive validity of personality information requires further investigation alongside other potential predictor variables such as severity of insomnia, cognitive style and sleep physiology. However, whether or not personality characteristics prove to be a cause of insomnia, or are simply correlates of disturbed sleep, the available evidence does point towards the appropriateness of assessing and managing insomnia from a psychological perspective.

Consideration of the role of life events in relation to insomnia may also be important. In one study, although the onset of insomnia was regarded as gradual by the majority of poor sleepers, major life events during the year in which insomnia started were evident in 70% of cases (Healey et al, 1981). Consistent with previous MMPI studies, poor self-concept and frequent health complaints were noted, and the authors proposed that their poor sleepers seemed prone to internalise stress reactions. It seems possible that if insomniacs are indeed prone to ruminative worry, they might be particularly vulnerable to react adversely to major life changes.

DAYTIME FUNCTIONING

The presence of daytime sequelae of poor nighttime sleep may be central to the diagnosis of insomnia (Dement, Seidel and Carskadon, 1984; Morin and Kwentus, 1988). Measurable effects upon daytime performance or mood may be sensitive demonstrations of the quantitative or qualitative insufficiency of sleep. Dissatisfaction with the sleep experience per se but without evident impact upon waking life has been given the term "insomnoid state" by one group of workers to differentiate this disorder from insomnia (Lichstein, 1984). Although it may be premature at this stage to introduce a simple categorical model of insomnia (i.e. with or without daytime effects), clinical experience does bear out considerable variation amongst subjects when it comes to daytime complaints.

For some, treatment goals are focused upon the functional outcomes, e.g. alert, refreshed, energetic. For others, attention to actual sleep parameters is of greater importance; and some of these subjects indeed may report no daytime tiredness or irritability associated with poor sleep. Therefore, it would appear to be both conservative and valid to regard insomniac complaints as varying along two dimensions—one to do with sleep time;

one to do with wake time. These dimensions may be seen to covary for the majority of insomniacs. Clearly the correlation will be higher for some subjects than for others, but it is just as unlikely to achieve 0.00 (i.e. no correspondence) as 1.00 (i.e. perfect correspondence). Sleep does not account for 100% of the variance in daytime performance even for the worst affected insomniac. It should be noted also that the existence of a correlation, even a strong one, does not imply causation. It is quite conceivable that poor daytime coping will adversely affect sleep through elevated anxiety levels and the development of a neurotic drive for sleep which can lead to performance failure, i.e. wakefulness.

With these provisos concerning the probable covariation of nighttime and daytime measures it may be useful now to outline the areas of daytime functioning which have received the greatest attention in the literature on insomnia. Three main groups of "next day effects" have been studied.

Firstly, Bootzin and Engle-Friedman (1981) have provided a helpful review of "performance measures" which appear to be sensitive to the effects of sleep loss. Sleep deprivation studies on normal samples have shown that subjects perform poorly on vigilance, reaction time and arithmetic tasks, making greater numbers of detection errors due to poorer attentional functioning, being slower to respond to both visual and auditory stimuli, and getting fewer problems correct in mental arithmetic exercises (Williams and Lubin, 1967; Poulton, Edwards and Colquhoun, 1974; Glenville et al, 1978). More recent work on insomniac patients has also revealed similar deficits on a variety of psychomotor and cognitive tasks, along with specific difficulties in semantic memory (Mendelson, Garnett and Linnoila, 1984; Mendelson et al, 1984). Inadequate sleep has been associated, therefore, with impairment of certain aspects of cognitive function.

A second area of concern is that of daytime fatigue. Dement, Seidel and Carskadon (1984) have reviewed the available evidence on the association between such fatigue and nighttime wakefulness. They reported the results of some of their own work which demonstrates a linear relationship between daytime sleepiness and sleep, in that fatigue increased as sleep was systematically reduced in experimental subjects. They recommended the use of the Multiple Sleep Latency Test (MSLT) as an objective measure of daytime tiredness since it is sensitive to the effects of relatively small reductions in sleep which may produce substantial and highly significant increases in daytime sleepiness (Carskadon and Dement, 1982; Roehrs et al, 1983).

In spite of insomniacs' subjective reports of daytime impairment, consistent differences in daytime functioning between insomniacs and normal control subjects have not been found. For example, Seidel et al (1984) compared large samples of chronic insomniacs and good sleepers and found no significant differences on the MSLT. Similar findings have been reported in other studies using smaller comparison groups (Mendelson et al, 1984; Sugarman, Stern and Walsh, 1985).

Stepanski et al (1988) compared 70 clinic-presenting insomniacs with 45 asymptomatic sleepers on sleep EEG and next day MSLT measures. They reported that whereas the insomniacs experienced significantly less nighttime sleep they were also significantly *more* alert than the control group during the following day. Stepanski et al interpreted these results in terms of a physiological hyperarousal model of insomnia where either increased alertness gives rise to a decreased sleep need or a chronic state of overarousal persists across the sleep–wake period. Schneider-Helmert (1987) also found that daytime performance was not generally impaired in insomniacs. Using the Multiple Relaxation Test (analagous to the MSLT) he found a greater spontaneous sleep tendency amongst normal sleepers. However, morning performance on auditory vigilance tasks was poorer amongst insomniacs, suggesting a "starting-up" difficulty relative to good sleepers. Interestingly, Haynes et al (1985) have provided a further demonstration of insomniacs' delayed sleep-onset on MSLT assessment relative to good sleepers. However, these workers do not regard this as evidencing lack of daytime fatigue amongst insomniacs. Rather they suggest that this finding is consistent with an initial insomnia problem which presents upon retiring to bed and/or a sleep maintenance problem comprising difficulty returning to sleep.

A third group of studies have reported disturbances in daytime mood in poor sleepers. Ratings of daytime irritability have been used as outcome measures and these have been found to reduce after psychological therapy (Nicassio and Bootzin, 1974). In another study insomniacs were found to differ from normal controls in that the former rated themselves as significantly more worried, upset, self-critical, hostile and depressed (Marchini et al, 1983). These insomniacs were also significantly less energetic, less physically active and considered that they "enjoyed themselves" less. It is of course possible that such features of insomniac mood state are a reflection of neurotic disposition, as previously described. If night to night variability in sleep pattern is indeed the norm it should be expected that similar and corresponding variations in daytime measures will be found. For example, Seidel et al (1984) found disturbed mood upon awakening, as measured by the Profile of Mood States, to be part of the presenting clinical picture. Further research is required, using a within subjects design, to clarify this.

There are good grounds, therefore, for adopting an individualised, 24-hour perspective in assessing clinical complaints of insomnia. Daytime variables require consideration alongside sleep variables. A further facet of the 24-hour perspective, however, is the predictability of sleep and waking based upon the individual's circadian cycle. Nighttime wakefulness and daytime fatigue may result from a sleep–wake schedule which is out of synchrony with the individual's lifestyle. It is a common experience, for example, for shift workers and aircrew to develop sleep problems when forced to obtain sleep at times when circadian rhythms favour wakefulness (e.g. Rutenfranz et al, 1977). Similarly, irregular, non-24 hour schedules, in which sleep and wake times are shifted frequently, have been found to decrease sleep efficiency and total sleep time and to increase time awake during the night and daytime sleepiness.

It should be noted at this point that DSM-III (revised) (1987) provides diagnostic criteria for Sleep–Wake Schedule Disorder which comprise "a mismatch between the normal sleep–wake schedule for a person's environment and his or her circadian sleep–wake pattern, resulting in a complaint of either insomnia ... or hypersomnia (the person is unable to remain alert when wakefulness is expected)". Sleep–Wake Schedule Disorder of course refers to an established pattern of impairment and not to transient schedule disruptions. It is suggested that differentiation between this disorder and primary insomnia lies in the typical improvement observed with Sleep–Wake Schedule Disorder when the person is allowed to follow her own schedule for a while. There is of course likely to be an optimal schedule for sleeping and waking for each individual. However, experience suggests that insomniacs may be unaware of their natural drive for sleep and are unable to harness it to their benefit.

ATTRIBUTION AND EFFICACY

It is the primary emphasis of this chapter to introduce the reader to the private and experiential world of the insomniac and to outline the concerns and characteristics she presents at the consulting room. Discussions of these areas would not be complete without consideration of causal attributions in insomnia.

What is meant by the term "attribution" is the extent to which an individual regards a behaviour as determined by internal or external sources. The behaviour, in this case sleep or insomnia, may be regarded as outwith personal control. An external focus may on the one hand increase emotional arousal and subjective concern as the person lacks a sense of mastery and feels helpless to effect change. On the other hand the facility to externalise responsibility for the sleep problem may liberate the insomniac from self-blame and lead to relaxation of efforts directly to control sleep. Similarly, internal attribution may be regarded as either arousing (being responsible for gaining and maintaining control) or de-arousing (feeling in control and able to act).

Studies conducted during the 1970s on attribution and insomnia yielded conflicting results. The pioneering study of Storms and Nisbett (1970) found that a manipulation of attributions from affect-laden personal feelings to external stimuli (placebo pills) led to an experience of less intense emotion concerning sleep, and to faster sleep-onset. Later partial replication studies, however, failed to reproduce these effects (Kellogg and Baron, 1975; Bootzin, Herman and Nicassio, 1976; Heffler and Lisman, 1978). Brockner and Swap (1983) have suggested that an individual-differences perspective may be central in resolving these discrepant results. Their own work lends support to the mediating effects of personality factors such as self-esteem. High self-esteem subjects are less likely to be manipulated by external cues and are more attentive to internal reactions. Subjects with low self-esteem, however, may be more suggestible.

What do these results imply for the practising clinician? Several salient points can be made. Firstly, the presenting insomniac will have an emotional reaction to her problem, otherwise referral is unlikely to occur. Secondly, attribution as to source and potential solution of the problem may vary along the internal/external dimension. Thirdly, self-esteem and self-efficacy dimensions are highly relevant and should be considered not only as trait (stable, relatively enduring) characteristics, but also as specific to insomnia per se. It is conceivable that an individual normally high in self-efficacy may, with respect to sleep, report low efficacy beliefs. This anomaly may heighten the emotional reaction considerably and either confirm or modify previous attributional beliefs.

The use of sleep medication is one particular source of external attribution which deserves special mention. It has been suggested that the insomniac who takes sleep medication regularly will attribute the sleep which she does get to the drug and to attribute to herself little capacity for falling asleep (Ribordy and Denney, 1977). Furthermore, the removal of hypnotic drugs is known to introduce physical rebound effects (Kales et al, 1974b) and these may give rise to even greater apprehension concerning ability to fall asleep on one's own. These apprehensions may appear to the insomniac to be confirmed by the withdrawal syndrome itself.

Clearly, attribution is a subjective phenomenon and may be invalid. Accurate attribution apportions sources of variation on the basis of objective information, or at least probability estimates. Unfortunately, many drug-using insomniacs continue to be ill-informed of the withdrawal consequences of hypnotic drugs. This may be in part due to a desire amongst doctors and patients alike to regard such medication as "mild" or "non-habit forming". The demand characteristics of the consulting room setting are such that treatment of the complaint and perhaps exploration of side effects *during* administration have precedence over discussions concerning withdrawal effects. Apart from the unavailability of such information to guide attributional beliefs, however, is the potentially deceptive effect of drug tolerance (see also Chapter 10). Many insomniacs quickly perceive the hypnotic drug to be ineffective in promoting sleep and this may reinforce internal attribution of even poorer sleep upon withdrawal since the drug apparently was not working.

An early experimental study investigated the causal attributions of insomniacs who had responded to a treatment package of a hypnotic drug, a relaxation procedure and the scheduling of bedtime behaviours (Davison, Tsujimoto and Glaros, 1973). Treatment responders were divided into two groups, half being told they had received an optimal dosage of the drug, and half being told they had received an ineffective, minimal dosage. The drug was then discontinued while subjects practised the other elements of the programme. Those who had been in the "minimal dosage group" and had been led to attribute improvement to their own resources were found to maintain improved sleep compared with the return to pre-treatment sleep latencies observed in the other group. Clearly, therefore, the attributional effects of drug-taking (psychological dependence) could interact with physical withdrawal effects to produce an even stronger dependency syndrome.

There is now a considerable body of research available which examines the importance of an individual's view of herself and her capabilities in effecting and maintaining behaviour change. Efficacy beliefs are regarded by Bandura as mediated (1) by direct experiences of success/failure, (2) by observation of others and their competencies, (3) by the persuasion and correction of competent commentators and (4) by the experience and interpretation of physiological symptoms (Bandura, 1986, 1989). Although actual mastery experience is perhaps the most effective, each of these four pathways may modify self-efficacy beliefs. Indeed it seems that it is the perception of oneself as *possessing* some control over a problem which may be therapeutic and anxiety-reducing, and not necessarily the actual exercising of that control (Bandura, 1989; Kent and Gibbons, 1987).

The relevance of self-efficacy beliefs to the complaint of insomnia has been recognised for some time (Killen and Coates, 1979) and successful behavioural treatment of insomnia has been associated with reports of increased mastery amongst our own subjects (Espie and Lindsay, 1985). Similarly, Lacks et al have observed marked increases in ratings of self-efficacy at post-treatment and now routinely advise appraisal of self-efficacy amongst treatment outcome measures (Lacks, 1987). A common thread running through research and clinical reports, therefore, is the importance of overcoming the client's sense of helplessness in the face of a threatening or aversive situation.

THE INSOMNIAC AT THE CLINIC

This chapter set out to put flesh on the bones of the condition which was defined and described in Chapter 1 as "insomnia". It may be of further help, therefore, to conclude the chapter with brief synopses of two cases. Hopefully, these case descriptions will reflect the chapter content and fairly represent the insomniac who presents at the clinic.

Case 1

L. was a 56 year old married lady who presented with a six year history of persistent initial and sleep maintenance insomnia. Her General Practitioner (GP) noted, however, "a long history of trouble with insomnia, anxiety and mild depression" which dated back to when L. was in her mid-30s. She had been prescribed anxiolytic and hypnotic drugs at various times but preferred to avoid using these. She worked part time as an office cleaner, commencing work at 8.00 a.m.

At interview L. admitted to having a nervous disposition, in this respect "taking after her mother". She denied having any substantive reasons for worry but appeared to be fretful, rushing and fussing about things, and always going out of her way to please other people. She complained of being kept awake by repetitive thoughts when lying in bed and of being easily aroused by the slightest noise during the night. L. experienced daytime tiredness but avoided taking naps. Although often very tired upon retiring to bed L. frequently felt "wide awake as soon as her head touched the pillow". This could lead to considerable frustration. She was conscious of not wishing to disturb her husband's sleep. He always fell asleep before L. and appeared to sleep soundly. L. and her husband enjoyed a close relationship. Their only son lived across the road with his wife and children.

Baseline sleep diary records were kept for three weeks which revealed an average sleep latency of 104 minutes, although this varied between 30 minutes and 160 minutes. Nine of the 21 nights exhibited SOL greater than two hours. Total sleep time varied between 3 hours 40 minutes and 8 hours with a mean of 5 hours 55 minutes. L. typically woke two or three times per night with difficulty in returning to sleep and reported low ratings of "restedness after sleep". She complained of not getting "a deep enough sleep".

Case 2

T. was a 41 year old single man who was referred by his GP because of the chronic nature of his sleep complaints and difficulties in withdrawing him from benzodiazepine drugs. At the time of referral he took Triazolam each night although he admitted to substituting two/three whiskies on a regular basis in an effort to promote sleep. T. was a capable man who worked as a consultant engineer. He did not mind working long hours if necessary, although he had other, mainly group-based social interests. He enjoyed sports and took part in "fun-runs". He requested a referral from his GP as he perceived his daytime performance, especially his concentration, was not as it used to be. He was also concerned that his use of medication and alcohol was becoming habitual yet without benefit to his sleep or his general ability to cope.

T. reported that he had never regarded himself as a good sleeper. He was first prescribed sleep medication around 10 years prior to this referral and had been on numerous preparations. Although he regarded his prescription of Triazolam as ineffective he had experienced acute withdrawal symptoms and had been unable to sustain the withdrawal programme. He felt angry that he could not succeed here and interpreted both the failure to persist without medication and the rebound effect symptoms per se as evidence of his personal inadequacy. He was someone who liked to set and achieve targets. He complained of tension in his arms and neck as well as an "inability to switch off mentally" when in bed.

T. spontaneously recognised variability in his sleep pattern which was later confirmed by monitoring via a sleep log. After medication was successfully withdrawn and alcohol intake controlled, a drug free baseline over two weeks revealed a mean SOL of 54 minutes. Night by night scores, however, comprised 10 nights with SOL less than 20 minutes, one night with SOL of 60 minutes, and three nights with latency from 2 hours 15 minutes to almost 3 hours 30 minutes. Duration of sleep varied correspondingly. T. was, in fact, *both* a good sleeper and a poor sleeper. Daytime irritability appeared more likely to follow a poor night's sleep. Equally, however, daytime stresses arose which could not validly be attributed to sleep loss. T. required help to recognise the need for development of daytime problem-solving strategies as well as behavioural management of his sleep pattern.

Chapter 3

Theoretical Models of Insomnia

Possible aetiological mechanisms in insomnia have been discussed by a number of reviewers (Coates and Thoresen, 1980; Turner and Di Tomasso, 1980; Borkovec, 1982; Lichstein and Fischer, 1985; Lacks, 1987). Insomniacs have been variously conceptualised; as somatically tense, mentally highly aroused, over-anxious in attitude and over-controlling of the sleep process. Other viewpoints have suggested that their sleep pattern is the result of faulty learning, a weak sleep-initiation system or a poorly balanced 24-hour sleep–wake cycle. These aetiological perspectives clearly vary widely, and may not be mutually exclusive. Furthermore, some may be better explanations of the *maintenance* rather than the cause of sleep problems. It is the purpose of this chapter to describe and discuss the most important of these models of insomnia, particularly those which give rise to the methods of psychological treatment which are introduced in Chapter 6 and following.

The concept of "arousal" plays an important part in most if not all understandings of the aetiology and maintenance of insomnia. Figure 6, therefore, presents an analysis of how different arousal mechanisms may contribute to sleep disturbance. Inspection of Figure 6 reveals that there are three routes by which arousal may be mediated.

Firstly, in the nervous system, arousal may be direct or indirect. The failure of Central Nervous System processes to promote sleep and/or to inhibit wakefulness constitutes a direct form of maintained arousal. High levels of autonomic activity associated with tension and problems in physiological relaxation, however, represent another, though less direct form of arousal which is potentially inhibitory to sleep.

Secondly, psychological processes may contribute towards overarousal. Here the problem is thought to be primarily cognitive or emotional rather than somatic. Mental alertness comprising thinking, rehearsing and planning may interfere with sleep, and sleep itself may become the subject of such mentation with consequent effects upon self-perception. Of course cognitive arousal per se need not imply irrational or neurotic thinking.

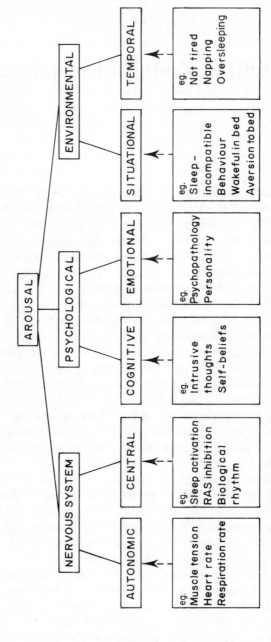

Figure 6   A schematic representation of models accounting for the aetiology and maintenance of insomnia

Emotional arousal, therefore, deserves separate consideration and refers to the presence of trait characteristics within the individual which may predispose to psychological upset and arousal, or of state characteristics which evidence rumination or worry.

Thirdly, arousal may have its source not in physiological or mental processes but in the environment: that is, in the place and not the person. Situational triggers may elicit arousal responses, either failing to predict sleep for the individual or predicting wakefulness. The de-arousal response also may be seen to operate under the behavioural principle of stimulus control. Furthermore, temporal cues may be inappropriately associated with sleep–wake patterns. Examples of this are daytime napping which contributes to nighttime wakefulness, and having an habitual bedtime which is unrelated to level of tiredness.

The remainder of this chapter provides more detailed description of each of the proposed aetiological systems and sub-systems. The research evidence for and against each hypothesised mechanism will be considered.

NERVOUS SYSTEM AROUSAL AND INSOMNIA

Central arousal

Although direct Central Nervous System (CNS) dysfunction may not be a major cause of clinically presenting insomnia, the role of the control processes of CNS arousal and sleep induction require consideration. Insomnia is known to result from thalamic lesion, that is damage to the sleep activation areas of the brain (Puca, Bricola and Turella, 1973), and from inhibition of the synthesis of the neurotransmitter serotonin (5HT) (Kales and Kales, 1984). The ascending Reticular Activating System (RAS), by comparison, appears to govern alert behaviour (Moruzzi and Magoun, 1949). Lesions to the locus coeruleus have been found to produce decreases in cortical arousal related to decreases in delivery of norepinephrine at thalamic and cortical terminals. Lesions of the posterior hypothalamus, however, produce the most typical cases of hypersomnia (Kales and Kales, 1984). There is evidence, therefore, from both neurochemical research and from studies of neuropathological states, to regard sleep as mediated by the action of a sleep-induction system and the inhibition of an arousal system. Insomnia may result from failure to switch off the alert system or failure to switch on the sleep system.

Some consideration will be given first of all to possible failures in central de-arousal. Coursey, Buchsbaum and Frankel (1975) suggested that insomniacs may have particularly sensitive sensory systems which are highly reactive to external stimuli. If this were so then de-arousal would be expected to take longer amongst insomniacs. A series of investigations on the effects of monotonous stimulation was conducted by Bohlin (1971, 1972, 1973) which indicated a relationship between orienting response habituation and the development of sleep-onset. In each of these experiments subjects achieved more rapid sleep-onset after monotonous stimulation (repetition of an audible tone every 20–40 seconds) compared with no stimulation control procedures, suggesting that orienting response habituation is a de-arousal process. Bohlin proposed that the rate of this habituation and subsequent sleep development interact with initial arousal level such that rapid habituation occurs when the subject is in a low state of arousal and slower habituation accompanies high arousal. The latter was hypothesised to be the case with insomnia. Borkovec (1979) raised the possibility that these findings may have some implications for the traditional psychological approaches to the management of insomnia and their underlying theoretical models. It is possible, for example, that repeated tension release cycles in relaxation therapy and the repetition of a "mantra" in meditation function as soporific stimuli within this habituation model. Similarly, techniques aimed at blocking out external stimulation and preclusion of intrusive thinking might significantly reduce initial arousal levels to facilitate habituation. Since attentional processes are of paramount importance in this theoretical analysis, any therapeutic procedure which overcomes the problem of dishabituating stimuli (overt or covert) might be of considerable value, and worthy of further investigation.

Deficiency in the functioning of the serotonergic sleep system is the alternative explanation for sleeplessness at CNS level (Hauri, 1975). Arising from an experimental animal study by Sterman, Howe and MacDonald (1970) which demonstrated that levels of sensorimotor rhythm (SMR), originating in the sensory motor cortex, could be strengthened and sleep enhanced by reinforcement schedules, attempts have been to apply SMR biofeedback to the treatment of insomnia. Hauri and his colleagues have reported a series of investigations suggesting that SMR may be weaker in insomniacs compared with normal sleepers, and that SMR biofeedback may effectively reduce sleep-onset latency and increase sleep efficiency (Jordan, Hauri and Phelps, 1976; Hauri, 1981; Hauri et al, 1982). The therapeutic effects in these studies were, however, associated with insomniac subjects who could be regarded as experiencing low anxiety and being non-tense, i.e. low levels of autonomic arousal. SMR biofeedback was not effective with tense insomniacs who improved only under EMG biofeedback training. The aetiological roles of cortical arousal versus autonomic arousal, therefore, require further research examination.

Reference is made in Figure 6 to a third component of CNS arousal associated with insomnia: that is, the typical biological rhythm which regulates the pattern of arousal and de-arousal (and other processes including body temperature, hunger and metabolism) for each individual, according to a 24-hour circadian clock (Aschoff, 1965; Czeisler et al, 1980; Johnson et al, 1981). The issue here is not so much one of arousal per se but more of timing. There may be synchrony or desynchrony between the individual's biological preparedness for making an alert response or for falling asleep. "Sleep readiness" at the CNS level appears to be of critical importance. Insomniacs may be poor at monitoring their sleep readiness and so develop an habitual sleep pattern which is undermined by conflicting biological rhythms. The behavioural issues of situational and temporal control form a separate area for consideration in terms of the arousal aetiology of insomnia and will be dealt with later on in this chapter.

Autonomic arousal

The conceptualisation of insomnia as resulting from physiological overarousal has enjoyed considerable popularity over the past 20 years. In 1967, Monroe conducted an extremely influential study comparing 16 good sleepers with 16 poor sleepers on a number of psychological and physiological variables. His results gave rise to the view that poor sleepers exhibit heightened autonomic arousal (higher rectal temperature, vasoconstrictions per minute, perspiration rate and skin conductance, body movements per hour) both prior to and within sleep. These results have only ever been partially replicated and several studies have failed to demonstrate any arousal differential between insomniac and control samples.

Higher levels of hormones indicative of higher adrenocortical activity amongst poor sleepers have been both supported (Johns et al, 1971) and denied (Frankel et al, 1973). One report of less rapid decline in heart rate associated with sleep amongst insomniacs (West et al, 1977) has to be considered against other reports where no significant relationship between sleep-onset and heart rate or frontalis muscle EMG has been demonstrated (Haynes, Follingstad and McGowan, 1974; Good, 1975; Browman and Tepas, 1976). These and other studies (some unpublished) have been carefully reviewed elsewhere with the general conclusion being reached that there remains inadequate evidence of autonomic hyperarousal amongst insomniacs (Bootzin and Nicassio, 1978; Coates and Thoresen, 1980; Borkovec, 1982).

Freedman (1987) has recently reminded researchers of his own research group's work which replicated some of Monroe's findings. Freedman and Sattler (1982) conducted a controlled comparative study on 12 chronic insomniacs and 12 normal sleepers using a wide range of physiological measures. Prior to sleep-onset, insomniacs were found to have significantly higher heart rates and frontalis and chin EMG levels, and lower skin temperatures, than non-insomniacs. Stepanski et al (1988) have suggested that their findings also are supportive of a physiological hyperarousal hypothesis. These workers found that, as well as a tendency towards nighttime wakefulness, their insomniacs were more alert during the day than control subjects (took longer to fall asleep on MSLT assessment). This, however, is a matter of interpretation since Haynes et al (1985), who obtained similar MSLT differences, regarded these simply as parallel data to the sleep latency differentials which are observable at night, i.e. insomniacs habitually take longer to fall asleep.

Given the equivocal nature of the literature on physiological hyperarousal, why did this theoretical model attain such popular approval? The answer here lies in three inter-related themes. Firstly, the ascendancy during the 1960s and 1970s of behavioural treatment approaches (especially relaxation methods) to psychological problems; secondly, the presentation of evidence (both objective and intuitive) that insomniacs experience higher than usual levels of anxiety and stress (see Chapter 2); and thirdly, a growing awareness that benzodiazepine hyponotics would not provide a lasting solution to the problems of chronic insomnia. The coming together of these three themes is well illustrated in an influential but largely pragmatic paper by Ribordy and Denney (1977). These workers presented behavioural treatments as an alternative to drugs in the management of insomnia. They quoted evidence against the long-term effectiveness of hypnotic medications and (based upon psychological treatment outcome work) provided evidence for the effectiveness of treatments such as systematic desensitisation, applied relaxation, attribution therapy and classical conditioning. The reported clinical utility of techniques such as relaxation training, which were *presumed* to operate via autonomic de-arousal, therefore, afforded a validity to the hyperarousal theory which was not justified by direct empirical study.

It is also noteworthy that a considerable number of studies reporting effective behavioural treatment for sleep-onset insomnia, by means of relaxation training and/or biofeedback methods (i.e. presumably de-arousing procedures) have failed to demonstrate post-treatment changes on physiological measures such as heart rate, respiration, and forearm and frontalis muscle EMG (Borkovec and Fowles, 1973; Freedman and Papsdorf, 1976; Haynes, Sides and Lockwood, 1977; Lick and Heffler, 1977; Borkovec et al, 1979; Coursey et al, 1980; Hauri, 1981).

A number of methodological difficulties with research reports also make it difficult to interpret the evidence for and against the autonomic arousal theory. Firstly, as Borkovec (1979) pointed out most reports have not differentiated adequately between good and problem sleepers in order to be convincing comparisons of two distinct groups. Even Monroe's original group of "poor sleepers" were not clinic-presenting insomniacs, and none was in receipt of medication for insomnia. Secondly, studies have approached insomnia as a unitary phenomenon and have failed to consider the possibility that specific sub-groups of insomniacs may exist. It is possible, for example, that following the Three Systems Model (Lang, Rice and Sternbach, 1972) some insomniacs may be more typically "physiological responders" than others. In any group study the commonalities across individuals tend to be emphasised at the expense of sometimes important inter-subject variability. The Three Systems Model could be fruitfully applied to the analysis of sleep disorders by careful consideration of each individual's characteristic behavioural, cognitive and physiological responses. Our own preliminary investigations of this area indicate that care must be taken to interpret responses made by insomniacs to questions of aetiology. For example, in rating the statement "I find it difficult to relax and let go" on the Sleep Disturbance Questionnaire (Espie, Brooks and Lindsay, 1989) insomniacs variously attributed this to mental and physical tension, when our intended emphasis had been purely the latter. Nevertheless, 45% of our sample did report bodily tension as a contributing factor to insomnia either "often" or "very often" (Table 2). Cognitive factors, however, appeared to play an even more important part in the aetiology of insomnia amongst these subjects (see later).

In conclusion, it is worth restating that the widespread use of relaxation-based techniques in the management of insomnia and other conditions does not in itself lend support to an autonomic de-arousal model, or to any other model for that matter. The role of a physiological mechanism in the aetiology and maintenance of at least a proportion of cases of insomnia awaits further innovative study.

PSYCHOLOGICAL AROUSAL AND INSOMNIA

The greatest rival to the physiological overarousal model of insomnia has been the mental overarousal model. Here the emphasis is upon thinking, styles of thinking and mood, and how these relate to sleep pattern and quality. In order to examine this model it may be helpful to recognise that there are two distinct yet complementary aspects to psychological arousal processes. Firstly, information processing in the brain may be associated with strictly cognitive arousal, i.e. mental acuity. Secondly, however, there may be emotional arousal which results from or directly causes mental processes. Here the cognitions are affect-laden. It may be reasonable then to think of a further two arousal models of insomnia, i.e. cognitive arousal and emotional arousal. These two are part of a "parent" psychological arousal model (see Figure 6).

Table 2 Summary of insomniac responses ($n = 42$) to items of the Sleep Disturbance Questionnaire. Figures represent the percentage of subjects rating an item at levels of response from "never true" to "very often true". (From Espie, Brooks and Lindsay, 1989, reproduced by permission of Pergamon Press PLC.)

	Never true	Seldom true	Sometimes true	Often true	Very often true
(1) I can't get into a comfortable position in bed.	24	37	34	5	0
(2) My mind keeps turning things over.	2	5	24	31	38
(3) I can't get my sleep pattern into a proper routine.	14	15	20	22	29
(4) I get too "worked up" at not sleeping.	12	21	36	14	17
(5) I find it hard to "let go" and relax my body.	7	14	31	12	36
(6) My thinking takes a long time to "unwind".	5	12	28	26	29
(7) I don't feel tired enough at bedtime.	19	17	29	20	15
(8) I try too hard to get to sleep.	25	22	32	8	13
(9) My body is full of tension	7	19	29	12	33
(10) I'm unable to empty my mind.	2	12	19	36	31
(11) I spend time reading/ watching TV when I should be sleeping.	32	17	17	12	22
(12) I worry that I won't cope tomorrow if I don't sleep well.	33	19	17	7	24

Cognitive arousal

There is a considerable body of research evidence which indicates that insomniacs are highly aroused cognitively. Reference was made in Chapter 1 to studies where insomniacs were awakened out of their sleep (as defined by EEG criteria) only to report that they had been awake (Agnew and Webb, 1972; Slama, 1979; Borkovec, Lane and Van Oot, 1981; Campbell and Webb, 1981). One likely explanation for this phenomenology is that continuing mental activity, even within stage 2 sleep, is interpreted by insomniacs as wakefulness. A cognitive arousal model of insomnia is certainly consistent with such findings.

There is also evidence from an experimental study by Gross and Borkovec (1982) that mental arousal can affect the sleep processes of good sleepers. These workers manipulated pre-sleep mentation by advising one group of subjects that they would have to present a speech on a given topic when aroused after a daytime nap. This group was subsequently found to require almost twice as long to fall asleep as other subjects, one group of whom were also asked to speak but no subject for the speech was provided. The clear inference here is that cognitive intrusion occurred when the instructional set facilitated active planning. A study by Haynes, Adams and Franzen (1981), however, provided results inconsistent with a hypothesised role of mental stress in sleep-onset insomnia. These workers found that a moderately difficult mental arithmetic task led to significant decreases in subjective and objective sleep latency compared to no-stress nights amongst insomniacs. They suggested that attributional factors may have been responsible for this finding. Where rational cause can be found for any wakefulness experienced, concern over that wakefulness may be reduced and sleep thereby facilitated.

When insomniacs have been asked to identify what they perceive to be the source of their sleep disruption they have indicated strongly in favour of cognitive determinants. Lichstein and Rosenthal (1980) asked 300 chronic insomniacs to weigh up somatic (restlessness, autonomic symptoms) and cognitive (planning, worry) elements to their arousal. They found that 55% of their sample attributed poor sleep to cognitive arousal with a further 35% stating that cognitive arousal was a factor of at least equal importance to somatic arousal. Clearly cognitive factors were perceived to be of much greater overall importance.

These findings are supported by our own studies (Espie, Brooks and Lindsay 1989). Some data on perceived contributory factors to insomnia were presented in Table 2. Reports on the Sleep Disturbance Questionnaire (SDQ) revealed that complaints such as "My mind keeps turning things over" (Item 2) and "I am unable to empty my mind" (Item 10) were the most highly rated questionnaire items. Over two-thirds of insomniacs regarded such cognitive intrusion as a frequent source of their sleep problem. Furthermore, principal components analysis of the SDQ led to the extraction of a first factor of "mental anxiety" which accounted for 40% of total variance.

Nicassio et al (1985) have developed a Pre-Sleep Arousal Scale and reported that the cognitive sub-scale was highly correlated with measures of sleep latency in their mixed sample of college students, adult insomniacs and adult normal sleepers. Van Egeren et al (1983) obtained time sampled "cognitive reports" from the pre-sleep period of 34 undergraduate students who complained of sleep-onset insomnia. Their data comprised audiotape recording of thoughts which had occurred immediately prior to a tone played over an intercom system in the sleep laboratory. A total of 255 reports were obtained and these were independently rated for content by three trained judges. Reports were also rated for affect. Regression analyses provided moderate support for a relationship between cognitive factors and the subjective experience of sleep-onset, especially where thought content was negative, related to physical sensations or environmental noise.

Further support for the relationships between sleep latency and cognitive factors comes from the experimental work of Shute et al (1986). Twenty-six elderly persons representing a range of sleep latency problems (5–75 mins) were required to complete three two-hour afternoon naps in a sleep laboratory. Measures of internal attentional control, i.e. the ability to attend selectively to internal cues, were correlated with objective and subjective sleep latency data. Results indicated that internal attentional control was significantly associated with sleep latency measures thus suggesting that cognitive processing of this type was a predictor of sleep latency.

Such findings, however, were not replicated by Sanavio (1988) who reported a very low correlation of only 0.09 between measures of pre-sleep cognition and self-reported sleep latency. Sanavio found that matching a cognitive treatment to subjects presenting with high cognitive arousal did not lead to superior outcome when compared with biofeedback treatment. Also, Borkovec (1982) quotes an example of failure to influence sleep parameters after a difficult mental arithmetic task was given to induce cognitive intrusions.

There is need for investigation of the relationship between pre-sleep mentation and daytime functioning during the preceding day (and evening). In particular, it seems possible that rehearsing and planning may occur during the bedtime period, by default, through lack of planned opportunity for "tying up loose ends" at other times earlier in the evening (cf. Espie and Lindsay, 1987). Interruption to sleep processes may be in such cases easily avoided. It is noteworthy, however, that so far from these intrusions being affect-laden and aversive, our own experience is that for a good number of insomniacs, this habitual pre-sleep routine of rehearsal and planning is in fact valued and enjoyed. There are then reinforcement contingencies operating which also require consideration.

Chapter 2 has included already a discussion of the concept of self-efficacy and its likely relationship to sleep processes for the insomniac. It is, nevertheless, worth recognising at this point that the individual who habitually experiences problems with intrusive thoughts is likely to develop a dysfunctional belief system in which she regards herself as "not in control". The regular interaction of cognitive intrusions, which at inception may be affect-free, with low self-efficacy beliefs may be responsible for generating more affect-laden thoughts which contribute not only to cognitive arousal but also to emotional arousal.

Emotional arousal

Much of the literature relevant to this section was reviewed in Chapter 2, particularly in the section on Personality Variables (pp. 29–31). Pertinent information was included also in the discussions of attribution and efficacy, and sleep pattern variability. It is only necessary, therefore, to provide a brief synopsis of the material which has been presented, along with some more detailed discussion on a number of points which have hitherto received cursory examination.

Insomniacs have been characterised as ruminative thinkers, presenting profiles of personality functioning which evidence some degree of psychopathology. Particularly in evidence are symptoms of anxiety and depression. Bedtime may be a time, in the absence of competing external stimulation, for selective attention to focus upon problems. It has been suggested that insomniacs internalise stress during the daytime which then emerges prior to and during sleep. Such affective responses may than combine with cognitive alertness and a vicious circle may be generated. The insomniac may seek but fail to interrupt this cycle and this may heighten anxiety even further.

It is a common clinical observation that insomniacs experience considerable anticipatory anxiety as bedtime approaches. A performance anxiety model has been formulated which proposes that anxiety responses may be conditioned not only to external, situational cues but also to the individual's own behaviour or performance (Ascher and Efran, 1978; Ascher and Turner, 1979; Espie and Lindsay, 1985). Fear of a performance failure and of the anticipated negative consequences of that failure is described as performance anxiety.

The victim of performance anxiety predictably attempts immediately to control and correct the deviant performance through deliberate coping efforts, but these efforts in turn may only contribute to longer term exacerbation of the original difficulty. The development of a vicious circle of performance fear and failure is particularly evident when related to the maintenance of control over physiological processes. A particularly useful review of this subject, and the therapeutic procedure known as paradoxical intention which has been forwarded to counter performance anxiety, is provided by Ascher (1980). The reader is referred also to Chapter 7 where cognitive treatments for insomniacs are discussed in detail.

A recent research study by Coren (1988) provides some evidence that insomniacs are predisposed to become aroused and alert. Coren devised and validated an Arousability Predisposition Scale in an attempt to quantify the probability of an individual reacting adversely to a poor sleep experience. It seems likely that this measure would correlate highly with measures of trait anxiety and perhaps with other measures of psychopathology. The suggestion appears to be that insomniacs have a reactive style in the face of presenting sleep difficulties. Inspection of the data in Table 2 affords further support to this view. Increased agitation at not sleeping, associated effort directly to control sleep, and worry about daytime consequences were regarded as significant elements of the presenting sleep problem for 20–30% of insomniacs in this study (Espie, Brooks and Lindsay, 1989).

The idea, then, going back to Monroe (1967), that insomniacs are characteristically overaroused has developed in more recent years into a prevailing model of mental hyperarousal in preference to physiological hyperarousal. This change in emphasis since the late 1970s has been supported by clinical and experimental study (e.g. Mitchell and White, 1977; Lichstein and Rosenthal, 1980; Gross and Borkovec, 1982) but also associated in more general terms with the ascendancy of cognitive theories and therapies across the spectrum of psychological processes and disorders (e.g. Mahoney, 1974; Beck, 1976; Meichenbaum, 1977). To conclude this section on psychological arousal and insomnia, attention is drawn to the need for further and more rigorous research evaluation. A number of specific points merit closer examination.

Firstly, reinforcement contingencies are not always negative. Thinking, planning and visualising may be intrusive but also may be valued and be enjoyable. Where such positive contingencies operate, preclusion of thinking from bedtime is likely to be more difficult. Secondly, a distinction should be drawn between cognitions which are responsible for delayed sleep-onset and those which are an inevitable result of wakefulness. After all it is hardly feasible to remain awake and maintain a blank mind. Issues of cause and effect have not been explained. Thirdly, the qualitative nature and impact of dysfunctional intrusive thoughts (usually affect-laden) need to be investigated and compared with those apparently incidental thoughts which may be related to simple mental acuity. Finally, the relationship(s) between mental models and cognitive treatments are far from clear. Techniques such as distraction, restructuring, paradox and suppression may be regarded as "cognitive" but each focuses upon a different solution to the mental problem. They represent variants of a psychological model of insomnia. Distraction emphasises *transfer* of thinking to another topic; cognitive restructuring emphasises *rational appraisal* of the thought content; paradox emphasises *enhancement* of the thought content; and thought stopping and articulatory suppression emphasise *blocking* of the thought content. It seems, therefore, that several cognitive models are available and each requires elucidation and evaluation. These issues will be taken up again in Chapter 7 when cognitive treatments are discussed.

ENVIRONMENTAL FACTORS ASSOCIATED WITH AROUSAL AND INSOMNIA

Theoretical models based upon nervous system functioning and psychological functioning imply that arousal and insomnia arise first and foremost *within* the person, whether body or mind or both. The view that insomnia may arise as a response to environmental (situational or temporal) events, or at least be a by-product of the interaction between the sleeper and her environment, merits separate consideration. In Figure 6, therefore, the third "parent" model of insomnia concerns *environmental* influences upon sleep and the sleeper. Within this framework, cues external to the individual are regarded as important mediators of arousal and de-arousal— the insomniac is not regarded as physiologically or cognitively overaroused but as situationally and temporally predisposed to wakefulness.

Although situational and temporal correlates of sleep pattern have in clinical practice been taken together, as part of the package of treatment advice comprising "stimulus control" therapy (see Chapter 8), from a theoretical viewpoint these components require separate consideration. Therefore, sections on situational factors and temporal factors follow. However, in keeping with the tendency for the two themes to be thoroughly interwoven in the relevant literature, the former section will contain the bulk of that literature, and the latter section will be confined to an extraction of the evidence for and against temporal factors.

Situational factors

Bootzin (1972) was the first to present an operant analysis of insomnia. He postulated that falling asleep is an instrumental act emitted to produce reinforcement (i.e. sleep). Stimuli associated with sleep thus become discriminative stimuli for the occurrence of that reinforcement. Difficulty in falling asleep, he suggested, may be the result of either failure to establish discriminative stimuli for sleep or the presence of stimuli which are discriminative of sleep-incompatible behaviour. Examples of appropriate discriminative stimuli for the occurrence of sleep are getting into bed, putting the light off and lying down to sleep. Examples of sleep-incompatible activities are reading, watching TV and mental problem-solving.

Bootzin conducted a number of treatment outcome studies on his stimulus control procedures (see Bootzin and Nicassio (1978) and Chapter 8 for review) which provided strong support for their effectiveness in markedly reducing sleep latency by 50–80% from pre-treatment values. However, in spite of continuing support over the past 10 years for the clinical effectiveness of stimulus control (Turner and Ascher, 1979a; Lacks et al, 1983a,b) including from our own research work (Espie, Brooks and Lindsay, 1989; Espie et al, 1989), there remains some uncertainty concerning the mechanism(s) by which stimulus control procedures achieve their effects.

Haynes et al (1982) have pointed out that such treatment outcome studies are not sufficient for validation of a construct such as stimulus control since alternative explanations for observed therapeutic effects cannot be excluded. In their own exploration of the stimulus control paradigm, Haynes et al compared insomniac and non-insomniac samples on self-reported sleep-incompatible behaviours. Interestingly, they found that only one out of 12 behaviours (listening to music) significantly differentiated between insomniac and non-insomniac groups and duration of sleep-incompatible behaviour was not found to be significantly related to measures of sleep-onset latency. These results confirmed some of their earlier work where no significant relationships had been observed between self-reported number of sleep-incompatible behaviours in the bed and bedroom and sleep-onset latencies or sleep difficulties (Haynes, Follingstad and McGowan, 1974). Haynes et al did concede, however, that theirs was not a clinical sample of insomniacs (students; mean age 23 years) and that generalisation to older adult, physician-referred groups could not be assumed. Nevertheless, the similarity in pre-sleep behaviour between good and poor sleepers does raise problems for the situational factors model.

Reference to the Sleep Disturbance Questionnaire data indicates that 34% of our clinic-presenting sample often read or watched TV in bed (Table 2). These individuals appeared to be continuing such bedtime "bad habits" at times when they felt they ought to have been asleep. There is evidence here, therefore, that at least in a proportion of clinical cases, poor stimulus control over sleep is maintained. Greater numbers of respondents, however, complained of lacking a proper sleep routine (51%), which may be attributable to either situational or temporal factors or both, and one-third or the group was simply not tired at bedtime, i.e. temporal arousal.

Two studies have attempted component analyses of stimulus control treatment. Tokarz and Lawrence (1974) separated the stimulus control components (those instructions focusing upon making the bed and bedroom more discriminative for sleep) from the temporal control components (regularising the sleeping pattern). They found that both sets of procedures equally and significantly reduced self-reported sleep latencies in their student sample. Zwart and Lisman (1979) conducted a more comprehensive study of 47 undergraduate subjects who were assigned to either stimulus control (all instructions), temporal control (lie down to sleep only when sleepy, rise at the same time every day, do not nap in the daytime), non-contingent control (a fixed number of arisings within 20 minutes of retiring), countercontrol (sit up in bed, read, watch TV, etc. if unable to sleep) and no treatment. Zwart and Lisman reported that the countercontrol strategy was as effective as the complete set of stimulus control instructions. One explanation which they proposed for the surprising effectiveness of the countercontrol procedure was that it ensured contingent disruption of bed and bedtime as cues for mental arousal. This preclusion of arousing cognitive events from the bedroom and immediate pre-sleep period finds some support also from a study by Turner and Ascher (1979b). These workers reported that subjects in their study found that stimulus control instructions served to "break up lying in bed and thinking behaviour". The countercontrol procedure then may act as a distraction technique by purposefully occupying the pre-sleep period for the insomniac. It is noteworthy that there may be parallels here also with paradoxical methods of treatment where attention is deliberately focused away from attempts to fall asleep (Ascher, 1980).

To summarise, therefore, evidence for situationally based arousal in the aetiology of insomnia is at best equivocal. Other explanations can be forwarded to account for the efficacy of stimulus control techniques. Indeed, Lacks (1987), who has based a treatment handbook upon the stimulus control principle, accepts that conditioned arousal at bedtime may be a maintaining factor of insomnia once the original causes of sleep difficulty, such as stress or illness, have abated. It is also evident from the research reports reviewed above that operant factors in insomnia have yet to be examined adequately amongst clinically presenting cases of chronic insomnia.

Some insomniacs do report an aversion to bed, comprising mounting anticipatory arousal and avoidance of going to bed even when tired. This may not seem surprising given that the sleep experience of many poor sleepers is unpleasant and frustrating. The relationship between situational stimuli and emotional responding merits further research study and there is the possibility that desensitisation to the bedroom environment may be an effective component of treatments for some individuals (see Chapter 6 for early studies employing desensitisation methods). We have also highlighted the relationship between "cognitive control" and stimulus control strategies in a short clinical report (Espie and Lindsay, 1987). It seems probable that sleep-incompatible cognitions occurring in bed, which bridge both psychological and situational arousal models, represent the most fruitful line for further enquiry.

Temporal factors

Lacks (1987) has commented that temporal factors "do not really fit with an operant paradigm, ... (nevertheless) the establishment of a regular

sleep schedule is also included in Bootzin's stimulus control methods".
It is important, therefore, to distinguish between stimulus control as a
behavioural construct with technical meaning and the same term more
loosely applied to describe a set of clinical procedures. The component
study of Zwart and Lisman outlined above is clearly valuable from this
conceptual point of view. The separate consideration in this chapter of
situational and temporal aspects of the environment appears then to be
justified. It may be helpful at this point to present a summary analysis of
these factors (Table 3).

Table 3   A comparison of situational and temporal factors associated with sleep
and the sleep environment

Situational influences upon sleep	Temporal influences upon sleep
(1) Being in bed with the light off	(1) Synchronising retiring to bed with "tiredness"
(2) Having a comfortable bed and a bedroom environment conducive to sleep	(2) Establishing a set time for waking and rising each day
(3) Avoiding sleep-incompatible activities in the bedroom	(3) Avoiding naps outwith the sleep period
(4) Rising from bed if wakeful and leaving bedroom	

A temporal model finds support in evidence to suggest that insomniacs
are not always sleepy upon retiring to bed, or at least are not optimally so.
Bootzin's first client treated with stimulus control therapy may be a typical
example. "His sleep pattern prior to treatment was to try to fall asleep at
about midnight, but to be unable to sleep until 3.00 and sometimes 4.00
o'clock in the morning" (Bootzin, 1972; Bootzin and Nicassio, 1978). One of
the obvious explanations of such sleep inefficiency is that too much time is
being spent in bed, rather than quantity of sleep per se being insufficient
(Dement, Seidel and Carskadon, 1984). Such individuals may try to go to
sleep too early, irrespective of sleep readiness. Responses to Item 7 of the
Sleep Disturbance Questionnaire (Table 2) are enlightening in this regard.
Only one in three of our insomniacs was reliably tired at the time of retiring
to bed and as many as 15% were habitually going to bed at times when
they were not tired.

Retiring to bed, therefore, may be triggered by factors such as faulty
habit or convention, absence of purposeful waking activity, and anxiety
to reinstate sleep loss from previous nights. Synchronising retiring with
biological preparedness may be the appropriate treatment here. Indeed,
Zwart and Lisman (1979) found temporal control instructions to be an

effective and sufficient treatment for insomnia, particularly after a positive demand expectation was generated. These improvements, achieved by means of temporal control instructions alone, parallel those of Tokarz and Lawrence (1974) and suggest that stimulus control therapy may function via improved harmonisation of the individual's circadian cycle rather than through reconditioning of responses to the environment.

The reader is referred back to evidence presented in Chapter 2 of considerable night to night variability within the sleep pattern of the insomniac. The temporal arousal model accommodates this view in stressing the need for a consistent sleep rhythm to develop which harmonises as part of the individual's 24-hour sleep–wake schedule. Anchoring waking time, and rising very shortly thereafter, ensures that the sleep period becomes predictable across nights. Furthermore this instruction along with the ban on daytime naps ensures that recovery sleep cannot be obtained outwith the optimal sleep period (Table 3). It is known that afternoon and early evening naps are associated with greater nighttime sleep latency and with significant reduction in stage 4 sleep during the night (Karacan et al, 1970; Lichstein and Fischer, 1985). Afternoon naps and "sleeping in" can also lead to partial reversal of the sleep and wake cycle (Kamgar-Parsi, Wehr and Gillin, 1983).

OVERVIEW OF AROUSAL MODELS

This chapter has presented an outline of three principal models of chronic insomnia, namely nervous system arousal, psychological arousal and environmentally based arousal. Each of these "parent" models was seen to subsume two second-level models. Each of these received full description and discussion.

A problem which arises in reviewing the literature in these areas is that most studies have addressed themselves to the task of identifying commonalities amongst insomniacs, that is, the pursuit of evidence for or against a single model. Since supportive evidence is available for each of the six models presented, and in some cases the evidence appears fairly robust, it would seem reasonable to conclude that more than one model may apply. This in turn suggests that attention needs to be paid to the dissimilarities amongst presenting insomniacs, recognising the probability that insomnia may arise for differing reasons across any random sample of insomniacs. Indeed there may be validity in more than one model for any given individual. Furthermore, a model which is valid in accounting for the development of insomnia may not explain the maintenance of that insomnia, and vice versa.

If one has to select a single model, then the cognitive arousal model would appear to be most favoured at the time of writing. In assessing and treating the presenting insomniac at the clinic, however, such a generalisation may be of limited practical value. In fact, it could be positively misleading. Rather, it would be fruitful for the practitioner to regard the assessment phase as a period of hypothesis-testing. Formulation of the insomniac's sleep problems should then predict treatment and hopefully maximise treatment benefit. The assessment of insomnia is described in the next chapter.

Chapter 4

The Assessment of Insomnia

The preceding chapters have made it clear that insomnia is not a simple clinical condition. Its presentation can be multifaceted; its parameters can be difficult to define; its aetiology can be complex; and in all these aspects there is considerable individual variability. Nevertheless, it is important now to consider how it is that insomnia can be assessed by the clinician. Given the above statements this may seem a daunting task. However, the assumption is made in this chapter, in keeping with what is typical in clinical practice, that the clinician in question is not a sleep specialist.

This chapter is designed to lead the clinician through an assessment protocol which is comprehensive yet at the same time has the facility to identify and pursue those aspects of a problem which are of critical importance for the given individual. Assessment should be concerned not only with producing accurate and reliably descriptive information, but also with achieving a formulation of the individual's sleep problem which predicts the form of intervention to be applied. It is only in this way that successful treatment can be promoted. Assessment, formulation and prediction must be intimately related to the selection of treatment goals and treatment strategies. The importance of this point cannot be overstressed. These matters will be addressed in some detail at a later point in the chapter.

Table 4 provides an overview of the content of this chapter. The clinical assessment of insomnia encompasses three dimensions. Firstly, there is need for what can be termed a "general assessment". This enables the clinician to place the sleep problem within the context of personal health and general functioning, both currently and historically. There follows, secondly, more *specific assessment* of sleep per se, of the individual's experience of sleep, and of associated daytime effects. Thirdly, and importantly, there is *predictive assessment* with the emphasis upon hypothesis-testing and designing effective intervention. These three areas will be considered in turn.

Table 4   Overview of assessment areas
providing the broad structure for content
of Chapter 4

GENERAL ASSESSMENT
History
Present State

SPECIFIC ASSESSMENT OF SLEEP
Sleep Pattern
Sleep Quality
Daytime Functioning

PREDICTIVE ASSESSMENT
Eliciting Treatment Goals
Appraising Treatment Goals
Agreeing Treatment Goals
Achieving Treatment Goals

GENERAL ASSESSMENT

Historical information

Background information should be gathered in the areas outlined in
Table 5. The three principal sources of this information are a detailed clinic
interview, examination of relevant health records, and discussion of such
case material with any clinicians who have more detailed knowledge of
the information to be obtained. It should be possible to collect the above
information comfortably within the context of an initial interview of no
more than 60 minutes. Indeed, in practice, it is usually possible to collate

Table 5   General assessment of insomnia: Part 1—collating historical
information

HISTORICAL INFORMATION
HISTORY OF SLEEP PATTERN
HISTORY OF SLEEP COMPLAINT(S)
MEDICAL HISTORY
HISTORY OF PSYCHOLOGICAL FUNCTIONING/PSYCHIATRIC ILLNESS
TREATMENT HISTORY—DRUG and OTHER
Sources: Interview
          Examination of case records
          Discussion with other clinicians involved

---

both historical and present state information within the intake interview and to review any necessary medical information at around the same time if that has not been completed beforehand. It is not necessary here to provide specific instruction on how to take a routine clinical history. The skills are similar across disciplines and the reader is referred to any major text book on the practice of physical medicine, psychiatry or clinical psychology. Readers requiring more specific guidance are referred to the protocol prepared by Lacks (1987) (Tables 5.1 to 5.4).

History of sleep pattern

It is useful to build up a picture of how an individual's sleep pattern has presented and developed over time, of how the pattern has withstood (or otherwise) times of change and pressure, and of the individual's perspective on sleep and herself as a good/bad/indifferent sleeper over time. Most insomniacs can report an approximate duration for their sleep problem. It is important, therefore, to elicit critical comparisons of sleep prior to and subsequent to that "pathological" change and to record any attributions and/or explanations which the insomniac can offer.

History of sleep complaint(s)

Logically, this is the next stage of the history taking. Periods of better and poorer sleep should be identified and consideration given to how the sleep complaint may differ now from previous episodes (if any) of help-seeking. Care should be taken to elicit information on the patient's concern over sleep loss and sleep adequacy and of the practical intrusiveness of the problem over time, as well as gathering quantitative data.

Medical history

The reader is referred here to the section in Chapter 1 on DIMS—Insomnia Associated with Medical Conditions (p. 19). A wide variety of disorders may affect sleep either directly, or indirectly through the production of pain or discomfort. The association of sleep problems with the presence of any such conditions in the patient's medical history should be noted and medical opinion should be sought as appropriate.

History of psychological functioning

The individual should be asked about any episodes of formal psychiatric illness or of treatment for mental health problems. In particular, episodes of depression may have presented, some of which may never have been reported to a family physician. A history of psychological functioning should also take account of levels of anxiety (both state and trait), panic disorder, and fluctuations in sleep patterns in relation to normal peaks in anxiety levels, e.g. examinations, pressure at work. Independent information should be sought from medical and other practitioners who may have been involved.

Treatment history

This is quite straightforward. All relevant prescribed medications and their pattern of usage should be noted. Case note records from the patient's family practitioner should be consulted whenever possible. Alternative medicines, treatments and self-help approaches which have been used should also be covered in the interview. Over-the-counter hypnotic preparations may have been used and, of course, alcohol which is the most widely self-prescribed hypnotic of all.

The patient's perceptions of the usefulness of these various approaches to treatment is important. Sometimes patients will use medicines in combinations which were not prescribed, and it is common for patients to retain supplies of old prescription medications for use on an ad hoc basis. For these reasons, it is not sufficient to derive information on drug-taking from clinical records alone.

In addition to these formal treatments, insomniacs invariably try out various behavioural, cognitive or environmental solutions to their sleep problem. It is enlightening, therefore, to enquire what has already been tried, for how long, and how it helped. Common examples of these are buying an orthopaedic mattress, staying up late before going to bed, trying to think pleasant thoughts, changing eating habits and taking more exercise.

Present State Information

Table 6 summarises the range of information to be included in the assessment of present functioning.

General health

The comments made above in connection with past medical history are relevant to the assessment of present health status and need not be reiterated. The value of a thorough medical examination, however, should not be underestimated. There is good evidence that a normal physical examination and prudent questioning is adequate for differential diagnosis

Table 6   General assessment of insomnia: Part 2—present state
information

PRESENT STATE INFORMATION
GENERAL HEALTH
CURRENT PSYCHOLOGICAL FUNCTIONING
PRESENT TREATMENT(S)
Sources: Interview of patient
　　　　　Examination of case records
　　　　　Discussion with other clinicians involved
　　　　　Medical examination
　　　　　Questionnaire/rating scale assessments

---

amongst various sub-types of insomnia. Guilleminault and Dement (1977)
reported that 85% of cases of narcolepsy, sleep apnea, nocturnal myoclonus
and restless legs syndrome were diagnosable via a physician's normal
physical examination. Given the probable rarity of these specific disorders,
at least when compared with insomnia, it seems likely that this would result
in less than two sleep-disordered patients per 100 being wrongly classified.
Other workers have also supported this view (Coates and Thoresen, 1980).

Furthermore, there has developed in recent years a reaction to what
some believe to have been an over-emphasis on physiological factors in
sleep laboratory studies of insomnia. For example, Kales and Kales (1984)
quoted from a pertinent editorial that "it is time to re-assess the value of
clinical judgement. It is time for the pendulum to swing the other way,
not only because of economic pressure but because of another lost art—
common sense" (Scott, 1979). Kales and Kales go on to say that the general
practitioner in the context of the office setting is best able to assess all aspects
of the patient's functioning in order to balance all of the contributory factors
towards an understanding of the patient's problems. Similarly, Oswald
(1981) concluded that the GP is the best person to diagnose and manage
most sleep disorders.

The reader is again referred to those sections of Chapter 1 which
describe insomnia problems associated with medical and/or physiological
disturbance where sufficient information is provided to enable the clinician
to construct a checklist of symptoms for application during the medical
consultation. For example, the checklist for sleep apnea would comprise
intermittent awakening, loud snoring, shortness of breath and abrupt
restoration of normal breathing. Episodes of the foregoing would occur
regularly across the night (interviewing the bed partner is often helpful
in establishing diagnosis). Daytime symptoms may include excessive
sleepiness, and morning headaches, and the subject may be overweight.

Current psychological functioning

Consideration of symptoms commonly found in anxiety and depressive disorders is an important element of the assessment of psychological functioning. Elevated levels of such symptomatology have been frequently reported in both research and clinical studies (see Chapter 2 pp. 29–31). It is noteworthy, however, that symptoms of depression may present in the absence of a formally diagnosable depressive illness. The reader is referred to the section on insomnia associated with psychiatric conditions in Chapter 1 (pp. 21–22) at this point. A wide range of rating scale and questionnaire instruments is available to measure anxiety and depressive symptoms. The following guidelines will help the clinician to decide which assessments are of greatest value for a particular clinical or research purpose.

The clinician is well advised to select an assessment device with which he is familiar. Although psychometric properties such as reliability and validity are of great importance, all widely used assessment procedures have both strengths and weaknesses. It is the practitioner's familiarity with a particular measure, and his knowledge of its strengths and limitations within a particular reference group, which ensure best use is made of the information distilled. The aim should be to achieve a congruent and conservative approach to assessment which balances clinical judgement with the "independent" assessment afforded by the selected scale. It seems reasonable to regard a clinical judgement as an hypothesis to be tested by the application of such a measure; and conversely an hypothesis raised via a pattern of rating scale scores should be tested out by prudent interviewing.

For the purposes of screening for significant psychological symptomatology, the General Health Questionnaire (GHQ) (Goldberg, 1978) and the Hospital Anxiety and Depression Scale (HADS) (Zigmond and Snaith, 1983) are amongst the most useful. Both have gained considerable popularity in the research literature and provide useful cut-off points determining the presence or absence of significant psychological morbidity. One disadvantage of the GHQ is its over-emphasis upon severe depression, which creates a rather all or nothing response to this factor. The HADS permits separate assessment of anxiety and depressive symptomatology against cut-off criteria. A further strength is the exclusion of somatic symptoms since these often confound assessment, particularly in medical populations and amongst the elderly.

Useful measures of generalised anxiety include the Taylor Manifest Anxiety Scale (TMAS) (Taylor, 1953), the State–Trait Anxiety Inventory (STAI) (Spielberger, Gorsuch and Lushene, 1970) and the Zung Anxiety

Scale (ZAS) (Zung, 1971). The TMAS is clinically sensitive; however, it is scored only on a true/false basis rather than the more discriminating Likert scaling of the other instruments. The ZAS has been used widely in research and clinical practice and has the advantage of providing a brief (20 item) assessment covering largely somatic and affective symptomatolgy. Its validity and reliability appear to be reasonably attested. The STAI, as its name implies, provides comparative scores on state and trait anxiety which can prove helpful in considering the insomniac's present and habitual mode of responding. Those aspects of anxiety response which may be regarded as stable and enduring aspects of personality may also be picked up by the MMPI.

The range of assessment measures for depression is also wide. Similar to the ZAS, the Zung Depression Scale (ZDS) is well established, also comprising 20 items rated on a four-point scale (Zung, 1965). The identical scaling properties of the two Zung Scales can ease administration and may form a useful assessment package. The ZDS represents an early attempt to provide quantification of depressive state and it has been found to be sensitive enough to mood change to be useful as a treatment outcome measure. The ZDS, in fact, has been preferred to other scales, notably the Beck Depression Inventory (BDI) (Beck et al, 1961) and the MMPI Depression Scale (Hathaway and McKinlay, 1942). Schaefer et al (1983) compared the validities of these three measures in relation to a number of clinical ratings, including psychiatric diagnosis based upon DSM III criteria. The ZDS emerged with the highest validity coefficients (range 0.71 to 0.79), and correlations with DSM III criteria were significantly greater than for either of the other scales ($p < 0.005$ in each case). Such comparisons, however, must be tempered by the recognition that all self-report inventories have limiting features. Indeed, Boyle (1985) has criticised the reliability and validity of seven commonly used self-report measures of depression (including the ZDS). Psychometric adequacy can be claimed by most familiar measures; it is where that adequacy combines with familiarity of use that the most salient clinical information is produced.

Aside from published scales, it is worth noting before leaving the issue of psychological assessment that purpose-made scales also have their place in assessment, particularly as "before and after" treatment measures of symptoms and complaints which are thought to be of clinical significance. For example, where a patient complains of intrusive anxious thoughts, a description of specific thought content, and its frequency and duration, may be more relevant than some general measure of anxiety disorder. There is a place, therefore, for the clinician and the patient to design a relevant assessment of psychological features which are correlated with insomnia. This approach enhances ecological and predictive validity.

Present treatments

Previously employed treatments and self-help methods were mentioned as part of history-taking. The assessment of strategies *presently* in use should be documented also. The clinical implications of pharmacological interventions require particular consideration since the use of both stimulant and hypnotic drugs can lead to tolerance, dependence and poor sleep (Kales et al, 1983b). Patients may have to be stabilised on medication, have it withdrawn or be safeguarded from the potentially deleterious effects of certain drug interactions. The impact upon sleep and upon general aspects of functioning of prescribed drugs, over-the-counter preparations and self-prescribed medications which an individual may be taking should be discussed with a knowledgeable physician. The reader is referred to Chapter 10 for detailed description and discussion of pharmacological treatments. Apart from medication as a formal treatment, most insomniacs will already be following or attempting to follow a self-management programme. This may be the distillation of long experience which suggests that certain routines and behaviours improve sleep, and/or advice from other sources on how to promote sleep. The clinician should establish what self-help measures are being adopted, at an early stage. It may be useful to get the patient to recount a typical night's routines, using prompts such as "...and what happens after that?", so that a detailed picture can be built up. The patient's free recall may be less reliable and less complete.

SPECIFIC ASSESSMENT OF SLEEP

Having considered general aspects of the patient's sleep complaint the next stage of assessment involves more detailed analysis of the sleep pattern per se and of potentially co-varying daytime functions. The crucial elements of assessment are presented in the 3 × 3 matrix of Table 7. Data on sleep pattern, sleep quality and daytime functioning are essential. There are then three *types* of data. The *sources* of these data are also threefold; namely subjective self-report, objective appraisal and informant/observer report.

Table 7 Comparison of utility of self-report, informant report and objective assessment across the three principal areas of sleep assessment

	Self	Informant	Objective
Sleep pattern	✓	?	✓
Sleep quality	✓	X	X
Daytime functioning	✓	?	?

Table 7 attempts to summarise the usefulness of each source of data against each data type. A tick ($\sqrt{}$) represents an "often useful" data source and a cross (x) a "seldom useful" data source. A question mark (?) appears where the data source is "sometimes or partly useful". A brief inspection of the table indicates that self-report measures are consistently supported in this analysis, whereas objective and informant report measures are not. This, of course, reflects the pre-eminence of subjective dissatisfaction with some aspect of sleep as *sine qua non* to referral and treatment.

The structure for the remaining part of this section on specific aspects of sleep assessment follows from the elements in Table 7 and the interaction between these elements. Firstly, each of the data sources will be examined in turn. Strengths and weaknesses in each will be identified. Secondly, there will follow description and discussion of actual assessment measures which may be used for recording each type of data.

Self-report

The two most commonly used self-report measures have been sleep questionnaires and sleep diaries. The sleep questionnaire is particularly useful where a large number of subjects is to be surveyed or screened. An example of this is the early descriptive study by McGhie and Russell (1962) where information was collected on the sleep pattern of many hundreds of subjects. More recently, Buysse et al (1989) have developed the Pittsburgh Sleep Quality Index as a screening instrument for use in clinical surveys. This measure has been found to have good diagnostic sensitivity in discriminating good from poor sleepers and evidences satisfactory test–retest reliability. The principal attraction of the sleep questionnaire is that it is quick, easy and inexpensive to administer. Factor analyses and normative data on sleep questionnaires have been reported (Johns, 1975; Evans, 1977), however, measures of sleep parameters have generally correlated poorly with both sleep diary and objective recordings of sleep pattern (Carskadon et al, 1976; Freedman and Papsdorf, 1976).

There are a number of other limitations to sleep questionnaire data. Estimates are inevitably a retrospective average of the individual's experience. They are not part of a process of ongoing specific monitoring but rather the data are artefactual and global. Reports are also likely to be highly reactive to the individual's mood state at the time of completing the questionnaire and/or to the individual's immediate prior experience of sleep. The respondent's attention may be particularly selective, recalling clearly nights of poor, disrupted sleep, and failing to place this in the context of more normal and acceptable sleep on other nights. Furthermore, the validity of an average figure can be called into question where night to night variability is high. Finally, where the insomniac hopes to receive treatment as a result of such assessment, there is likely to be reporting bias in the direction of exaggerating sleep disruption. In spite of these drawbacks, sleep questionnaires may serve as useful adjuncts to continuous sleep records, and Bootzin and Engle-Friedman (1981), in their review of assessment methods, consider that the sleep questionnaire still has a valuable role.

Most of the influential treatment studies have preferred the sleep diary to the sleep questionnaire. The general use of such daily sleep logs, based upon the work of Monroe (1967), has led Bootzin and Nicassio (1978) to describe these as "the staple of assessment procedures in insomnia treatment outcome research". The sleep log is completed each morning upon wakening and includes variables such as: number of minutes to sleep onset, total time slept (hours and minutes), frequency of intermittent wakenings and proportion of time in bed spent asleep. Qualitative ratings of, for example, "sleep satisfaction" and "restedness" may also be incorporated into the diary. The sleep log, therefore, makes the subject's task more specific and less ambiguous than the questionnaire and diminishes the problem of response bias, although it does so incompletely. Some researchers have required subjects to return diaries each day by mail to counteract the tendency of some retrospectively to complete the logs on the day prior to their next appointment (e.g. Lick and Heffler, 1977; Lacks et al, 1983a). Steinmark and Borkovec (1974) have also developed an experimental design which controls for therapy-induced expectancy effects and demand characteristics, thus improving reliability of self-report. This "counterdemand" manipulation will be described at a later point (Chapter 6, p. 121). Further inaccuracies in reporting via sleep logs may be overcome by means of training procedures which ensure the achievement of certain reporting criteria before the acceptance of data as valid. These training procedures will be described in the section on "the assessment of sleep pattern" which follows shortly.

An investigation by Coates et al has been quoted as evidence for the reliability of sleep log measures (see Bootzin and Engle-Friedman, 1981). These workers obtained an average test–retest correlation for sleep-onset latency of 0.93 for poor sleepers and 0.58 for good sleepers. The comparable test–retest figures for EEG assessment were only 0.70 and 0.58 respectively. Overall sleep log reliabilities were 0.69 and 0.35 while EEG reliabilities were 0.66 and 0.60 for poor and good sleepers. From this work, therefore, it seems reasonable to conclude that the insomniac's sleep diary report has reliability at least comparable to that of EEG assessment. Measures of validity have been equally encouraging. Sleep log estimates have been found to correlate highly with observer estimates of the same night's sleep ($r = 0.84$; Turner and Ascher, 1979a). For further description and discussion on the validity of self-report data the reader is referred back to Chapter 1 (pp. 17–19) when this issue was dealt with at some length.

Apart from reasons of convenience, and independent of attested reliability and validity, there is one other compelling reason for the clinician to utilise self-report data. Such data are simply indispensable given that it is invariably verbal complaint of insomnia which initiates help-seeking. Verbal and written statements, whether in the form of a questionnaire or night by night diary, must be of primary evaluative importance. If this is true of the actual parameters of sleep such as sleep latency and the number of hours slept, it is even more true of the qualitative and attributional aspects of sleep. Reports which are independent of the subject (whether via an observer or via objective monitoring devices) have no contribution to make to the assessment of sleep quality. Sleep quality is entirely "felt", it is experiential not tangible, and it is often central to the clinical complaint. Similarly, although daytime performance conceivably may be measurable (e.g. reaction time tests, selective attention, work output efficiency), it is often the subject's perceptions of daytime performance which mediate concern. Furthermore, variation in mood, particularly negative mood state, is often experienced, but may be only sometimes observed. The sleep log proves to be the most useful self-report format for information on sleep quality.

In summary, self-report data are essential for any adequate assessment of insomnia. The insomniac alone can provide information on all three salient aspects of sleep pattern, sleep experience and sleep effects. It seems reasonable, therefore, to regard self-report as the primary data source, with objective and observer measures as corroborative rather than criterion measures. Sleep diary measures are preferred and are most useful when taken continuously on a night by night basis, and after satisfactory training.

Informant/observer report

A number of workers have made use of nurses' (Erwin and Zung, 1970; Kupfer, Wyatt and Snyder, 1970) and spouses' or room-mates' (Nicassio and Bootzin, 1974; Turner and Ascher, 1979a; Lacks et al, 1983b) observations to provide a measure of sleep pattern independent of the sleeper's self-report. The observer has been asked to attend to criteria such as: subject's eyes closed, absence of voluntary movement, deep respiration and failure to respond to probe questions (e.g. "Are you asleep?"). On the basis of such information the observer has been required to make a decision as to whether the subject was awake or asleep.

In the hospital ward setting, time sampling procedures have been used from which estimates of sleep latency, sleep time and frequency of wakenings have been derived, although data from available studies have produced very different results for the reliability of these observations. Erwin and Zung (1970) consistently obtained reliability coefficients greater than 0.90, whereas Kupfer, Wyatt and Snyder (1970) reported that less than 25% of estimates were "accurately determined" compared with EEG criteria. It should be noted, however, that subjects sampled in the latter study were psychiatric in-patients, many of whom had depressive illnesses, and may not be considered as necessarily similar to primary insomniacs. Furthermore, in the Kupfer et al study almost one-third of the observations themselves precipitated sleep stage changes suggesting that the monitoring process itself may be unacceptably intrusive. A further serious limitation to nurse observation is that subjects need to be hospitalised, which raises the question of whether data gathered in a controlled environment can be taken as a representative sample of insomniac sleep, which typically occurs at home.

Although the involvement of spouses or room-mates as home-based observers overcomes some of these latter difficulties, there remain significant shortcomings to this approach. Such observers are seldom able to provide consistent data unless they too are poor sleepers, or are willing and able deliberately to remain awake and vigilant. For the assessment of moderate to severe insomnia, observer report appears then to be impractical for other than corroborative evidence of self-report data on sleep pattern.

Having recognised that informant report has little to offer in the measurement of actual sleep indices, consideration must be given now to those other types of data which are required for assessment of sleep (Table 7). It is clear that quality of sleep cannot be measured independently of the experience of sleep itself. Observer report on sleep quality, therefore, is not feasible other than through inference based upon observation of daytime performance, alertness, fatigue, mood and so on. Data from an observer of such daytime functions, however, may be of considerable value as more direct evidence of the impact of insomnia over the 24-hour period. This has been a seriously neglected area in research studies and clinical reports to date. The section on the assessment of daytime functioning, which follows later in this chapter (pp. 84–87), provides examples of items and scales which could be completed both by the insomniac and by an independent witness. Care would have to be taken to minimise collaboration in reporting, and from this point of view, intermittent "spot checks" by telephone might give more reliable information than continuously recorded charts. Again it seems inevitable that self-report should form the core data source with verification sought from such independent assessment. Another possibility would be a structured interview assessment with the independent witness at pre- and post-treatment. The interview would provide the clinician with the opportunity to test out the strength and clinical importance of changes in daytime functioning which were reported.

In summary, informant-report has severe limitations and cannot be regarded as a primary data source. It may offer, however, useful corroboration (or otherwise) of sleep itself and of sleep-related information. In particular, the assessment of daytime performance and functioning could be imaginatively and usefully addressed through greater use of observer reports. Clearly, selection and training of appropriate observers will be of paramount importance and efforts must be made to ensure that data derived are criterion-based and are truly independent of self-reported information.

Objective assessment

Undoubtedly the most widely known and the most widely used objective method of sleep evaluation is electroencephalography. However, other objective measuring devices are available and these have appeared in the behavioural literature in recent years. These differing approaches to objective assessment are best dealt with separately.

EEG assessment

Interest in all-night polygraphic recording of sleep was initially aroused by the discovery of neurophysiological changes from wakefulness to sleep (Loomis, Harvey and Hobart, 1937) and the milestone discovery of REM sleep (Aserinsky and Kleitman, 1953). There has emerged comprehensive definition of various sleep stages (Rechtschaffen and Kales, 1968). Over the past 30 years in particular, a vast research literature has developed describing sleep patterns, stages and disorders in terms of the objective definitions of the EEG. Much of this work has been the product of numerous Sleep Disorders Centers set up since the mid-1970s, particularly in the USA. Sassin and Mitler (1987) have provided an interesting and readable account of the historical development of these centers and of the growth of "sleep disorders medicine" in general.

Although the term EEG refers only to electrophysiological recording of brain activity, via standard electrode positions, in practice, EEG is recorded through a polygraph, different channels of which are used also to measure eye movement (EOG) and muscle activity (EMG). Concurrent recording of EEG, EOG and EMG result in polygraphic traces which are output to a printer, and may be visually scored in segments of 20 or 30 seconds. These segments can be assigned to stages of sleep according to the recognised criteria devised by Rechtschaffen and Kales (1968). Objective data are generated, therefore, on the various stages within sleep, and the EEG is uniquely appropriate for detailed descriptive analysis, and for the definitive diagnosis of the less commonly presenting sleep disorders.

There has been some debate over the role of polysomnography in the assessment and management of *chronic insomnia*. Jacobs et al (1988) reported on a review of 123 consecutive patients who had received comprehensive clinical interview evaluations, completed self-report sleep logs and undergone two nights of polysomnographic assessment in the laboratory. Raters independently reviewed each patient's evaluation, in particular to determine whether or not the laboratory findings confirmed the initial clinical impression, refuted it or failed to support it. To summarise their findings Jacobs et al reported that in 49% of cases polysomnography added to, refuted or failed to support the clinical impression. Regestein (1988), however, has disagreed strongly with Jacobs et al's methodology stating that some cases were inappropriately included (e.g. sleep studies of depression) and others exhibited sleep disturbances which were doubtful causes of insomnia. Regestein considers that Jacobs et al may have considerably exaggerated the diagnostic importance of the sleep assessment. Nevertheless, there is some agreement that polysomnography should be applied after careful clinical evaluation and appropriate educative and behavioural treatment have been attempted unsuccessfully, or where there is suspicion, from initial appraisal, of specific disorders such as sleep apnea (Billiard, Besset and Passouant, 1981; Jacobs et al, 1988; Regestein, 1988).

The relationship between self-reported information upon sleep and EEG-derived data was discussed fully in Chapter 1 in the context of the DIMS categories of Psychophysiological and Experiential insomnia (pp. 17–19). The case was made at that point for the relative reliability and validity of sleep log information. It may be helpful for the reader to review that discussion at this point. It is further noteworthy, however, that there are a number of practical and methodological problems associated with the use of EEG assessment.

Firstly, EEG recording is a highly technical procedure and is seldom routinely available to the consulting clinician. Given the high presentation rate of insomnia in general practice, the use of EEG assessment as a treatment outcome measure appears to be out of the question. Even in research studies evaluating psychological and pharmacological treatment, sleep laboratory measures have seldom been taken for more than three consecutive nights within a treatment phase. Furthermore, EEG recording is very expensive, not least in terms of the sheer volume of recorder paper (300 to 700 meters per subject night). Resource costs are also high in terms of operative and support services.

Secondly, during the first night in the sleep laboratory, subjects are known to take longer to fall asleep, to awaken more often and to have more total wake time than on subsequent nights when they are found to have adjusted better to their new sleep environment (Agnew, Webb and Williams, 1967; Rechtschaffen and Verdone, 1964). For this reason, it is now commonplace for an adaptation night to be included routinely in sleep studies in order to obviate such a "first night effect". Although subsequent nights may be less reactive, it should be remembered that a stimulus control hypothesis would predict rather less transitory alterations in the sleep pattern of chronic insomniacs, and the directionality of any change might also vary; that is, sleep pattern might be expected to improve rather than deteriorate. The removal of the subject from the home environment is, therefore, a confounding variable, particularly where it is recognised that the study of insomnia is not simply a biological science but also a social/behavioural science. From this point of view it should be noted also that changes in physical and mental relaxation may also modify the problem under observation. The attachment of numerous electrodes and the novelty of the laboratory environment may occupy the subject's thinking and preclude intrusive worry or produce anxiety in a naive subject who is uncertain of the procedures and their purposes.

Thirdly, a further methodological problem arises where researchers have required subjects to sleep only within the limits of predetermined recording periods. This has been done at times to cater for attempts at between group comparison, and at other times to comply with the workshifts of support staff. Such experimental manipulation is certainly invasive of the sleep process itself on the recording nights, but might also modify the sleep pattern on forthcoming nights by rescheduling wakening time. The rather more flexible "ad lib" design is to be preferred and has the advantage of permitting subjects to remain in bed for as long as they wish.

The development of home polysomnography, where polygraphic data are transmitted over a single telephone line (Coates et al, 1982a), partially overcomes some of the above methodological constraints. Home recording does allow for assessment within the natural environment, but remains expensive and intrusive, and technical failure may result in the loss of considerable amounts of data (Ancoli-Israel et al, 1981). Of course technical advances will continue to reduce such difficulties. For example, ambulatory EEG monitoring systems, which record signals to audiocassette tapes for subsequent decoding, have now been adapted successfully for sleep assessment and sleep stage analysis.

In summary, therefore, EEG assessment offers extremely valuable diagnostic and descriptive information. Where facilities are available they should be utilised. However, EEG assessment is not indispensable in the routine assessment and treatment of primary insomnia. It does not reliably predict complaints about sleep pattern and offers nothing to the assessment of sleep quality. EEG assessment will continue to play an important role in research studies but it is not feasible to include polygraphic assessment as part of routine clinical practice.

Other recording devices

Behavioural scientists also have recognised the value of obtaining independent objective evidence of sleep pattern, and this has led to the presentation in the research literature of a number of recording devices. Most of these are based upon the premise that the sleeper's response to external stimuli will reduce as arousal reduces and as sleep deepens. That is, awakening threshold increases and greater intensity stimulation is required to produce arousal. The detection (or not) of a cue stimulus, therefore, should reveal the presence or absence of sleep. For the purposes of assessment, of course, it is important that the selected cue is perceptible, but not intrusive.

One of the most useful devices currently available, and for which there is most support in the research literature, is the "Somtrak" Sleep Assessment Device (SAD). This is the objective measure which we have employed in our own research work. The SAD was introduced in a research paper by Kelley and Lichstein (1980). It generates a brief, soft tone at pre-set intervals throughout the night and tape records verbal responses to these cues. The tone generator is linked to a cassette recorder for this purpose. If the subject is awake, the tone will be heard and the criterion response of "I am awake" is recorded. Conversely, if no response is recorded the interpretation is made that the subject was sleeping. Volume and pitch of the tone can be adjusted for the individual to ensure that it is perceptible while awake but not intrusive upon sleep. The usual inter-tone interval of 10 minutes is not sufficiently frequent to render it soporific or to cause habituation (Lichstein et al, 1983), and comparisons with EEG recordings have demonstrated levels of agreement greater than 90%, with no significant differences in measures of sleep latency, total sleep time and sleep efficiency (Lichstein et al, 1982). The measurement of intermittent awakening, however, has proven less valid (Lichstein et al, 1982; Espie, Lindsay and Espie, 1989). This is because the time sampling procedure utilised by the SAD inevitably forfeits data. The reader is referred back to Table 1 and its associated text (Chapter 1, p. 20) where some of our own research results using the SAD were presented.

In a review paper, Lichstein and Kelley (1979) helpfully identify the most important criteria against which to evaluate an objective assessment method. These criteria are (a) portable to the natural environment, (b) self-administered, (c) non-intrusive, (d) relatively inexpensive and (e) very accurate. Apart from the SAD other behavioural devices have been reported in the literature which meet some of these criteria. Webster et al (1982) used an activity-based system which monitored wrist movements. Ogilvie and Wilkinson (1988), in an experimental study, programmed a computer to generate faint tones and to record subjects' reaction time responses (and the absence of responses) across the night. Behavioural responses were made by pressing a miniswitch sewn into a squash ball and attached by a strap to the sleeper's palm. Morin has made use of a similar device, devised by Franklin (1981) in a treatment outcome study (Morin and Azrin, 1988). Franklin's device comprises a switch-activated clock where the sleeper sustains thumb pressure upon a lever. This pressure is relaxed upon sleep-onset and the clock is automatically de-activated. Morin and Schoen (1986) reported an 86% agreement coefficient between this device and EEG defined sleep-onset. Holborn, Hiebert and Bell (1987) have used a similar mechanical device but with computer interfacing which enables continuous assessment of sleep.

The assessment of sleep pattern

Having considered the merits of the three potential data *sources* (patient, informant, objective measure) the remaining elements of the matrix in Table 7 now require detailed consideration. These are the three *types* of data to be gathered as part of a comprehensive sleep assessment: data on sleep pattern, sleep quality and daytime functioning. First of all the assessment of sleep pattern will be considered and comprises three sub-sections. Firstly, the daily sleep log itself will be described; secondly, training procedures to improve its application will be introduced; and thirdly, advice will be presented on the interpretation of data derived from sleep log assessments.

The daily sleep log

The great majority of psychological treatment studies have relied largely or exclusively upon sleep log reports of sleep pattern. The sleep log is a self-report measure completed upon rising as a summary record of sleep parameters from the preceding night's sleep. Various versions of the daily sleep log are available having the same or similar item content. The information to be recorded upon a daily sleep log is summarised in Table 8.

Sleep-onset latency (SOL) is the length of time which the subject takes to fall asleep after retiring to bed. For most subjects the time at which the bedroom light is switched off signals intention to fall asleep and represents the best starting point for calculation. Depending on the individual's routine, it may be useful to take into account the period of time between retiring to bed and putting the light out, particularly when a stimulus control formulation is under consideration. Subjects should be required to

Table 8 Item content for a daily sleep log

Item	Comment
Sleep-onset latency (SOL; min.)	To nearest 5 minutes
Total sleep time (hr/min.)	To nearest 15 minutes
Frequency of awakenings	Total across night
Return to sleep time (min.)	To nearest 5 minutes
Wake time after sleep-onset (WASO; min.)	To nearest 5 minutes
	Total across night
Bedtime	Retiring and lights out
Waking time	Final awakening
Rising time	If different from above
Nap time (hr/min.)	Outside of sleep period
Sleep efficiency(%)	Calculated as: $\dfrac{\text{total sleep time}}{\text{total time in bed}} \times 100$

estimate SOL to within five minutes in order to obtain accurate data. If this is not stressed subjects will tend to approximate and to be less careful in their retrospective judgements.

Total sleep time is the quantity of sleep obtained across the night, adding together time slept between awakenings (if these occur). Sleep duration should be estimated to the nearest quarter hour. In addition to a measure of total duration, more detailed analysis of episodes of sleep across the night may be useful. For example, subjects commonly report they sleep best during the first third of the night. The sleep log, therefore, may be adapted in order to provide the information which is most salient for the individual case. Another measure of sleep duration which may be used is a report of the longest period of continuous sleep on a given night since this often seems to be related to the subjective experience of having had a "good" or "deep" sleep.

The recording of awakening frequency is less straightforward than sleep latency and sleep duration. This is because the definition of an awakening can be imprecise and/or the individual may be unable to discern discrete awakenings within a period of restless sleep. Knab and Engel (1988) compared perceptions of waking and sleeping in 14 insomniacs compared with matched control subjects. These workers found that many arousals not perceived occurred during the first REM–NREM cycle. Insomniacs also had difficulty detecting arousals which occurred outwith periods of consolidated sleep: that is, they tended to perceive continuous wakefulness compared with controls who tended not to perceive wakefulness at all. Subjects, therefore, will often report that sleep was disjointed or that they were "tossing and turning". Nevertheless, an estimate of the total number of awakenings provides an index of the degree to which sleep is interrupted. Supplementary items may be included on the sleep log. For example, a question such as "How many of these awakenings were longer than 10 minutes?" aids the identification of intrusive arousals. The time taken to return to sleep may be measured where there is a regular pattern of intrusive arousals. This amounts to a supplementary measure of sleep latency.

It is often helpful to associate items on quantitiative aspects of intermittent sleep disturbance with qualitative ratings of items such as "restlessness during the night" (see pp. 80–84). A measure of wake time after sleep onset (WASO) has become increasingly popular in the more recent treatment outcome studies. This may offer an alternative approach to the assessment of intermittent wakefulness, particularly where the overall quantity of sleep intrusion is an important component of complaint rather than discrete episodes of wakefulness per se. WASO should also be recorded accurately to the nearest five minutes.

The foregoing items comprise the most commonly recorded aspects of sleep pattern for the monitoring of treatment process and the evaluation of treatment outcome. A further assessment measure, however, is recommended; namely sleep efficiency. As the term suggests, sleep efficiency represents the proportion of time in bed which the subject spends asleep, expressed as a percentage. Sleep efficiency per se would not be included as an item in the daily sleep log but should be calculated by the clinician on the basis of information on the parameters of sleep which the subject has reported. From Table 8 it can be seen that reports of bedtime, waking time and rising time should be included in the sleep log. The denominator of the sleep efficiency equation (i.e. total time in bed) is calculated by subtracting rising time from bedtime. (The separate inclusion of waking time can be helpful to identify occasions when the subject lies on in bed resting but not sleeping.)

Finally, the sleep log should include a measure of daytime napping. At the simplest level this may be a single total of time spent asleep outside of the designated sleep period. This could be napping during the daytime and/or evening. As before, depending upon the presenting routine of the individual, more detailed reporting of nap periods may be important.

The author stresses the importance of tailoring the assessment of sleep pattern in order to quantify those aspects of sleep pattern which are most descriptive of the sleep problem from the individual's perspective.

Training procedures

It is not adequate simply to provide the subject with a sleep log and hope that she will complete it accurately. It has been our experience that time must be spent going through the sleep log item by item with the subject *and* in providing a one week practice opportunity for the insomniac prior to accepting baseline sleep pattern data. This first week provides the clinician with the opportunity to examine the early reports of the subject on the sleep log and to further the training process until certain criteria of recording are achieved (cf. Table 8). In this way the subject also has opportunity to discuss any problems which have arisen during monitoring. Table 9 summarises the elements of the tailoring and review process.

Table 9   Components of the Daily Sleep Log Training Procedure

---

Explanation of purpose of sleep log recording
Discussion of item content and detailing same
Discussion of recording criteria and recording procedure
One week home practice then review

Checklist for review: All items completed
                       Accuracy criteria achieved
                       Within night consistency achieved
                       Inspection for "tell tales"

The clinician must be prepared to take time to explain the importance of sleep log recording to the patient. It is worth emphasising that the sleep log will provide initial information on sleep pattern which cannot be obtained at interview and that it will help to identify exactly where the sleep pattern problems lie. This is likely to lead to more effective treatment. The patient should know that the sleep log records will be used to evaluate changes which occur as a result of treatment. A sample, completed sleep log can be helpful to show the insomniac what is required and to illustrate the type of information which will be derived.

At the feedback/review appointment the clinician must inspect the completed sleep log in some detail and be prepared to probe question the subject. Quite apart from the importance of obtaining accurate data on which to base a treatment intervention, issues of credibility arise when insufficient time is spent at the training stage. This can easily be illustrated. If a patient has hurriedly, or belatedly, or in other respects unsatisfactorily, completed the daily sleep log then she will be conscious of the limitations of the data which are presented to the clinician. The demand characteristics operating in the consulting room, however, are likely to lead the patient to report compliance in self-monitoring. If the clinician then accepts the data uncritically and uses these data as the basis for a formulation of the sleep difficulty, the insomniac can be caught in the invidious position of being unsure about the validity of the formulation and any treatment offered resultant from that formulation but unable to comment otherwise. At all times, therefore, it should be emphasised that the training procedures are permissive of misunderstandings and errors. Indeed, expectations should be set up that at the review appointment it will be necessary to iron out teething problems which will undoubtedly have arisen.

The elements of the review procedure are noted in Table 9. Firstly, the clinician should check for gaps in the sleep log against any of the items, and clarify which items were easier to complete and those which were more difficult. Discussion can then follow to improve reporting of the latter. Secondly, completion of each item should be checked against the accuracy criteria which were outlined in Table 8 and which would have been explained to the subject prior to the practice week. Some subjects may find the accuracy criteria difficult to achieve. However, the clinician should remember that the issue of relative accuracy across nights and across treatment phases may be as important as absolute accuracy. In any event, having strict accuracy criteria only highlights to the subject the value which the clinician places upon the information in the log and is likely to maximise reporting accuracy and credibility. Thirdly, the clinician should check the consistency of the data which are recorded within each night. In other words, the various measures of sleep pattern should approximately tally when considered arithmetically. Data for a subject night are complementary. Lastly, the clinician should look for certain "tell-tale" signs which may indicate inaccuracy in self-reporting. For example, forms which are returned in pristine condition, which are unfolded, and have been completed with uniform neatness using the same pen may have been completed retrospectively prior to the appointment. Usually such logs will evidence an unlikely level of consistency in sleep pattern across nights and/or a tendency to round off data too generously in comparison with the accuracy criteria. Probe questions should be employed to check with the subject that forms were completed at the agreed time, soon after rising, and it can be helpful to identify an exact time with the subject which can then be fitted into the morning routine.

The importance of adequate training in the use of sleep logs is underlined by our own experience. We have found that data recorded during the first (training) week after a sleep log is issued are unsatisfactory in as many as 40% of cases (Espie et al, 1989). The feedback/review appointment, however, has proven invaluable since it does prove satisfactorily corrective for the vast majority of cases. Some research workers have required subjects to return sleep logs immediately by mail to ensure that retrospective guesswork does not become a problem. This appears to be a useful research strategy but may be less practical in clinical settings. Regular contact with patients in the early stages of assessment and therapy can provide weekly returns and in most cases this proves adequate.

Interpretation of scores

Once data considered to be reasonably reliable are being presented the next task facing the clinician is that of data interpretation. Until recently every treatment outcome study utilising sleep logs assessed treatment benefit by comparison of *mean scores* either before and after intervention, or across the phases of treatment. In our own work, however, we have stressed the importance also of considering alternative summary descriptive statistics as outcome measures. There is good reason for doing so given the role which variability in sleep pattern may play in the complaint of insomnia. Both the summary description of a problem and the analysis of change may be incomplete where a mean value alone is taken as a representative statistic descriptive of "typical" sleep pattern. For example, an average SOL of 60 minutes for a given patient suggests that this individual takes around one hour to fall asleep per night. Raw score *variance*, that is night to night variability in SOL, however, is likely to be considerable (see Chapter 2). On occasions the patient will fall asleep quickly; at other times SOL may be very lengthy. It is often this unpredictability of sleep which is of concern to the insomniac. It seems then that a measure of range or standard deviation would be useful as an index of variability which permits consideration of potentially important clinical change. The reader is referred to Espie et al (1989) for further information. The recognition that a measure of variance may be important is, however, just one aspect of a wider issue: that is, how can the clinician effectively measure *clinical change*?

There has developed in recent years (since Bergin and Strupp, 1972) a considerable literature reflecting the concern of some practitioners that strictly "scientific" analyses fail to tackle material of clinical importance. As Barlow (1981) has put it, "at present clinical research has little or no influence on clinical practice". Jacobsen, Follette and Revenstorf (1984) in reviewing the question of statistical versus clinical significance, have made two major criticisms of psychotherapy outcome data reporting. Firstly, they comment that statistical comparisons between experimental conditions are generally based on average improvement scores which provide no information on therapy changes for individuals; and secondly, that "significance tests" impose criteria for determining treatment effects which often have unestablished clinical relevance. Hence studies may over-estimate or under-estimate the clinical significance of the results obtained. Kazdin (1977) has argued that a change in therapy is clinically significant when the patient moves from the dysfunctional to the functional range on whatever variable is used to quantify the clinical problem. With such a "distributional" model it should be possible to deduce the relative proportion of subjects who return to normal functioning after intervention. This approach does of course presuppose that normative data are available to establish cut-off points for the functional and dysfunctional distributions.

Reconsidering in the light of these comments the within subject variability outlined above, it seems likely that a proportion of the nights of sleep which the insomniac subject has will be within normal limits, i.e. SOL is already within the target (normal) range. The clinical task, therefore, would be to effect change in SOL (or whatever variable) in such a way that the residual nights also conformed to the normal range. The clinician who is examining the sleep log of the insomniac patient should, therefore, along with the subject, identify those nights scores which are reflective of the sleep complaint, i.e. the problem nights, and define the functional range within which sleep may be deemed acceptable. In this way therapeutic goals can become more specific and outcome assessment can become more clinically meaningful.

An alternative approach, in the research literature, to the establishment of suitable cut-off points for functional and dysfunctional distributions has been the determination of the proportion of subjects who improved at post-treatment compared with the proportion who did not improve. This approach tackles the issue of individual variability in response. Yet another approach has been to define significant improvement as a change over baseline of greater than 50% (e.g. Lichstein and Fischer, 1985).

In our own research work we have applied three criteria for the evaluation of clinical significance of outcome in terms of sleep-onset latency. These criteria are listed in Table 10 and may be found to be useful not only in the evaluation of the individual case but also for use in group comparison research studies.

Table 10 Criteria for the evaluation of clinically significant change in sleep onset latency (SOL) as applied in Espie, Brooks and Lindsay (1989)

(1) Absolute (i.e. any) reduction in SOL at post-treatment
(2) 50% reduction in SOL at post-treatment
(3) Final post-treatment SOL less than or equal to 30 minutes

It is clear, therefore, that valid interpretation of sleep log information depends upon careful analysis of the "shape" of the data over time. Raw score values should not be summarised into mean scores too readily lest essential descriptive information be sacrificed. The insomniac may be in a general sense dissatisfied with her sleep but it is likely that good nights are interspersed with bad nights. It is the contribution of the latter which predicts complaint. One of the goals of assessment should be to identify the boundaries of functional and dysfunctional ranges of sleep pattern variables so that treatment can be validly targeted and its effectiveness validly measured. Researchers and clinicians alike would do well to remember that data analyses may be statistically robust and significant without necessarily being of great clinical importance.

The assessment of sleep quality

The appraisal of sleep quality is certainly the most subjective element of the sleep assessment. Here objective measurement has little direct relevance (Table 7). For example, although EEG recordings can provide data on the nature of sleep, perhaps allowing comparison of "light sleep" (stages 1 and 2) with "deep sleep" (stages 3 and 4), the relationship between such information and the insomniac's sense of restedness and sleep satisfaction remains unclear. Indeed, numerous studies comparing insomniacs and normal sleepers have produced ambiguous results with some evidencing deficiencies in slow wave sleep in insomniac groups (Coursey, Buchsbaum and Frankel, 1975; Frankel et al, 1973; Galliard, 1978) and others evidencing no such deficiency (Monroe, 1967; Karacan et al, 1971). Clearly the electroencephalogram does not discriminate reliably between insomniac complainants and non-complainants even in terms of sleep pattern. Inferential connections which some workers have endeavoured to make between objective sleep pattern and subjective sleep quality, therefore, remain speculative. Similarly, when it comes to independent informant report, the measurement of sleep quality may be attempted only by inference based upon observation. For example, the observer may notice daytime fatigue, impoverished concentration or a change in mood, but in reality these are observations of daytime functioning and performance and not valid measurements of the sleeper's sleep quality.

It is evident, then, that sleep quality can be measured only by insomniac self-report. In spite of the widely recognised importance of such perceptions of sleep quality, however, the vast majority of psychological treatment outcome studies have failed to report on the effects of treatment upon such variables. A number of studies have employed rating scale measures of qualitative aspects of sleep, and have reported such in the methodology of the studies, but outcome reporting in the results sections of these same papers has almost always concentrated upon changes in sleep pattern, particularly sleep-onset latency. Major review papers on psychological treatment have also reflected this emphasis upon quantitative measurement (e.g. Bootzin and Nicassio, 1978; Lichstein and Fischer, 1985) although Morin and Kwentus (1988) in their recent review have commented appositely, "...variables such as sleep quality, mood, performance efficiency, and alertness reflect on insomnia complaints. These parameters tend to discriminate poor from good sleepers more reliably than sleep latency alone and are therefore prime variables for assessing treatment outcome".

Before going on to consider in what ways sleep quality may be appropriately assessed, it should be noted that there is a dearth of literature on the assessment of sleep quality in normal populations. Of course, many studies have required participants to categorise themselves as "good" or "poor" sleepers, to enable between group comparisons to be completed. This is not, however, the same as requiring subjects on a night by night basis to comment on sleep quality. It seems possible, even probable from anecdotal reports, that some non-insomniacs (i.e. good sleepers) will rate themselves low on variables such as "feeling rested after sleep" if required to make a judgement within one hour of rising. These matters will be dealt with in greater detail at a later point in this section.

Table 11 suggests some of the self-report items which may be useful in the assessment of sleep quality. Although sleep quality is a construct which is difficult to define, clinical experience suggests that there are three principal components to a good quality sleep. Firstly, there is the association of quality sleep with *"sufficiency"* for the forthcoming day. That is, subjects require sleep to have restorative powers and wish to feel "refreshed" and "satisfied" that they have had "enough" sleep. Secondly, good quality sleep may be associated with the actual *experience of sleep* itself. Here, subjects look for sleep to be "enjoyable", a positive rather than a negative experience. "Restlessness" is often associated with poor quality sleep whereas "deep sleep" or "a proper sleep" indicates a good experience. Thirdly, subjects equate quality in sleep with having a *"normal sleep"*. Clearly this is again highly subjective, and individuals differ in the criteria which they apply to define what to them is "satisfactory" sleep, but categorical distinctions are made by insomniacs and the quality often desired is something to do with "getting back to normal". In summary, good quality sleep appears to be related to the individual's perception of sleep as enjoyable, restorative and non-pathological.

The comments made above are not intended to be provocatively vague.

Table 11 Sample item content for an assessment of sleep quality

---

"A restful sleep"
"Refreshed after sleep"
"Satisfied with sleep"
"An enjoyable sleep"
"A deep sleep"
"A good sleep"

Rather, they are a true reflection of the clinician's experience in trying to define what are the critical qualitative judgements made by the individual at the clinic. The ambiguity of the terminology only serves to underline the importance of tailoring assessment measures specifically to address the needs of the individual. Many of the terms used in Table 11, and others mentioned in the text, will appear to the reader to by synonomous, but may not be so to the insomniac. It is essential, therefore, that the practitioner uses in the assessment of sleep quality those terms which have immediate personal meaning to the insomniac and which to her describe the most salient aspect(s) of sleep quality. Thus, and for example, if a patient regularly refers to having or not having "a sound sleep" then this semantic construct should be adopted. It is then the practitioner's task to define this term as clearly as possible so that both patient and clinician have a shared understanding. The alternative to accepting the patient's semantic sphere is to teach the patient the equivalence of other terminology. It seems likely that in most cases this would be a less valid procedure. A comprehensive assessment of sleep quality *from the patient's perspective* is very important. Just because a concept is elusive and appears less scientific it cannot be dismissed, especially when it has fundamental clinical validity.

After suitable description(s) of sleep quality has been agreed the next task is to select a suitable response format. In most studies items on sleep quality have been incorporated into the daily sleep log. This is the approach we have used in our own research work (e.g. Espie et al, 1989). The clear advantage in doing so is that the subject completes both quantitative and qualitative aspects of assessment simultaneously and in immediate response to the preceding night's sleep; typically within one hour of rising. Figure 7

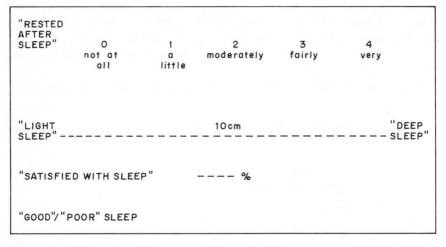

Figure 7   Sample response formats for assessment of sleep quality

illustrates a number of sample scales which might be used by the clinician, or serve as useful models.

Likert Scales ensure that the subject makes a forced choice between a small number of graded responses from an extreme negative to an extreme positive. As in the example given, such scales do not need to be overtly numerate but can retain a verbal description. It is always possible to assign numbers to such ordinal scales at a later point. The second example is a linear analogue scale, 10 centimetres long with, in this case, the poles of "light sleep" and "deep sleep" identified. The subject's task is to place a cross (x) at any point along the line. Analogue scales act similarly to a thermometer, and may be sensitive to rises and falls of relatively small magnitude across the treatment period. In similar vein the third example requires the subject to assign a percentage score (0 to 100), in this case in response to the statement "satisfied with sleep". A percentage value like this may be helpful also in helping the subject to judge how close to her "target" a particular night's sleep was. The final example is of a dichotomous choice. Here the categories are simply stated as "good" and "poor" sleep and the subject is required to allocate the night's sleep to one or other category on balance. As was mentioned earlier, many subjects appear to think in terms of simple categories rather than linear scales. Such dichotomous forced choices may get round the tendency of some patients to "hug" the middle ground of linear scales and to fail to use the breadth of ratings available.

To summarise so far, the clinician is urged to select items for an assessment of sleep quality which are of immediate relevance to the presenting individual, which cover adequately the three aspects of sleep quality outlined above (perceived restorative value, acceptability of the sleep experience, perceived normality of sleep) and to use response formats which are accessible to the individual and which the clinician can interpret.

The next point to consider is the timing of such assessments. It was mentioned earlier that most studies have required subjects to complete ratings of sleep quality soon after rising. Doubts were expressed at the likelihood of ratings made at this time discriminating successfully between insomniacs and normal sleepers. It may be that more valid assessment of sleep quality would be achieved through ratings made some while later, perhaps mid-morning, when people are better able to judge the value of the previous night's sleep in relation to performance. This is particularly so when it comes to qualitative ratings referring to the dimension of "sleep sufficiency" or sleep adequacy (for daytime purposes). On the other hand, there would appear to be less reason for delaying assessment of sleep quality in terms of "sleep enjoyment".

Satisfaction with the sleep process may also be measured by including items which primarily concern the *pre-sleep* period. For example, individuals who regularly experience intrusive thoughts upon retiring to bed and/or upon awakening during the night may be asked to rate items such as "worrying while in bed" or "difficult to empty my mind". Some studies have also asked subjects to rate "difficulty in falling asleep" which might be regarded both as a quantitative correlate of sleep latency and as qualitative in terms of the (pre-) sleep experience.

Assessment of daytime functioning

Dement, Seidel and Carskadon (1984) have emphasised the necessity of "thorough enquiry about daytime symptoms and their relation to night time sleep". These workers are rightly concerned that in clinical practice, daytime symptoms may be taken for granted as occurring after poor sleep. This is certainly not always the case. Some insomniacs report no significant daytime impairments yet complain of unsatisfactory sleep. Furthermore, it is clear that where daytime sequelae are recognised, these may present in differing ways amongst insomniacs. Therefore, both the intensity and the range of daytime effects require to be assessed. Finally, the co-existence of a sleep problem with some form of daytime impairment cannot be taken as evidence of causality. For example, an individual who is troubled by irritable moods during the day may wrongly attribute these to insufficient sleep. Assessment of daytime functioning, therefore, must take account of the range of symptoms experienced, their intensity and intrusiveness, and the attributions which the subject makes concerning these symptoms taken against competing hypotheses of symptom presentation.

There are four major categories of daytime functions which should be included in any comprehensive assessment of insomnia (Table 12). Firstly, daytime *tiredness* may be expected where sleep is disturbed. Periods of recovery sleep may occur, i.e. napping, or the individual may feel drowsy and on the verge of sleep. Secondly, and related to the first point, the individual's ability to attend to and respond appropriately to relevant signals may be impaired. That is, there may be problems with selective *attention* and/or subsequent concentration. Thirdly, there may be effects

Table 12   Aspects of daytime functioning for inclusion in sleep assessment

---

Sleep readiness/fatigue
Attention span—information input
Task performance—information processing
                    —work output
Mood

---

upon daytime work *performance*. Reasoning and decision-making may be affected, and work rate or efficiency may be reduced. Fourthly, there may be changes in aspects of emotional control such as heightened anxiety or there may be greater fluctuation in daytime *mood*. Each of these four areas deserves more detailed consideration.

Table 7 suggested that the insomniac herself would prove to be the best source of information relating to these daytime functions. Objective measurement and informant report do, however, have a part to play, albeit not a primary role, in routine clinical practice. As far as the assessment of sleep readiness is concerned the Multiple Sleep Latency Test (MSLT) has been developed as an objective measure of daytime tiredness (Richardson et al, 1978). The MSLT is based upon the simple premise that the speed with which a subject will fall asleep during the day, given the opportunity so to do, is a direct measure of sleep readiness, i.e. fatigue. The MSLT has been widely used in research studies where a sleep laboratory has been available and has been found sensitive enough to detect significant increases in daytime sleepiness associated with relatively small reductions in prior nighttime sleep (Carskadon and Dement, 1981; Roehrs et al, 1983). Detailed discussion of MSLT-produced data can be found in Chapter 2 (pp. 32–33). For most practical clinical applications, however, an alternative and more accessible measure of sleep readiness must be found. Fortunately, this can be readily and simply achieved by requesting subjects to record on a daily basis the amount(s) of time which they spend napping. This should be done both in terms of frequency and duration of nap periods. Such information can be collected by including an item on napping in the daily sleep log. Subjects should be requested to estimate the duration of each nap to the nearest five minutes. Furthermore, unlike the measurement of nighttime sleep parameters, independent informants are often able to provide some corroborative evidence of the time which insomniacs spend napping during the day and in the evening prior to bedtime. Other measures of reporting daytime tiredness may be useful, such as Likert type rating scales or analogue measures (cf. Figure 7). These prove essential where subjects do not permit themselves any daytime naps, but complain nonetheless of significant levels of fatigue during the day. For example, the Stanford Sleepiness Scale is a self-rating method for quantifying sleepiness where the subject can provide self-assessments on a simple seven-point scale at intervals as small as 15 minutes (Hoddes, Dement and Zarcone, 1972; Hoddes et al, 1973).

Insomniacs frequently complain of concentration difficulties and of impoverished performance and efficiency in day to day tasks. Illustration of these information-processing deficits was presented in Chapter 2 (pp. 32–33 & 38). Once again, the primary source of these data must be the insomniac herself since independent assessment, either objectively or through an observer, will be seldom available and at best corroborative. Selective attention refers to an individual's ability to discriminate the presence of a target stimulus within the context of general background distraction, and attention span refers to the period of time for which attention can be maintained. One consequence of insufficient nighttime sleep can be impairment of this input stage of the information processing chain. Subjects frequently complain of distractibility, of finding it hard to get started on a task, and of losing concentration. As with the measurement of sleep quality, such constructs may become labels for a rating scale assessment to be completed on a daily basis. If an objective measure is required, particularly for research rather than for clinical purposes, this could be based upon standard experimental psychology tasks of vigilance, scanning or reaction time.

Independent evidence of deficiencies in work performance may be more forthcoming. It is often possible to quantify an individual's work rate as a measure of treatment process and outcome. For example, the relationship between the number of hours worked and some appropriate measure of output can produce an index of productivity. A secretary could calculate the number of words per minute typed or number of letters completed; a factory worker could collate information on pieces of work processed or assembled; a teacher could report on the number of examination papers marked or on preparation time required for a piece of classwork. The most relevant measure to apply will be the one which validly describes the individual's complaint of daytime performance deficit. We have found it useful to use self-rating scales of the analogue type to cover fatigue, attention, performance and mood variables. A series of around 10 self-rated items provides an achievable descriptive profile on a day to day basis. This core assessment of daytime functioning can be supplemented as required, for example, using an objective measure of performance.

The section on General Assessment at the beginning of this chapter discussed the practice of assessing insomniacs for symptoms of both anxiety and depression, and outlined some of the more useful measures which are currently available. Few of these, however, are suitable for the regular monitoring of mood on a day to day basis such as is necessary to consider the relationship between nighttime sleep and daytime consequences: hence the utility of the rating scale "amalgam" of items on daytime functions, including those aspects of daytime mood which appear to be most relevant. Common examples of such items would be "irritable", "agitated", "tense" and "feeling flat" (low). It is worth nothing at this point that the drugs most commonly prescribed for insomnia (benzodiazepines) are, apart from their hypnotic function, also tranquillisers. They are basically Central Nervous System depressants. Assessment of daytime mood, therefore, may also help to assess the impact of drug administration, drug change and drug withdrawal. For example, the withdrawal of benzodiazepine hypnotics has been associated with significant increases in daytime anxiety (Kales et al, 1983b).

Apart from constructing, along with the insomniac, an appropriate assessment of relevant daytime functions, the clinician should be concerned to test out *alternative hypotheses* for the presentation of daytime symptoms. The conviction with which an insomniac may attribute daytime symptoms as sequelae of sleep should not be taken as sufficient evidence of a causal link. Chapter 2 (pp. 29–31) demonstrated that people presenting with insomnia are prone to anxiety and stress disorders and may have mildly obsessional personality traits. It follows, therefore, that anxiety management per se may be required for certain individuals *in addition to* treatment of sleep disorder. In other words, management of insomnia may be a necessary but not a sufficient treatment for daytime symptoms in some individuals. For others, lifestyle change, time management or stress reduction may be what is primarily required to improve daytime factors. The ingenuity and problem-solving skills which an individual applies to work-related tasks is not then entirely or even mainly a function of sleep adequacy. It may be convenient and less threatening, however, to attribute such difficulties to an "external" source (i.e. sleep) rather than recognising limitations to personal resourcefulness and ability. To take one final example, selective attention will be compromised where an individual approaches work in an unstructured and undisciplined manner. The principles of stimulus control apply to the daytime environment too. The clinician should not be tempted to accept possibly remote causes, both temporally and situationally, for an observed daytime effect, when more immediate and sometimes more probable precipitants are evident.

PREDICTIVE ASSESSMENT

Near the start of this chapter Table 4 identified three broad areas of assessment: namely, *general* assessment of the insomniac, *specific* assessment of sleep and sleep correlates, and *predictive* assessment of appropriate goals and treatments. The chapter will conclude, therefore, with consideration of this third aspect to assessment.

We have suggested before that there are four key stages of predictive assessment and programme design which, if dealt with carefully, are likely to produce the most effective treatment outcomes from the patient's *and* the therapist's viewpoint (Espie, 1989; Espie et al, 1989). These stages have been implicit throughout this chapter on assessment procedures, but are now deserving of explicit consideration. What is meant by the term "predictive assessment" is the means by which an agreed formulation of the sleep problem is achieved which satisfies both the patient and the practitioner, which identifies those variables which ought to change as a result of successful treatment, and which predicts the critical components of that treatment intervention which are most likely to contribute towards those outcomes. The four key stages are as presented in Table 13.

Table 13   Four key stages of predictive assessment and programme design

Content	Task	Function
(1) The patient's definition of insomnia and what she hopes to gain from therapy	Eliciting treatment goals	Assessment
(2) The validity and accessibility of the patient's goals	Appraising treatment goals	Assessment
(3) The information and educational needs of the patient	Agreeing treatment goals	Teaching
(4) The specific psychological treatment(s) to be applied	Achieving treatment goals	Treatment

Eliciting treatment goals

The critical question here is "What constitutes improvement for this patient?". The practitioner must establish what it is the individual hopes to gain from therapy and what difference(s) will be made by effective treatment. It is not uncommon in clinical practice with a wide variety of presenting problems to find that patients appear satisfied with progress in therapy when their therapists can in all honesty discern little change. Equally, clinicians can be dismayed by the lack of satisfaction shown by other patients whose progress to their way of thinking, or as measured by standard instruments, has been considerable. Why should there be such poor correlation? What is it that predicts outcome?

Such disharmonies arise out of a fundamental problem. Many practitioners do not spend long enough at the "contractual" stage in the therapeutic process. A failure to establish what the patient's goals in therapy are, and what will be necessary to affect "complaining behaviour", evidences inadequate assessment. For a clinician to be unaware of what specifically the patient regards her needs to be is tantamount to saying that he does not really know why the patient has come along for help in the first place. It follows that neither does he know what will stop her coming along in the future. One reason for this form of assessment neglect may be the development within clinical professions of a "technician mentality" towards treatment to the extent that in many cases it appears not to matter what the detail of a particular problem is, or the reason for its presentation, since ultimately the treatment package is going to be the same in any case. The practitioner must take care not to become a diagnostician, but must remain an applied scientist practitioner.

To move back from generalities to the specific task here; what is it that constitutes "improvement" for this insomniac patient? As has been stated the essence of the definition of insomnia is subjective dissatisfaction. It is something to do with not getting "enough" of a "proper" sleep. Consequently, the severity of insomnia varies in relation to the degree of subjective concern and this may or may not correlate well with objective parameters of sleep disturbance such as sleep latency or time spent awake while in bed. We have suggested that the improvement which the individual aims for is something to do with one or more of the goals identified in Table 14 (Espie, 1989).

Table 14 Categories of treatment goal presented by insomniac patients

More sleep
A more satisfying sleep
A more restorative sleep
A more reliable sleep
A more normal sleep

The individual may seek improvement in the sleep pattern itself. Basically, this insomniac perceives a need for *more sleep* and this may be presented in terms of a wish to fall asleep more quickly, to stay asleep for long and/or to be less restless and wakeful during the night. Other insomniacs, however, may be more concerned with sleep quality than sleep quantity. The desire here is likely to be for a *more satisfying sleep*. The individual may hope to enjoy sleep more and for it to change from being a somewhat negative to a positive experience. Apart from concerns over sleep quantity and quality, there are insomniacs who present primary goals in terms of improved daytime functions. Here the desire is for a *more restorative sleep* and the individual may wish to become more alert, to be better at problem-solving, to cope better emotionally and to have improved performance in waking life. Still others may seek a *more reliable sleep*; that is, for sleep pattern to become more stable and predictable on a night by night basis over time. Such an insomniac may not feel in control of the overall pattern and may have concerns about "bad nights" and otherwise "good nights" which vary unpredictably. (There appear to be many non-complaining "normal" sleepers who have a poor but stable sleep pattern.) Finally, some insomniacs wish to achieve a *"normal"* sleep. Often, the reference point for this is the individual's previous experience of satisfactory sleep, or the sleep pattern of the bed partner (see Chapter 2, pp. 27–28). Experience suggests that most people have some knowledge of the normal distribution across the population of sleep parameters such as duration of sleep. However, this may not translate readily to recognition of its implications for their own sleep pattern over time and with advancing age.

The practitioner, therefore, must attend to and assess those particular facets of sleep complaint which comprise the subjective experience of insomnia. The individual who complains of daytime fatigue will not necessarily value a reduction in sleep latency; similarly, an attested improvement in average ratings of sleep enjoyment may not satisfy the insomniac who wishes to sleep from 11.00 p.m. until 7.00 a.m. every night.

Appraising treatment goals

Once the practitioner has elicited the subject's initial hopes and expectations of treatment, it is necessary to conduct an appraisal of these stated goals. The key question here is "is improvement in these terms a valid and achieveable goal?" (Table 13). It is the therapist's job to consider the individual's personal definition of insomnia, the various "meanings" which may be ascribed to sleep, and the individual's aspirations for future sleep against what is known about normal variation in night to night sleep, developmental changes in pattern, attributional aspects of sleep in relation to daytime functioning and so on. The practitioner will be unable to design a sensible treatment programme without sufficient background knowledge in these areas. The preceding chapters in this book provide such background information. One or two examples, however, may be helpful at this point.

Case 1

A 35 year old business man complains of delayed sleep onset. He often takes longer than 90 minutes to fall asleep and becomes very frustrated. He works long hours, often under pressure of time, and reports increasing problems in managing his workload. His stated goals for treatment are firstly, to fall asleep within 15 minutes of retiring to bed; and secondly, to experience less daytime tiredness resulting from an improved sleep pattern.

Clinical appraisal of these goals, however, established that they could be only partially achieved through behavioural management of initial insomnia per se. The primary problem appeared to be poor time management during the day which resulted in working well into the evening. Invalid attributions were made to sleep. The patient's goals could become valid only when made accessible through management on a 24-hour perspective.

Case 2

A 60 year old woman complains of light sleep which is interrupted by frequent wakenings. She does not feel tired in the morning or during the day but becomes anxious when awake during the night. She feels that sleep has become an unpleasant and even at times aversive experience for her. Typically she retires to bed at around 12 midnight and rises at 7.30 a.m. She hopes that treatment will provide her with a continuous sleep period (i.e. around seven hours) similar to her husband, who sleeps well.

Baseline data of sleep duration indicate an average total sleep time of five and a half hours. Considerable variability in sleep is evident with her target criterion being achieved only occasionally and usually during "recovery" nights after a prior poor night's sleep. Continuous, unbroken sleep of this length is not regarded as a viable therapeutic goal and comparisons with the husband's sleep pattern are invalid. A measure of sleep efficiency is regarded by the therapist as a more appropriate statement of the presenting problem.

Appraisal of the patient's outcome objectives, therefore, can identify significant gaps in knowledge and understanding which have to be addressed if the clinician wishes to present acceptable and effective treatment to the individual.

Agreeing treatment goals

The key question here is "what information and education is required" as the first phase of intervention? The eliciting of the patient's goals in therapy and the appraisal of these by the clinician is, of course, part of a dialogue between patient and therapist which logically leads on to an agreement about the treatment outcome measures to be adopted. Although reference has been made to this as a "contractual" aspect of therapy, this should not be taken to imply that the agreement of goals is a matter simply for negotiation. Agreeing on outcome measures must not be a matter of compromise. Rather, it is the clinician's task to perform a teaching function which assists the patient to formulate her sleep difficulty accurately yet retaining wherever possible the parameters and constructs which the individual herself supplied as being most descriptive and clinically relevant.

This is the pivotal stage in the patient/practitioner interaction. It is the point at which assessment merges with treatment, albeit didactic treatment. The function here is an important teaching one and a separate chapter (Chapter 5) is devoted to the consideration of the various components of didactic and other non-specific intervention which may be useful.

Achieving treatment goals

The key question here is "which psychological intervention(s) predict the best outcome for the agreed goals?". Once the above three stages have been worked on and achieved it is appropriate to decide upon any further treatment which may be required. By this point, however, the treatment should be clearly goal directed, and the practitioner and patient should have agreed upon the goals. The practitioner must use his knowledge base of treatments and their effectiveness to introduce the correct therapeutic elements towards the desired outcomes. Chapters 6 to 8 in this book, therefore, review the treatment outcome literature on relaxation-based therapies, cognitive treatments and behavioural (operant) approaches respectively, and Chapter 9 presents an overview of comparative studies. Differences amongst treatments in their impact upon measures of sleep quantity, sleep quality and daytime function will be highlighted to help the clinician in designing the most appropriate programme.

In summary, it is always the case that the patient and the therapist wish treatment to be successful. In order to achieve successful outcome, however, there needs to be a shared understanding of what the needs of the individual are. These must be explored, and achievable goals must be contracted upon. This is likely to involve an educational process, which should be regarded in itself as a therapeutic procedure. The available psychological treatments offer different types of benefit and should be selected as appropriate to address the assessed needs of the individual.

Chapter 5

Information and Advice for Insomniac Patients—Non-Specific Treatment

The distinction between *advice* and *treatment* is and perhaps must remain somewhat arbitrary. Before considering the case of the insomniac, it may be helpful to illustrate this point with a couple of examples from other fields of study.

After suffering a myocardial infarction a person will be, in all probability, offered general guidance on for example appropriate levels of exercise, diet and weight control, smoking cessation and so on. The aim is to increase knowledge, influence attitudes and by these means to change behaviour. Another individual, however, may be offered a formal cardiac rehabilitation programme. Exercise tolerance tests may be undertaken, diets monitored and weights recorded, group discussion meetings may be arranged and homework assignments allocated and reviewed. The literature usually would regard the latter as a behavioural intervention or treatment, but how, if at all, does the package of advice differ from the treatment programme? Are they categorically different or is treatment simply an extension of information and general advice with possible improvements in compliance? To take another example, the stressed and anxious client may be regularly and from various sources exhorted to "ease off, learn to relax, stop overworking and get things in perspective". Such direction may not constitute cognitive or behavioural therapy but neither is it necessarily inconsistent with such treatments. A training course in techniques of stress management may simply get more of the same message home to the person.

It is the purpose of this chapter to consider "non-specific treatment" for insomnia, i.e. the role of information and advice. It is felt that this term is the most descriptive since it emphasises the clinical importance and potential effectiveness of advice per se, yet also recognises the multifaceted nature and general applicability of much of the advice to all cases of insomnia. Thus non-specific treatment points the way to the employment of one or more of a number of specific treatments—if required. In introducing the importance of didactic intervention in Chapter 4 emphasis was placed upon the critical stage of assessment/planning where the practitioner and client agree or contract upon goals for treatment and thereby agree upon the means by which treatment effects will be measured. As will become clear shortly such didactic intervention forms a central part of the non-specific treatment of insomnia. The practitioner's roles as teacher and therapist are, therefore, complementary ones just in the same way as learning and behaviour change should be complementary aspects of the individual patient's response to treatment.

The first part of this chapter describes the various elements of non-specific treatment for insomnia which have been recommended in the literature and which are commonly used. The research evidence associated with each element will be reviewed. The remaining part of the chapter comprises an evaluation of the impact and clinical effectiveness of non-specific treatment per se. Treatment outcome comparisons which have compared non-specific treatment with formal specific treatments will be reviewed although the research literature in this area is sparse.

A PACKAGE OF NON-SPECIFIC TREATMENT TECHNIQUES

The term "sleep hygiene" has been used in the literature to describe an individual's preparation of herself and of the sleep environment for sleep. The assumption is that good sleep hygiene will be associated with optimal sleep, both quantitatively and qualitatively. Conversely, poor sleep hygiene is likely to be correlated with poor and inconsistent sleep. In this book the terms "non-specific treatment" and "sleep hygiene" may be regarded as synonymous, although the former is preferred for reasons outlined above. Furthermore, the term "sleep hygiene" has limited semantic appeal and is only obliquely descriptive of some of its component parts.

A summary of the typical elements of non-specific treatment for insomnia is presented in Table 15. It can be seen from the table that non-specific treatment covers three areas. Firstly, it is concerned with the patient's understanding of sleep processes, functions and needs and with relating such information to the individual's own experience of past and present sleep and sleeplessness. Secondly, non-specific treatment seeks to overcome behavioural practices which may have an adverse effect upon sleep; or on the positive side to promote sleep through healthy living. The term "sleep hygiene" is most apt to this section. Thirdly, non-specific treatment guides

Table 15 Elements of a typical non-specific treatment programme for insomnia

Assimilation of knowledge	Self-management of behaviour	Environmental planning
Sleep patterns and stages	Exercise regime	Comfortable bed
Sleep functions and effects	Typical diet	Comfortable temperature
Sleep variability over time	General health	Minimal distraction (noise, illumination)
Insomnia—facts, figures and effects	Use of non-prescribed drugs (stimulants, e.g. caffeine; depressants, e.g. alcohol)	

the individual towards preparing a sleep environment which is conducive to sleep. The individual should be warm and comfortable in bed and the environment should not be overly arousing to the senses. Each of these three aspects of non-specific treatment will be considered in turn.

Assimilating knowledge about sleep

The person who regards herself as insomniac is usually interested in the topic of sleep. This may appear to be a self-evident statement. The individual has a need to talk about the problem and her understanding of it, and has a need for information to help her test out her own formulation and amend it if required. However, busy primary care physicians seldom have the time or take the time to discuss sleep needs and sleep processes with the insomniac. The demand characteristics of the consulting room setting appear to operate in such a way that both practitioner and patient move too quickly towards deciding upon a treatment strategy. It is essential, therefore, that the practitioner recognises that the first task is not a prescriptive one but an educative one.

It is usually necessary to teach the insomniac about normal sleep processes, normal sleep patterns, the functions of sleep, the normal variability in night to night sleep and developmental changes which occur in sleep with age. Such information should be presented methodically and there should be opportunity for the patient to rehearse and assimilate what has been said in relation to her own personal situation. As in any teaching programme, effectiveness may be measured in terms of the individual's learning of the presented information. It is the assimilated input which is important and not the teaching output. Clearly if the therapist concentrates on the latter then teaching may be deemed to have taken place in the absence of satisfactory learning.

Of course, many poor sleepers already have a considerable degree of understanding about sleep. Indeed their knowledge may be greater than their counterparts who are good sleepers (Lacks and Rotert, 1986). Nevertheless, the provision of sleep information is important for three reasons. Firstly, and most straightforwardly, it is encouraging to have knowledge confirmed and poor sleepers by virtue of their poor sleep may be more likely to doubt the accuracy of what they know. Secondly, awareness of certain facts may not correspond with the application of that knowledge in practical ways. In that same study quoted above Lacks and Rotert (1986) reported that insomniacs instituted known desirable behaviours less often in their daily lives than did good sleepers. Thirdly, gaps generally do exist in knowledge itself and it is these which require to be specifically addressed by the therapist. This is so particularly where the gaps are not only of academic importance but play an important role in the individual's (mis)understanding of her problem.

It is not necessary here to reiterate the format or content of the didactic programme to be followed. The components are identified in Table 15 and the reader is referred back to the relevant sections in Chapter 1 which introduced sleep processes and sleep disorders. The visual material presented there may be useful also in the teaching process. Chapter 4 underlined the achievement of an agreed contract between therapist and patient as a critical outcome of the didactic process. Thorough assessment should help the practitioner to select from the "menu" of sleep information areas in keeping with the educational needs of the presenting patient.

Self-management of behavioural habits

Knowledge about sleep processes and needs comprises one element of the non-specific treatment package. Inspection of Table 15 reveals that a second element is concerned with the self-management of everyday behavioural habits which are known to have some impact upon nighttime sleep, either to promote sleep or to inhibit or disrupt sleep. Although these habits are seldom root causes of clinically presenting cases of chronic insomnia, advice aimed at eliminating even contributory difficulties can be helpful. Furthermore, since drinking coffee, taking exercise and so on are high in public awareness as correlates of sleep, it is necessary to deal with such matters to foster credibility and compliance. Dealt with as part of the non-specific intervention the insomniac is enabled to make her first therapeutic response to her problem, yet at the same time she gains an accurate perspective of the relatively limited importance of such habits relative to other factors to be managed more specifically at a later point.

The possibility of there being a significant relationship between *physical exercise* and nighttime sleep has considerable intuitive appeal. Insomniacs frequently report attempts to "tire themselves out", and also report astonishment that even high levels of fatigue may not reliably induce sleep for them. Such intuition concerning the role of exercise is not without empirical evidence. Certainly, the restorative hypothesis of sleep would predict that such physical activity would increase the total time slept, particularly in slow wave sleep (NREM stages 3 and 4). The earliest evidence for this view was provided by Baekeland and Lasky (1966) who obtained significant increases in slow wave sleep especially following afternoon exercise in their sample of 10 athletes. By comparison, evening exercise was associated with more disturbed sleep characterised by more frequent, brief wakenings and increased stage 1 sleep. These authors, therefore, identified the importance of the timing of exercise, and suggested that the later the exercise the greater its potential as "a stressor producing

CNS activation". Horne and Porter (1976) have also provided some evidence that late daytime exercise intrudes upon sleep.

A comprehensive review by Torsvall (1983) considered 20 research reports of the association between sleep and exercise. Half of these studies were found to support the hypothesis that activity facilitates deeper and longer sleep, and three of these reports also found reductions in sleep-onset latency. However, the remaining studies were categorised as either inconclusive or unsupportive of the theory. Torsvall concluded that the strongest weight of evidence for the positive impact of exercise on sleep was amongst already physically fit subjects. The optimal level of this activity is yet to be investigated. He also stressed the need for longitudinal studies incorporating sufficient numbers to compare trained and untrained subjects during an exercise programme.

The impact of exercise within the insomniac population has not been examined systematically. Marchini et al (1983) did find that the daytime behaviour of insomniacs and good sleepers differed in that the good sleepers had busier and more active daytime lives than their insomniac counterparts. These workers proposed that "increased activity, especially in the mornings and early evenings may be helpful in treating insomniacs". Clearly, controlled research would be required to establish firstly, whether significant changes in insomniac sleep pattern can be obtained by exercise methods alone; and secondly, whether or not such improvements are of clinical importance. Lichstein and Fischer's (1985) review of psychological management issues in insomnia strongly supports Paxton, Trinder and Montgomery's (1983) conclusion that "the relationship (between sleep and exercise) is unreliable and subject to alternative explanations. Clinical prudence demands that the sleep effects of exercise be judged on an individual basis."

The practitioner's advice to the insomniac concerning exercise, therefore, should take account of two factors. Firstly, exercise may have a primary role in promoting fitness and general health but may be of little benefit to sleep pattern until a training effect is achieved over a prolonged period. Secondly, there are strict limitations to the intuitive idea that exercise produces fatigue and that fatigue produces sleep. Paradoxically, exercise taken near bedtime may exacerbate sleep problems. The insomniac should be advised to exercise regularly as part of a daytime or early evening routine.

Bootzin and Engle-Friedman (1981) have stressed the importance of considering all aspects of drug use and diet in the assessment of insomnia. Probably the most commonly taken drug in daily use is *caffeine* which is contained in coffee, tea, "cola" drinks and certain analgesic and weight control substances. Research indicates that caffeine can be a powerful CNS stimulant drug capable of disturbing sleep and may be associated with racing, worrisome thoughts (Goodman and Gilman, 1969; Regestein, 1983). Bootzin and Engle-Friedman (1987) also note that complaints of both insomnia and anxiety may be due to excessive ingestion of caffeine. They state that since caffeine has a plasma half-life of around six hours, older adults in particular may continue to experience effects long after it was ingested. It follows that reducing or eliminating the intake of caffeine, particularly in the afternoon and evening, might be expected to contribute towards sleep improvement. It should be noted, however, that there is little evidence to indicate that insomniacs habitually drink coffee to excess. Indeed, in a recent epidemiological survey Cirignotta et al (1985) reported that poor sleepers drank significantly less coffee than good sleepers.

Sleep disturbance associated with caffeine has been found to be dose-related. In one study, the equivalent of four cups of coffee induced a reduction in total sleep time of 0.4 hours and increased sleep latency by 13 minutes, whereas one cup of coffee taken 30 minutes prior to bedtime had no significant effects. A report by Brezinova, Oswald and Loudon (1975), however, found that caffeine 15 minutes prior to bedtime produced more frequent and longer wakenings in their subjects. In addition, Bolton and Null (1981) have suggested that heavy, regular consumers are more likely to develop a tolerance to caffeine and, therefore, to suffer less ill-effects on their sleep than sporadic consumers.

In summary, therefore, the evidence concerning caffeine indicates that insomniacs should be advised to limit caffeine intake or to take decaffeinated drinks throughout the day and evening, although the final effect upon sleep pattern may be small. Before leaving the subject of stimulant drugs, it should be noted also that nicotine acts as a CNS stimulant and may be a contributory factor to insomnia for some subjects (Soldatos et al, 1980). Modest improvement may be effected in sleep pattern if cigarette smoking is ceased, particularly amongst heavy smokers.

Other non-prescribed drugs may be used by insomniacs in an effort to promote sleep. *Alcohol* acts as a CNS depressant and as a self-prescribed hypnotic agent may promote more rapid sleep-onset. However, alcohol acts upon the nervous system in a manner similar to benzodiazepine hypnotic drugs. It disrupts sleep from its natural rhythm by decreasing REM sleep and deep sleep and by producing greater fragmentation of sleep with frequent awakenings (Pokorny, 1978). Problems arise with alcohol particularly with habitual heavy use and the typical withdrawal syndrome, again similar to other hypnotic drugs, includes REM rebound, fitful sleep and elevated daytime anxiety. Furthermore, the combination of alcohol and sleeping tablets may exacerbate side effects and withdrawal problems and such a combination should be avoided (Institute of Medicine, 1979).

Safe and sensible use of alcohol should involve, therefore, only irregular use (if at all) as an hypnotic agent. It should be noted also that the traditional "night cap" will be less well tolerated by the older than the younger adult since clearance rates of toxic substances are slower amongst older people (Bootzin and Engle-Friedman, 1987). Regular use of alcohol at bedtime will lead to sleep disruption and a loss of facilitative effect upon sleep latency as drug tolerance increases.

"*Over-the-counter*" sleep medications containing antihistimines also act as depressants and may potentiate the effects of other depressant drugs. The hazards with these medications are, therefore, similar and there is little evidence of therapeutic benefit (Kales et al, 1971; Bootzin and Engle-Friedman, 1987).

Other aspects of *diet* may be worth considering in giving general advice to the insomniac patient. The ingestion of "Ovaltine", "Horlicks" or warm milk has been found, in laboratory studies, to improve sleep, especially during the last third of the night (Brezinova and Oswald, 1972). Fletcher (1986) has discussed the scientific basis to the old wives' tale about drinking a glass of warm milk before going to bed. Milk contains the amino acid L-tryptophan which, as a precursor of the neurotransmitter serotonin, has been shown to promote natural sleep, in particular increasing the proportion of stages 3 and 4 sleep (Hartmann, Cravens and List, 1974; Hartmann, Spinweber and Ware, 1983). Such findings, however, have been disputed and Adam and Oswald (1979) reported that one gramme of L-tryptophan failed to alter time taken to fall asleep. Similar reservations have been expressed by Nicholson and Stone (1979). As far as bedtime snacks are concerned it seems that these may not adversely affect sleep providing they are relatively light and are part of the individual's usual routine (Adam, 1980b). Lacks (1987) also stresses the importance of maintaining the existing habit so long as it is not excessive. Additionally, however, Lacks comments that insomniacs should not eat a snack in the middle of the night lest they train themselves to wake up at that time to eat. Large fluid intake in the evening should also be avoided for subjects who awaken in order to urinate.

Physical disorders which may interfere with sleep were reviewed in Chapter 1 and do not require to be reiterated here. It is relevant, however, to recognise that subjects may not understand fully the relationship between their illness state and present sleep pattern and any didactic intervention should seek to cover such an eventuality. Similarly, disease processes, as an initial primary cause of sleep disturbance, may give rise to secondary habitual sleep disruption, and the insomniac may require help to appreciate how differing components of treatment will address the overall situation.

Environmental planning

Most people are aware of the importance of a comfortable night's sleep. However, advice on planning the bedroom environment to ensure that it facilitates sleep is an important element to non-specific treatment (see Table 15). Bootzin and Engle-Friedman (1987) commented on the adaptability of most individuals to sleep comfortably in differing environments, whether the variation is in terms of temperature, mattress firmness or background noise. It may be therefore the *familiarity* of the setting which is of critical importance in predicting good quality sleep. Nevertheless, workers such Hauri (1982) have recommended a background room *temperature* of 65 to 70 degrees Farenheit, and Lacks (1987) quotes the early work of Monroe (1969) suggesting that a restless *bed partner* or one who is a snorer may contribute to the individual's sleep problem. For others, however, even a temporary alteration in sleeping arrangements may prove counterproductive due to the unfamiliarity of the sleep environment. Bed manufacturers are both aware of and partly responsible for public consciousness of the importance of a suitable bed and *mattress*, matched to individual requirements. Apart from the distribution of body weight over the mattress, cervical-support pillows have also been recommended (Fletcher, 1986). *Discomfort* in bed, however, may be a relatively rare contributory factor to insomnia. Reporting upon perceived aetiological factors of poor sleep on those nights when they slept poorly, only 5% of the insomniacs in one of our studies stated that they were often uncomfortable in bed (Chapter 3, Table 3). This result was in marked contrast to all the other aetiological factors tested.

The effects of *noise* upon sleep have been researched more thoroughly than the environmental factors mentioned above. Noises which are loud, sudden and infrequent appear more likely to produce an orienting or arousing response than predictable and minimally disruptive sounds. Where possible, therefore, the sleep environment should be free from such intrusive distractions. Although clinical experience suggests that people can become used to noise in the environment (e.g. passing road or rail traffic, a chiming clock in the hall) and there is experimental evidence of response habituation to audible stimuli (Bohlin, 1972; 1973), Sanchez and Bootzin (1985) have indicated that people who habitually sleep in noisy environments adapt to the noise incompletely.

Reference was made in Chapter 3 to the potentially therapeutic impact of monotonous stimulation which has a de-arousing effect, presumably by reducing the sensitivity of the reticular activating system. One clear example of this has been the presentation of monotonous audible tones (Bohlin, 1971). Other techniques, however, may operate by a similar route. The sub-vocal repetition of a mantra in meditation, the rhythmical pattern of muscular tension-release in progressive relaxation (Borkovec, 1979) and the repetition of semantically neutral words in Levey et al's (1991) articulatory suppression technique may be other examples of a similar phenomenon. Advice to patients may also include the production of background "white noise" which has the dual effect of both masking out potentially intrusive sporadic noises, and being in itself soporific (Hauri, 1982; Lacks, 1987; Golden and James, 1988). Equipment is available commercially which generates white noise but tape recordings can readily be made to produce a similar effect (e.g. noises generated by a central heating boiler, an extractor fan, a television set which is not tuned to receive a signal). Fletcher (1986) in his resource list of sleep aids also includes reference to a sound generator that reproduces tranquil sounds of nature such as surf, rain water and waterfall. With such stimuli there may be potential for both white noise equivalence and monotonous visualised stimulation.

In summary, therefore, the sleep environment, to be optimally facilitative of sleep, should be maintained at a physically comfortable and minimally distracting level. Factors such as temperature, illumination and noise should be adjusted to suit the individual and should then remain stable. The environment should be, at least, non-contributory towards insomnia and could be, at best, moderately therapeutic in promoting sleep.

Before concluding this discussion of the elements of non-specific treatment, it should be noted that elsewhere in the literature some descriptions of non-specific treatment or "sleep hygiene" have been more wide ranging than suggested here. In particular, simple relaxation advice, sleep scheduling (e.g. rise at the same time each morning, including weekends), advice on pre-sleep routines and activities, and the exclusion of sleep-incompatible behaviours from the bedroom environment (e.g. reading, watching TV) have been variously included as part of non-specific treatments (e.g. Walsh, Sugerman and Chambers, 1986). This perhaps illustrates the point which was made at the beginning of this chapter, that the distinction between non-specific and specific treatment must remain ambiguous. However, within the context of this and subsequent chapters in this book such elements will be considered as part of specific treatment. That is, relaxation based approaches will be considered in the next chapter and specific cognitive and behavioural techniques in the subsequent two chapters.

The importance of examining such ingredients from within a conceptual framework should not be underestimated, notwithstanding the clinical appeal of an overall package of treatments. It may be far better to ensure that an individual complies with one or two critically important and specific therapeutic instructions than to achieve compliance with half a dozen less important suggestions. There will be situations where the most important instructions will be the hardest to follow. These should not be "lost" within a package of general advice which allows the patient to demonstrate compliance on a selective basis.

Before turning to these specific forms of intervention, the important issue of the effectiveness of non-specific treatment will be addressed.

THE CLINICAL EFFECTIVENESS OF NON-SPECIFIC TREATMENT FOR INSOMNIA

In recent years most major text books and review papers on insomnia have included description and discussion of non-specific treatment. In their 1984 book Kales and Kales devoted an entire chapter to "general measures for treating insomnia". These workers commented that "the physician should neither under-emphasise nor over-stress their importance. . . . Nevertheless, patients with chronic insomnia can assume more responsibility for obtaining healthful sleep by identifying and maintaining habits and lifestyle patterns that are best for them" (p. 87). In similar vein, Lacks (1987) reported that "we take the stance that good sleep hygiene is essential to establish before we move on to other approaches. We always begin the first session by teaching the client to set up consistently ideal circumstances for sleeping" (p. 89). Lacks and her colleagues also recognise that "some participants have found that implementing the recommended sleep hygiene and scheduling practices was sufficient to improve their sleep" (p. 90). Morin and Kwentus (1988) have summed up the value of sleep hygiene interventions by stating that "education will often help to modify cognitive appraisal of the patient's sleeping problem but may not be enough to prompt behaviour changes in sleep habits".

It seems, therefore, that non-specific treatment has achieved an accepted status in routine clinical practice with insomniacs. Clinicians regard the education and advice package as a useful starting point in the therapeutic relationship, and although changes in sleep pattern and behaviour may not be expected necessarily to accompany the non-specific treatment, compliance appears to be enhanced and more fertile ground prepared for further specific treatment to proceed. The reader will recall that the introduction to this chapter placed non-specific treatment within the context of the assessment evaluation and the agreement of therapeutic goals.

One reason for the limited effectiveness of non-specific treatment has been identified by a study by Lacks and Rotert (1986). These workers developed the Sleep Hygiene Awareness and Practice Scale (which is reprinted in Lacks, 1987) and compared two sizeable groups of insomniacs, approximately half of whom had difficulties falling asleep and half had the primary problem of sleep maintenance insomnia, with a control group of good sleepers. Lacks and Rotert found that sleep hygiene knowledge and practice was in fact generally high for both good and poor sleepers alike. The insomniacs exhibited somewhat better hygiene knowledge than the good sleepers, a difference which was modestly significant upon statistical testing, but practised that knowledge significantly less, particularly in the case of the sleep-onset insomniacs. They reached the conclusion that poor sleep hygiene practice is not a major determinant of insomnia. Nevertheless, Lacks and Rotert felt that this element in treatment may reduce the likelihood of chronicity and the development of exacerbation cycles.

This same research group followed up on their descriptive study with a treatment outcome evaluation comparing sleep hygiene training with a conventional stimulus control treatment programme and a meditation technique in a sample of 65 adult media recruits who complained of significant sleep-maintenance insomnia (Schoicket, Bertelson and Lacks, 1988). Outcome analysis on the variables wake time after sleep onset (WASO) and number and duration of nighttime awakenings revealed that improvements over baseline were achieved with all three treatment interventions with no statistically significant between group differences emerging. Schoicket et al reported on treatment efficacy also in respect of a follow-up questionnaire which asked subjects whether or not they considered themselves still to have insomnia. Interestingly, 50% of the subjects in both the stimulus control and meditation groups considered themselves no longer to have insomnia in comparison to 20% of the sleep hygiene subjects. Furthermore, an assessment of treatment credibility revealed that subjects in the sleep hygiene group would be the least likely to recommend or repeat the treatment. Consistent with the study by Lacks and Rotert, some of the sleep hygiene subjects were found already to have good knowledge to which treatment added little. Given that the results for these subjects are likely to have contributed both to dissatisfaction with the treatment and potentially to poorer treatment outcome, it would have been interesting to consider the results for the sub-set of sleep hygiene subjects who had relatively poorer initial knowledge and practice. Unfortunately, Schoicket, Bertelson and Lacks did not present such an analysis.

There are only two other treatment comparison studies available which have included non-specific treatment as a single intervention. A study by Ladouceur and Gros-Louis (1986) reported on the effects of paradoxical intention, stimulus control, "sleep information" and a control procedure upon sleep-onset latency across a total sample of 25 insomniacs. Results showed that the paradoxical intention and stimulus control groups were equally effective but significantly superior to both the sleep information and control groups. It is noteworthy also that Ladouceur and Gros-Louis reported that the information group "showed less motivation to continue therapy at the end of therapy".

A more comprehensive evaluation using larger groups has been reported by Bootzin and his colleagues (Bootzin, Engle-Friedman and Hazlewood, 1983; Engle-Friedman, 1985; Bootzin and Engle-Friedman, 1987). Subjects for this study were 53 older insomniacs (age range 47 to 76 years) with either sleep-onset or sleep-maintenance insomnia. Three active treatment groups and a no treatment control group were employed in the study and all of the active treatments included a significant component of support and sleep hygiene instruction. These workers were concerned to evaluate the effects of adding more active treatments to the non-specific treatment. Thus the comparison comprised support and information alone, support and information plus progressive relaxation training, and support and information plus stimulus control treatment over four weeks of weekly individual sessions. Bootzin et al reported significant improvements on both quantitative and qualitative ratings under all three active treatments. Differential treatment effects were relatively few; however, the addition of either stimulus control or relaxation to the non-specific treatment was found to result in improved sleep efficiency. Adjusted means were found to be 77% for stimulus control, 78% for progressive relaxation and 60% for non-specific treatment.

In conclusion, collation of comments made by various writers, along with the results of more formal treatment comparisons, lead to the conclusion that non-specific treatment alone is unlikely to provide a satisfactory clinical outcome for cases of chronic insomnia. Nevertheless, non-specific treatment may serve a facilitative function through enhancing compliance. Potentially, it may accelerate the insomniac's response to conventional treatments and may contribute to longer term treatment gains. These issues have not been formally investigated so far. Given the relatively high levels of sleep knowledge already possessed by many insomniacs it would seem sensible for clinicians firstly to appraise pre-existing knowledge and practice in order to identify gaps in understanding and to concentrate upon these during the educational/didactic intervention. This should get round the potential problem of loss of motivation mentioned above which is likely to be associated with unnecessary repetition and rehearsal of known information. Patients should be encouraged to regard the non-specific treatment as a preparatory phase during which time outcome measures can be agreed and self-report sleep diaries and other measures devised and practised.

Chapter 6

Relaxation-based Treatments of Insomnia

This chapter on relaxation-based treatments of insomnia, and the subsequent two chapters on cognitive and stimulus control treatments respectively, attempt to achieve two principal goals. Firstly, each chapter aims to describe the elements and techniques which comprise treatment in such a way that the practitioner will be enabled to implement the treatment in clinical practice. Secondly, each chapter includes a comprehensive literature review of outcome studies pertaining to the treatment approach, and presents evidence for the effectiveness of the intervention under consideration. In other words, as a result of reading the chapter, the reader should have an understanding of the treatment and of how well it works and for whom. Chapter 9, however, provides an important overview of *comparative* outcome research studies where relaxation treatments have been evaluated against other behavioural and cognitive interventions. The reader is strongly advised, therefore, to regard Chapter 9 as a logical continuation of the discussion contained within each of the three preceding Chapters 6, 7 and 8.

This chapter is concerned with techniques of relaxation and anxiety reduction. Although the largest part of the research literature has centred on the application of progressive relaxation therapy, other methods such as desensitisation and variants of relaxation such as autogenic training and meditation have been described and evaluated. Biofeedback techniques can also be included here since these generally have appeared either in conjunction with or in comparison with relaxation training. These various treatment methods will be described prior to consideration of their effectiveness.

PROGRESSIVE RELAXATION TRAINING

The early development of progressive relaxation is credited to Jacobson (1929) who found that the sequential tensing and relaxing of the main muscle groups was associated with considerable decreases in muscle activity, blood pressure and heart rate. The advent of behaviour therapy many years later, and particularly the proposition that relaxation could provide an effective competing response to phobic anxiety (Wolpe, 1958), however, was largely responsible for a renaissance of interest in the technique. Over the past 30 years relaxation has become one of the mainstays of clinical behaviour therapy and various workers have produced abbreviated forms of Jacobson's procedures. Perhaps the best known of these has been Bernstein and Borkovec's (1973) manual.

Table 16 presents a descriptive summary of abbreviated progressive relaxation training, henceforth to be called simply "progressive relaxation" in keeping with the research literature on insomnia. Jacobson's techniques as originally presented involved a formidable list of tension-release cycles requiring very many practice sessions over many days. The reader will find Jacobson's (1970) text helpful. It contains many useful illustrations of tension-release procedures. For most clinical purposes, however, progressive relaxation can be taught by concentrating on the major voluntary muscle groups in order (Table 16). Indeed, it is possible to combine some of the exercises to abbreviate the procedure further, e.g. hand/forearm and biceps by clenching fist and simultaneously bending

Table 16 Descriptive summary of a progressive relaxation training procedure

Muscle groups (in order)	Instructional sequence for each muscle group
Dominant hand/forearm	
Dominant biceps	(1) Focus attention upon muscle
Non-dominant hand/forearm	group
Non-dominant biceps	
Forehead, upper cheeks and nose	(2) Tense muscle group upon
Lower cheeks and jaws	command
Neck and throat	
Chest, shoulders and upper back	(3) Maintain tension at constant
Abdominal/stomach region	level for 5–7 seconds
Dominant thigh	
Dominant calf	(4) Relax muscle group upon
Dominant foot	command
Non-dominant thigh	
Non-dominant calf	(5) Maintain focus of attention
Non-dominant foot	upon muscle group as it relaxes

arm at the elbow. A relaxation practice session will typically last around 20 minutes and the set of exercises should be practised twice daily, either lying down or sitting (the former is preferable for insomniac patients). Generalisation is an important aspect of applied relaxation practice. That is, instructions in the consulting room must generalise to home-based practice. Tape recordings of clinic sessions can be extremely helpful here. Also, however, the practical application of relaxation may be facilitated by the development of cue control where the subject learns to produce a relaxation response to the self-controlled presentation of a cue such as the word "relax" repeated sub-vocally.

Researchers have investigated the individual components of the progressive relaxation procedure in some detail. Reports such as those of Benson, Beary and Carrol (1974), Davidson and Schwartz (1976) and King (1980) provide a good general perspective on relaxation treatments. King's review paper in particular is an excellent resource. He concludes that it may be the processes which maintain the presenting problem which are of greatest importance in determining whether or not component procedures are essential to the overall package. More specifically, however, Borkovec and his colleagues have conducted a series of studies investigating critical factors in the relaxation procedure with respect to the treatment of initial insomnia (Borkovec, Kaloupek and Slama, 1975; Borkovec and Hennings, 1978; Borkovec and Sides, 1979; Borkovec et al, 1979). Summary results from these studies are included in Table 17. In each case the total relaxation programme produced the lowest sleep-latency scores at post-treatment and follow-up when compared with the attention-focusing component alone (Borkovec, Kaloupek and Slama, 1975; Borkovec et al, 1979) and the tension-release component alone (Borkovec and Hennings, 1978). Commenting on his own work Borkovec (1982) points to the fact that the attention-focusing component was significantly inferior to progressive relaxation on both subjective and objective sleep measures when counterdemand strategies were in operation to control for expectancy effects. He suggests, therefore, that the muscle-tension release component may play some particularly important role. However, consideration of the results of the studies from a *clinical* point of view, by considering final outcome scores, suggests that both individual components can produce a considerable therapeutic effect and that these effects do not appear to be greatly different from those obtained with the total package. The only negative finding was in fact the Borkovec et al (1979) study where attention focusing alone had little impact on objective SOL.

The component analysis study of Woolfolk and McNulty (1983) is of considerable interest. These workers compared progressive relaxation, progressive relaxation without tension-release (somatic focusing), imagery training with tension-release, imagery without tension-release and no treatment in order to compare the relative contributions of tension-release and focus of attention. Unlike the Borkovec studies which employed undergraduate students, Woolfolk and McNulty recruited adult insomniacs from the community (mean age 43 years). These subjects proved to have chronic and severe insomnia with a mean duration of symptoms of 15 years and on average initial SOL was 104 minutes at baseline. Their results indicated that all four treatment groups were effective in reducing SOL compared with the control group. Interestingly, the presence of muscle tension-release was unrelated to outcome. Not a single tension-release/no tension-release comparison was significant for any dependent variable. There was a trend, however, for visual imagery treatments to be superior to somatic-focusing treatments in reducing sleep latency. Woolfolk and McNulty tentatively concluded, therefore, that their data "appeared to indicate that changes in cognitive activity prior to sleep are more likely to facilitate reduction of sleep-onset latencies than is reduction of bodily tension". They suggested further that the success of other attention-focusing treatment for insomnia (Carr-Kaffashan and Woolfolk, 1979; Nicassio and Bootzin, 1974; Woolfolk et al, 1976) may lie in directing attention away from obsessive pre-sleep mentation. The Woolfolk and McNulty study also included a six month follow-up. Data collected at this time indicated that whereas progressive relaxation and somatic focusing had relapsed to pre-treatment levels, the imagery training groups had not only mantained improvement but had further reduced sleep latencies from post-treatment levels.

AUTOGENIC TRAINING

Bootzin and Nicassio (1978) in their review include autogenic training as one of a number of "cognitive relaxation strategies". Nevertheless, it has been decided to include description and discussion of autogenic training, and indeed also meditation, in this chapter rather than Chapter 7 on cognitive treatments. The decision is somewhat arbitrary but in historical terms such treatments emerged in the literature at a time when the mediational role of physiological arousal was to the fore. Hence, it seems reasonable to regard these as relaxation variants rather than as treatments designed to obviate cognitive arousal, although the latter may be in fact a more important mechanism of effect.

Schultz and Luthe (1959) have described the autogenic training procedure. The subject is taught to rehearse simple, standard phrases referring to experiences of warmth and heaviness in the extremities (e.g. "my right arm feels warm and heavy"). The subject, therefore, basically instructs her body towards the achievement of a state of low physiological arousal and attends to the sensations which are associated with the self-instruction. There are standard exercises also for respiratory regulation. Autogenic training is similar to progressive relaxation in having the component of somatic attention-focusing. However, progressive relaxation is an active technique involving cycles of muscle tension-release. In autogenic training the subject's responses are more passive although self-observation does provide feedback on the body's responses to suggestions about weight and heaviness in a manner similar to progressive relaxation where the subject is encouraged to observe the difference between tense and relaxed muscles. Autogenic training may be regarded as a form of self-hypnosis where the subject's self-talk and concentration is used to elicit bodily changes. Suggestions that limbs are tired are commonly used also in hypnosis.

MEDITATION

Various forms of meditation are practised (e.g. yoga, transcendental meditation), but these techniques have in common the employment of a repetitive stimulus word or "mantra" as the focus for concentration. The aim is to transfer attention from the external to the internal and to narrow that focus selectively upon the repeated mantra. Mention was made earlier that such a stimulus is likely to prove soporific, which may be one explanation for the de-arousing effects of the procedure. Alternatively, repetition of the mantra may act to block competing mental activity. The subject may also be required to remain immobile and have his eyes closed (Woolfolk, 1975; Woolfolk et at, 1976). Woolfolk et al required subjects to sub-vocalise the mantra "in" and "out" associated with inhaling and exhaling. The cue-control command "relax" associated with tension-release and exhaling is in fact commonly included in progressive relaxation packages. Meditation may also be regarded as similar to autogenic training although the primary focus is upon the bodily sensations associated with breathing rather than upon limbs and skeletal muscles.

HYPNOSIS

Lichstein and Fischer (1985) referred to the paucity of studies on hypnosis for insomnia, and Kales and Kales (1984) referred to two practical problems in applying hypnotic procedures to insomnia. Firstly, not all subjects are easily hypnotiseable and the unavailability of the therapist to the patient at bedtime compounds this problem; and secondly, sleep is not generally achieved during or following a hypnotic trance. Thus the patient's acquisition of some skill in relaxing may be the principal and non-specific benefit of hypnosis. In their study of relaxation and hypnosis in the treatment of insomnia Graham et al (1975) reported that subjects scored relatively low on a test of hypnotic susceptibility and that this factor correlated poorly with outcome measures.

Techniques of hypnotic induction vary considerably, e.g. one common technique is eye fixation where the subject is required to fixate a small dot or point on the ceiling which is above and behind her field of vision. With eyes remaining open it is inevitable that suggestions to the effect that the eyelids are becoming heavy will be fulfilled and thus initial induction to the hypnotic state may proceed. There is an interesting parallel with this method of hypnotic induction in the cognitive technique of paradoxical intention. Here the subject is required to lie with her eyes open in a darkened room and to attempt passively to resist signals of the encroachment of sleep (as signalled by eyelids closing) (see Chapter 7, pp. 136–139, for further information on paradoxical treatments).

BIOFEEDBACK TRAINING

It is appropriate also to include biofeedback techniques in this chapter on relaxation-based treatments of insomnia. An early paper by Budzynski (1973) set out the goals of biofeedback training very clearly. These were firstly, the development of increased awareness of relevant internal physiological functions or events; secondly, the establishment of control over these functions; and thirdly, the transfer or generalisation of that control from the training site to other areas of the subject's life. In the context of insomnia, and the early interest in muscular relaxation as a treatment, the internal physiological event which has formed a prime focus of interest has been muscle tension. The technique of EMG biofeedback, therefore, has been applied in a number of studies.

Most commonly the subject's awareness of present level of muscle tension has been provided by indicative levels of forehead tension via electrodes placed on the frontalis muscle and auditory feedback through an electromechanical counter (e.g. Coursey et al, 1980; Nicassio, Boylan and McCabe, 1982; Freedman and Papsdorf, 1976). During EMG biofeedback training sessions the subject is instructed to decrease the frequency of the sound by concentrating on sensations and thoughts which appear to reduce the rate of biofeedback signal. In this way successful relaxation is rewarded by auditory feedback and a technique of muscle relaxation is learnt. EMG biofeedback may be regarded, therefore, as a means to the same end as other relaxation techniques, i.e. a state of physiological relaxation. Budzynski has described biofeedback as "a mirror reflecting some aspect of physiology".

Given the importance of the EEG in the investigation and assessment of sleep it is not surprising that feedback of electrical activity in the brain has been studied also by a number of researchers. The production of theta waves, that is drowsy brain rhythms, by means of electroencephalogram feedback has been one approach. EEG-theta biofeedback has generally followed initial training in EMG biofeedback (e.g. Stoyva and Budzynski, 1972; Hauri, 1981; Hauri et al, 1982). The prior EMG training reflects the importance of eliminating EMG artefacts from the EEG channel as well as possible facilitative benefits of the adjunctive treatment. EEG-theta biofeedback refers to perceptible signals such as an amber light being displayed when EEG waves of 4–7 Hz present in the EEG trace. Since such lowering of arousal from alpha rhythm to increasing theta activity is associated with sleep-onset the training up of some voluntary control over such changes may be therapeutic particularly for the sleep-onset insomniac.

An alternative approach to affecting central arousal has been the employment of biofeedback targeting the sensorimotor rhythm (SMR). This form of biofeedback attempts to strengthen the 12–14 Hz SMR, which is a low amplitude EEG rhythm measured over the sensorimotor cortex during wakefulness. This SMR is related to sleep spindling which characterises stage 2 NREM sleep (see Chapter 1, p. 4). SMR biofeedback emerged as a possible treatment for insomnia after Sterman, Howe and Macdonald (1970) reported that longer epochs of undisturbed sleep and more sleep spindles were achieved in their experimental study on cats by increasing the frequency of SMR during wakefulness. Since then a number of research evaluations have been completed on human subjects and insomniacs (e.g. Feinstein, Sterman and Macdonald, 1974; Hauri, 1981; Hauri et al, 1982).

One practical disadvantage to biofeedback training, by whatever method, is the reliance upon sophisticated technical equipment. The treatment outcome studies to be described later all involved sleep laboratory-based training, at least initially. Thus, there may be limitations to the general application of biofeedback in non-specialised clinic settings. Also Budzynski (1973) has highlighted the subject's ability to understand and verbalise the learned control strategies as a critical factor to enhance the transfer of learned strategies to real life situations. He suggested that patients should be encouraged during the training phase to describe sensations and the associated successful strategies with the aim of conditioning a phrase or series of phrases to desired physiological patterns. It is not clear, however, whether or not such recommendations have been followed by the majority of research workers. Rather, more general advice on relaxation methods appears to have been provided.

EFFECTIVENESS OF RELAXATION-BASED TREATMENTS

Investigations of the effectiveness of relaxation-based treatments of insomnia reflect the emergence of behaviour therapy techniques as applied to other disorders, such as phobic and obsessional states. A number of the earliest reported studies employed a desensitisation paradigm. These studies conducted in the late 1960s and early 1970s were paralleled by early investigations of progressive relaxation training. Table 17 provides a summary of the available treatment outcome studies. Some information on subject sampling and the principal treatment outcome comparisons is presented in the table and more detailed discussion will follow at appropriate points in the ensuing text. The table is confined largely to the presentation of SOL data since this has been the principal outcome measure employed. Where this is not the case other information is presented. It should be noted that Table 17 does *not* include studies comparing outcome across diverse therapeutic strategies since these will be dealt with in Chapter 9. Rather the emphasis is upon relaxation-based treatments and comparisons within this sphere of management.

Desensitisation treatment has been evaluated both with single cases (Geer and Katkin, 1966; Evans and Bond, 1969) and with larger groups (Hinkle and Lutker, 1972; Borkovec, Steinmark and Nau, 1973; Gershman and Clouser, 1974; Steinmark and Borkovec, 1974). Geer and Katkin (1966) reported that a treatment comprising initial sessions in progressive relaxation followed by nine sessions of single-item desensitisation led to subjective improvement in sleep which was maintained at 8 month follow-up. By comparison, the single case study of Evans and Bond (1969) found that the same treatment produced no improvement in hours slept whereas a subsequent classical conditioning treatment involving the pairing of methohexital sodium injections with counting up from 1 to 28 improved the client's total sleep time from around two hours to between five and six hours. Hinkle and Lutker (1972) treated seven student subjects with a combined relaxation and desensitisation programme which led to a 50% reduction in sleep latency for the group as a whole although five of the seven subjects improved considerably more than the remaining two.

The first study to compare the effectiveness of desensitisation with a relaxation procedure was that of Borkovec, Steinmark and Nau (1973). Twenty-three recruited insomniacs (ages not specified) received either progressive relaxation (alone), single-item desensitisation plus relaxation or desensitisation alone. Baseline sleep latency scores were used to rank subjects in terms of severity, with subsequent random assignment within bands to one of the three treatment conditions. Borkovec, Steinmark and Nau reported that all three treatments resulted in significant improvements in SOL (average reductions from 40.6 to 25.1 minutes

Table 17 Relaxation-based treatment studies of insomnia. Outcome data reported are subjective sleep log ratings of sleep-onset latency (SOL; min.) unless otherwise stated

Authors	Sample	Total N	Age (mean years)	Duration (mean years)	Treatment(s)	SOL Pre (mean min.)	SOL Post (mean min.)	SOL F.up (mean min.)	F.up (month)
Borkovec and Fowles (1973)	S	37	NA	NA	Progressive relaxation	46	25	NA	NA
					Hypnotic relaxation	43	24	NA	NA
					Self-relaxation placebo	42	24	NA	NA
					No treatment	44	44	NA	NA
Borkovec and Hennings (1978)	S	44	NA	NA	Progressive relaxation	34	*CD/PD* 23/19	NA	NA
					Progressive relaxation (tension release only)	47	29/26	NA	NA
					No treatment	37	37/35	NA	NA
Borkovec and Weerts (1976)	S	36	NA	NA	Progressive relaxation	40	28	27	12
					Desensitisation placebo	53	39	58	12
					No treatment	47	37	NA	NA
Borkovec, Kaloupek and Slama (1975)	S	56	NA	NA	Progressive relaxation	46	*CD/PD* 25/23	16	5
					Prog. rel. (attention focusing only)	38	28/26	23	5
					Desensitisation placebo	42	35/25	32	5
					No treatment	35	32/33	NA	NA
Borkovec, Steinmark and Nau (1973)	R	23	NA	NA	Single-item desensitisation Progressive relaxation Desensitisation plus relaxation	41	25 (global reporting)	NA	NA

						EEG	EEG		
Borkovec et al (1979)[a]	S	29	NA	NA	Progressive relaxation	50	33	"maintained"	12
					Prog. relaxation (attention focusing only)	46	45	"maintained"	12
					No treatment	51	59	NA	NA
Budzynski (1973)	P	11	NA	NA	EMG + theta biofeedback	6	"improved"		
Carr-Kaffashan and Woolfolk (1979)	R	30	40	11	Progressive relaxation (moderate insomnia)	59	40	49	6
					Progressive relaxation (severe insomnia)	150	80	49	6
					Desensitisation placebo (moderate insomnia)	50	35	66	6
					Desensitisation placebo (severe insomnia)	112	62	66	6
Coursey et al (1980)	P	22	38	14	EMG biofeedback	3 of 6	"meaningful improvement"	NA	NA
					Autogenic training	2 of 6	"meaningful improvement"	NA	NA
					Electrosleep	0 of 10	"meaningful improvement"	NA	NA
Evans and Bond (1969)	P	1	45	7	Single item desensitisation	2	"no change"	NA	NA
					Classical conditioning	2	5.5 (hours of sleep)	NA	NA
						EEG	EEG		
Freedman and Papsdorf (1976)	R	18	23	>0.5	EMG biofeedback	42	13	NA	NA
					Progressive relaxation	43	20	NA	NA
					Exercise control	43	40	NA	NA
Geer and Katkin (1966)	P	1	29	1	Single-item desensitisation	-	"sleeping well"		8
Gershman and Clouser (1974)	S	20	NA	NA	Systematic desensitisation	75	30	18	12
					Progressive relaxation	55	37	15	12

Table 17 (*continued*)

Authors	Sample	Total N	Age (mean years)	Duration (mean years)	Treatment(s)	SOL Pre (mean min.)	SOL Post (mean min.)	SOL F.up (mean min.)	F.up (month)
Graham et al (1975)	S	22	NA	NA	Progressive relaxation	5.9	3.1	NA	NA
					Hypnosis	5.9	3.1 (rating of severity)	NA	NA
Hauri (1978)	P	37	NA	NA	Frontalis EMG biofeedback	*EEG/LOG* 60/94	*EEG/LOG* 50/64	NA	NA
					Frontalis + EEG theta biofeedback	31/64	26/45	NA	NA
					SMR biofeedback	34/86	26/54	NA	NA
					Control (discussion/advice)	47/103	64/70		
Hauri (1981)	P/R	48	41	8	Frontalis EMG biofeedback	91	63	52	9
					EEG theta biofeedback	48	30	40	9
					SMR biofeedback	64	41	26	9
					No treatment	94	NA	76	9
Hauri et al (1982)	P/R	16	49	NA	EMG plus EEG theta biofeedback	*EEG/LOG* 16/27	*EEG/LOG* 15/24	*EEG/LOG* 15/12	9
					EMG plus SMR biofeedback	28/35	33/32	20/18	9
Haynes et al (1974)	S	14	18–21 (range)	5	Progressive relaxation	61	34	"maintained improvement"	9
					Discussion placebo	53	40	NA	NA
Haynes, Sides and Lockwood (1977)	R	24	29	7	Passive relaxation	51	26	16	12
					EMG biofeedback	49	23	26	12
					Self-relaxation control	48	45	51	3
Hinkle and Lutker (1972)	S	7	NA	2 (median)	Relaxation plus desensitisation	70	34	23	2 weeks

Study					Treatment	52 (median)	22	15	11
Kahn, Baker and Weiss (1968)	S	13	NA	NA	Autogenic training	52	22	15	11
Lick and Heffler (1977)	R	40	48	12	Progressive relaxation	63	30	NA	NA
					Progressive relaxation + tape	62	38	NA	NA
					False biofeedback placebo	69	66	NA	NA
					No treatment	60	63	NA	NA
Nicassio and Bootzin (1974)	R	30	45	NA	Progressive relaxation	131	73	47	6
					Autogenic training	109	46		6
					Self-relaxation placebo	119	117	112	6
					No treatment	122	99	NA	NA
Nicassio, Boylan and McCabe (1982)	R	40	44	11	Progressive relaxation	97	42	31	6
					EMG biofeedback	84	31	52	6
					Biofeedback placebo	97	60	34	6
					No treatment	92	84	NA	NA
Pendleton and Tasto (1976)	S/R	29	NA	>1	Metronome-conditioned relaxation	49	34	32	6
					Progressive relaxation alone	55	25	11	6
					Metronome-induced relaxation alone	51	27	27	6
					No treatment	60	79	NA	NA
Shealy (1979)[b]	S	70	20	NA			CD/PD		
					Passive relaxation	46	44/28	24	6
					Passive relaxation + stimulus control	47	28/32	29	6
					Self-monitoring	47	48/38	43	6
					Discussion placebo	41	39/29	31	6
					No treatment	59	NA/41	48	6

Table 17 (continued)

Authors	Sample	Total N	Age (mean years)	Duration (mean years)	Treatment(s)	SOL Pre (mean min.)	SOL Post (mean min.)	SOL F.up (mean min.)	F.up (month)
Steinmark and Borkovec (1974)	S	52	NA	>0.5	Progressive relaxation	39	CD/PD 28/27	19	5
					Relaxation + desensitisation	36	25/24	18	5
					Desensitisation placebo	42	40/24	30	5
					No treatment	32	35/42	NA	NA
Traub, Jencks and Bliss (1973)	P	7	42	NA	Autogenic training (+ elements of progressive relaxation)	EEG 27	EEG 11	NA	NA
Weil and Goldfried (1973)	P	1	11	NA	Tape-recorded relaxation	120	15	"no sleep difficulty"	6
Woolfolk et al (1976)	R	24	44	14	Progressive relaxation	65	29	27	6
					Meditation	74	34	25	6
					No treatment	67	67	NA	NA
Woolfolk and McNulty (1983)	R	44	43	15	Progressive relaxation	98	CD/PD 76/73	90	6
					Imagery training	108	40/50	35	6
					Imagery training + tension release	101	51/55	35	6
					Somatic focusing	104	67/68	84	6
					No treatment	110	119/109	NA	NA
Vander Plate and Eno (1983)	S	24	20	1.4	EMG biofeedback	30	16	10	2
					Pseudofeedback	40	17	10	2
					No treatment	28	26	NA	NA

Notes. [a] Data presented are extrapolated from original graph.
[b] Total sample = 70; data presented are for "moderate insomnia" group only.

Key. CD = counterdemand instruction; PD = positive demand instruction; S = student; R = recruited subject; P = patient were the only sleep latency data presented), rated difficulty in falling asleep and number of awakenings (which reduced from 1.15 per night to 0.69 on average). Gershman and Clouser (1974) also employed a group comparison design but like the previous study, control groups were not available. Gershman and Clouser compared group treatments which utilised tape-recorded instructions of systematic desensitisation and progressive relaxation respectively. Treatment was over eight therapy sessions. Post-treatment measures of sleep latency were similar for the two groups and were similarly maintained at one year follow-up (see Table 17). Interestingly, these workers also reported that there were trends towards improved emotional stability and self-reliance as measured by 16 PF assessment, after desensitisation treatment. The effectiveness of a similar tape-recorded relaxation procedure was reported in a study by Weil and Goldfried (1973) where dramatic reductions in sleep latency were achieved in an 11 year old girl. These authors also noted that there was marked generalisation to daytime function with parents reporting that she was more rested and relaxed and that her piano performance had improved.

In keeping with the classical conditioning paradigm, Pendleton and Tasto (1976) investigated the effectiveness of metronome-conditioned relaxation training, progressive relaxation training alone and metronome-induced relaxation alone. They reported that subjects in all three groups improved and maintained improvements six months later relative to an untreated control sample. The addition of the metronome conditioning did not add anything to the effects of progressive relaxation. Indeed, inspection of the data in Table 17 indicates that the combined condition had the lowest pre-treatment sleep latency of the experimental conditions, but had the highest sleep latencies at post-treatment and follow-up. In contrast, progressive relaxation alone was associated with the greatest absolute reduction in sleep latency across treatment and at follow-up. The effectiveness of the metronome only condition raises the possibility that the one second interval rhythmic beats had a soporific effect.

Early studies on autogenic training and progressive relaxation were also poorly controlled, but nonetheless, proved to be influential (Kahn, Baker and Weiss, 1968; Traub, Jencks and Bliss, 1973; Haynes et al, 1974; Graham et al, 1975). Kahn, Baker and Weiss's student sample reduced median sleep latency by 30 minutes after four group sessions of autogenic training. Traub, Jencks and Bliss had seven older adults in their study of autogenic training, which also included elements of progressive relaxation. However, these workers reported upon EEG changes associated with treatment rather than using anecdotal or self-report measures of change. All seven subjects reported overall sleep improvement, although only three demonstrated significant therapeutic change in either EEG-defined SOL or total sleep time. A measure of delta sleep (NREM stages 3 and 4) was also employed but demonstrated improvement in only two subjects. Although this study is severely limited in terms of numbers, the relatively short (12 night) experimental period and the heterogeneity of pre-treatment sleep patterns, it is commendable as an early effort more systematically and objectively to evaluate treatment outcome.

Haynes et al (1974) randomly allocated 14 young subjects to either progressive relaxation group treatment or a group discussion placebo. Both treatments led to reduced sleep latency, although percentage change was considerably greater after the active treatment. Gains were maintained amongst those contactable at follow-up. Haynes et al also reported that awakening frequency reduced markedly in both treatments but significantly more so in the relaxation group where the baseline average was 2.8 wakenings per night and final outcome was 0.7 wakenings per night. Graham et al's (1975) comparative study investigated a relaxation procedure, which combined elements of relaxation and autogenic training, with a simple hypnosis treatment. Subjects were not required to keep a daily sleep log in this study. Rather, pre- and post-training ratings were made on a 10 point scale of insomnia severity. Interestingly, identical mean scores were achieved at both pre-and post-treatment for both therapies. Reduction in severity rating approached 50%. However, a measure was taken also of the proportion of nights on which insomnia occurred. Comparison on this variable revealed a significant post-training reduction for the relaxation treatment but not for the hypnosis treatment. From Graham et al's data, it seems likely that this difference arose because of considerable elevation of pre-training scores in the relaxation group rather than absolute between group differences at post-treatment.

Studies by Borkovec and Fowles (1973) and Nicassio and Bootzin (1974) demonstrated improved methodological controls, since both employed "relaxation placebo" and no treatment interventions within a random allocation design. Borkovec and Fowles compared progressive relaxation and hypnotic relaxation with these control treatments in a student sample of 37 female college students with relatively mild sleep-onset problems (average SOL at baseline was around 45 minutes). After initial baselines were recorded, subjects were matched on SOL and randomly assigned out of groups of four into one of the experimental conditions. Borkovec and Fowles found that the relaxation placebo procedure was as effective as the two active interventions, and that all three relaxation groups were superior to no treatment in reducing sleep latency (see Table 17). Very similar results were obtained for number of nighttime awakenings and ratings of morning restedness. Interestingly, however, Borkovec and Fowles found that measured physiological changes during therapy were unrelated to outcome. They commented that the non-specific, active ingredient in the interventions may have been that of focusing upon pleasant internal feelings; a response incompatible with cognitive activity.

Nicassio and Bootzin (1974) by comparison found that this self-relaxation placebo treatment was ineffective when applied with a group of older adults with severe initial insomnia who were recruited from the community. In their study, progressive relaxation and autogenic training led to reductions in sleep latency of 58 and 63 minutes respectively, and post-treatment gains were maintained in a combined follow-up group six months later. Nicassio and Bootzin also employed measures independent of insomniacs' subjective reports. Evidence from spouses or room-mates confirmed the subjective estimates obtained from sleep diaries, and pupillography demonstrated less pupil restriction (a correlate of drowsiness) after active intervention. Other sleep pattern measures, however, such as total sleep and number of awakenings were not affected significantly by any of the treatments.

Borkovec and his colleagues conducted a further series of influential investigations. The first of these compared progressive relaxation, systematic desensitisation (incorporating progressive relaxation), a quasi-desensitisation placebo and a no treatment control group (Steinmark and Borkovec, 1974). The study was designed, however, not simply to compare treatment effectiveness but to quantify the influence of non-specific factors in therapy such as expectancy effects and demand characteristics. Steinmark and Borkovec employed a counterdemand instruction for the first three weeks of therapy which encouraged subjects to believe that no improvement would occur during this time. The issuing of a positive demand instruction, however, led subjects to expect dramatic improvement after the fourth session. An assessment of treatment credibility (Borkovec and Nau, 1972) was also completed. Subjects received four sessions, one per week in small groups. The results from this study in terms of sleep latency are presented in Table 17. Both relaxation conditions were found to be significantly superior to placebo and no treatment in reducing initial sleep latency during the counterdemand period. The presentation of the positive demand instruction, however, produced comparable improvement in the placebo group although this was seen to diminish at follow-up compared with the active interventions.

The main contribution of the Steinmark and Borkovec study, therefore, was the demonstration that relaxation had therapeutic effects upon sleep latency which were independent of demand and placebo influences. The fact that all three treatments were regarded as highly and equally credible lent further weight to this conclusion. Steinmark and Borkovec reported that there were no significant effects from analysis of the number of times which subjects awoke during the night or in their rated difficulty in returning to sleep once awakened.

Borkovec and Weerts (1976) conducted a partial replication of the above study, but on this occasion employed electroencephalographic assessment of sleep pattern as the dependent variable. The results from this study were more ambiguous. Progressive relaxation was not shown to be superior to control groups during counterdemand, although progressive relaxation alone produced significant linear decreases in stage 1 sleep-onset over the experimental period from pre-treatment to the end of positive demand. Thus, some confirmation of the effectiveness of progressive relaxation using objective assessment methods was forthcoming from this study. Furthermore, the lengthy (one year) follow-up also pointed to the persistency of relaxation treatment gains whereas placebo subjects had returned to baseline levels.

Studies by Borkovec, Kaloupek and Slama (1975), Borkovec and Hennings (1978) and Borkovec et al (1979) were discussed in some detail earlier in this chapter. Borkovec was concerned to investigate the effectiveness of component parts of the relaxation procedure and has discussed and summarised his principal conclusions in a later paper (Borkovec, 1979). His overall conclusion was that subjective improvement in sleep latency is due to the muscle tension-release component of relaxation training. Attention focusing on the other hand appears to have a secondary function and may contribute through the preclusion of cognitive intrusions or the provision of monotonous stimulation. Summary data from these studies may be found in Table 17. It may be helpful, however, to make one or two further points in addition to what is stated above and what has been said earlier.

Firstly, in each study, student samples were used and sleep latencies at baseline were on average mild. Indeed, at one year follow-up in one of the studies, the seven no treatment subjects who were contacted had achieved reductions in sleep-onset latency of a magnitude comparable to the improvement originally obtained by the treated relaxation groups (Borkovec et al, 1979). Secondly, apart from changes in sleep latency, other treatment effects were noted. Borkovec, Kaloupek and Slama (1975) found that awakenings and difficulty in returning to sleep positively improved for the total group of subjects actively treated, although there were no between group effects. Thirdly and interestingly, they also reported a significant inverse correlation between a measure of restfulness prior to sleep and practice of the relaxation procedure. This suggests that a proportion of subjects may regard treatment as a palliative procedure to be used in a reactive fashion rather than a training technique where practice is essential in order to learn a skill. Borkovec and Hennings (1978), however, found that subjects in both their relaxation-treated groups reported greater success in eliminating daytime tension. Thus there is also an indication of potential generalised benefits from relaxation training. This point will be taken up again later in this chapter. Finally, in this same study both progressive relaxation and tension-release exercises were associated with reductions in ratings of bedtime intrusive thoughts, which provides further evidence that relaxation procedures may operate via cognitive de-arousal (see Chapter 3).

In spite of some evidence that muscle tension-release is an important therapeutic element in progressive relaxation training, a number of studies have demonstrated that more passive approaches to relaxation such as meditation, autogenic training and imagery training can be highly effective.

Woolfolk et al (1976) compared standard progressive relaxation with meditation and no treatment in a sample of 24 moderate insomniacs. The meditation treatment comprised elements of both Zen meditation and Yogic meditation (transcendental meditation). Subjects practising meditation were required to lie immobile with eyes closed. They were instructed at first to maintain a passive focus upon the physical sensations associated with breathing. Later they were told to focus attention upon their respiration and to rehearse sub-vocally the mantras "in" and "out" in accordance with their breathing. The meditation procedure was thereafter generalised to incorporate some imagery training. Woolfolk et al found that their insomniacs responded equally well to the meditation and progressive relaxation treatments and that both were superior to an untreated control group on measures of SOL and rated difficulty in falling asleep. Treatment gains were maintained at six month follow-up.

In a further study, Carr-Kaffashan and Woolfolk (1979) investigated the effectiveness of relaxation procedures separately in moderate and severe insomniacs compared with a quasi-desensitisation placebo treatment. They reported that their relaxation training programme (which combined aspects of meditation and progressive relaxation) led to improvement during a counterdemand period which was not found with the placebo intervention. A 46% average reduction in SOL was obtained with active treatment.

Woolfolk and McNulty's (1983) influential component analysis study was introduced in Chapter 3 and also earlier in this chapter. Treatment outcome data on sleep latency, however, are presented in Table 17. Woolfolk and McNulty randomly allocated their severely insomniac sample to one of four active treatments or a no treatment control group. Subjects were treated in groups of five receiving four, weekly one-hour sessions. Two of the active treatments involved visual focusing techniques. Imagery training (alone) comprised visualisation of common, neutral objects but avoided concentration upon somatic sensations. Imagery training plus tension-release relaxation comprised sequential progressive relaxation but substituted the above object imagery in place of somatic focusing. The other two treatments involved somatic-focusing techniques. These were standard progressive relaxation and a treatment, named somatic focusing, in which subjects were instructed to become aware of and focus upon bodily tension and to allow that tension to go. No prior muscle tensing was involved here and there was no visualisation element.

Woolfolk and McNulty's results have proven supportive of the cognitive hyperarousal view of insomnia since only the visual focusing treatment groups reduced SOL significantly more than the control group under counterdemand instruction. Significant gains were also made under counterdemand in subjective ratings of ability to control intrusive thoughts. Interestingly, however, no significant differences were found across treatments on global anxiety assessments at post-treatment which suggests that the treatments effects were specific to bedtime intrusive thinking. The two visual focusing treatments also exhibited further post-treatment to follow-up gains compared with the somatic-focusing techniques on measures of sleep latency, sleep duration, quality of sleep, ratings of restedness and control of thoughts.

Haynes, Sides and Lockwood (1977) reported that a passive relaxation procedure where subjects were told to focus on various muscle groups, to allow these muscles to become relaxed, and to focus on changing proprioceptive feedback and pleasant feelings, was equally effective to a frontalis EMG biofeedback group in reducing sleep latency and times awake during the night. Both groups were superior to a control group where subjects were told simply to practise relaxing but had no specific instruction. Intervention effects were maintained to a greater degree, however, in the passive relaxation group (compared with biofeedback) at 12 month follow-up. Haynes, Sides and Lockwood quote this evidence, and the economic benefits of the passive relaxation procedure, to suggest that this may be a preferred treatment compared with biofeedback.

Shealy (1979) reported on a large, student sample of mild and moderate insomniacs and considered comparative treatment effectiveness within each of these two severity sub-groups. Since the mild insomniacs as a group had an average baseline sleep latency of less than 30 minutes, only the data from the moderate insomniac group are included in Table 17. Shealy reported that a treatment group which combined automated passive relaxation with stimulus control instruction was the most effective intervention, being superior to various control groups (self-monitoring, discussion placebo and no treatment) but also superior to passive relaxation alone under counterdemand. The issuing of a positive demand expectancy, however, led to equivalent improvement in this passive relaxation group which was still evident at six month follow-up. Shealy suggested that a plausible explanation may be that passive relaxation alone requires more time to yield significant reductions in sleep latency compared with the combination treatment.

Toler (1978) also compared the effects of adding stimulus control to relaxation in a study of 24 prisoners in a federal penitentiary. Subjects were assigned to either progressive relaxation, relaxation plus stimulus control instruction or no treatment. After a brief, two week treatment period both treated groups had demonstrated substantial reductions in sleep latency, although post-treatment latency was still quite high (see Table 17). At eight week follow-up, however, SOL scores had returned close to pre-treatment levels in both groups. Toler suggested that the high stress environment in which these subjects lived may have mitigated against long term treatment gains. Furthermore, the brevity of intervention may have contributed to the ephemeral benefit. Toler also reported results in terms of nightly wakenings. Again both treated groups demonstrated post-treatment reductions in frequency of awakenings, but only the augmented treatment (relaxation plus stimulus control) produced a significant reduction from pre- to post-treatment.

Although a number of different relaxation-based treatments have been investigated, most have involved some consulting-room instruction and home practice. However, in routine clinical work, for reasons of efficiency and generalisation, many practitioners make use of audiotaped instruction. Lick and Heffler (1977) have made a systematic study of the benefits of using audiotapes for home practice. These workers compared a progressive relaxation group who were provided with six sessions of training and written instructions for home practice with another relaxation group who, in addition, were provided with a tape for home practice. No additional benefit was conferred by the addition of the audiotaped instructions although both relaxation groups improved relative to placebo and no treatment in terms of sleep latency, number of hours slept and quality of sleep as rated upon wakening. Both actively treated groups also achieved significant reduction in sleep medication. The main advantage of audiotaped instruction, therefore, may be to obviate the need for protracted treatment at the clinic. Indeed in some cases it appears that automated instruction alone may have beneficial effects (e.g. Weil and Goldfried, 1973).

The earliest clinical investigations of biofeedback procedures were conducted by Budzynski (1973) and Feinstein, Sterman and Macdonald (1974). Budzynski reported briefly on a sample of 11 sleep-onset insomniacs who were treated with a combined biofeedback procedure of EMG training followed by EEG-theta feedback. Outcome data were not provided; however, Budzynski stated that six of the 11 subjects improved (three dramatically), but five demonstrated no improvement. He suggested that the facilitative effects of EMG feedback were particularly useful for tense subjects. Feinstein, Sterman and Macdonald considered the effects of biofeedback training using four different EEG frequencies. Subjects received 25 sessions of EEG biofeedback training consisting of three, one-hour feedback periods over five weeks. The subject received reinforcement in the form of lights and tones for production of the appropriate EEG pattern. These workers reported that the four subjects receiving SMR training showed a decrease in sleep latency and in number of movements during sleep, an increase in percentage REM time and improvement in cyclicity of sleep stages. A mixed control group who received training of other EEG frequencies (occipital 10 Hz, i.e. alpha, central 10 Hz, central 15 Hz) did not show similar improvement. Early investigations of biofeedback, therefore, were encouraging and controlled studies followed which considered both EMG feedback and EEG feedback.

Freedman and Papsdorf (1976) conducted an influential controlled comparison of EMG biofeedback and progressive relaxation in a sample of 18 university students who complained of difficulty falling asleep. The investigation included a control group who were instructed to repeat a series of physical exercises such as touching toes and sit-ups. Six subjects were allocated per experimental group, each receiving six 30-minute training sessions in one of the three procedures, spaced over a two week period. Both prior to and after treatment subjects were required to sleep overnight in the sleep laboratory so that objective records of sleep pattern could be made. Freedman and Papsdorf reported that the only significant treatment by time interaction effect was for SOL where both biofeedback and progressive relaxation groups improved significantly more than the control procedure but were not significantly different from each other. Both active treatment groups also demonstrated significant decreases in heart rate as well as frontal masseter and forearm extensor EMG, while changes in the control group where minimal. However, no significant relationships between physiological levels and sleep-onset time were found, indicating that muscle relaxation alone was not responsible for the subjects' improvements. In discussing this matter Freedman and Papsdorf reported that at the initial interview the vast majority of their subjects had claimed that repetitive cognition kept them awake at night.

It is also noteworthy that in this study subjects' self-report of sleep latency correlated highly ($r = 0.75$) with EEG sleep-onset time for the final night's sleep in the laboratory. Freedman and Papsdorf reported that this correlation steadily increased throughout the study, implying that the subjects had become more accurate in their estimations of how long it took them to fall asleep. Such improvements in accuracy of self-report information, however, may also reflect the point made in Chapter 1 (p. 19), in the discussion on subjective/objective concordance, that since sleep latency was actually reducing as a function of treatment, the subject's task was simply becoming an easier one.

Hauri (1978) reported on a study of referred patients with chronic, severe insomnia where initial sleep latencies were of the order of 60 to 90 minutes. These compare with relatively moderate SOL difficulties in the Freedman and Papsdorf study. Hauri compared a conventional frontalis EMG feedback group with a combined group where EMG training was followed by EEG-theta feedback, and an SMR training group. The number of sessions of training received by patients varied between 15 and 60 and each feedback session usually lasted 45 minutes.

The results of this study indicated that frontalis EMG feedback yielded significant improvements both in sleep latency and total sleep time according to sleep logs kept by subjects, but little improvement was obtained according to sleep laboratory assessment. EEG-theta feedback produced no significant improvement, either subjectively or objectively. However, SMR feedback yielded significant improvement in subjective sleep latency, in sleep efficiency according to laboratory measurement, and in the amount of stage 2 sleep. Control subjects showed no significant objective change on any sleep parameter although they did reduce sleep latency by 33 minutes from a high initial baseline value on the sleep log measure (a non-significant reduction). SOL data from both sleep log and EEG assessment are presented in Table 17. It is clear from inspection of these data that there were considerable mean baseline differences between treatment groups in this study and also intragroup variability may have accounted for either failure to achieve statistical effect or indeed for some of the significant effects which were demonstrated.

In order to explore his data further, Hauri conducted a further analysis of results on the basis of appropriate/inappropriate assignment to biofeedback group. This judgement was based upon intake data, such that evidence of psychological tension, EMG muscle tension and excessive sleep latency were taken as indices of "excessive arousal" and indicative of EMG or EEG-theta feedback as the appropriate treatment. Low arousal, frequent wakenings and poor sleep spindling during stage 2 were taken as indices of a poor sleep system, for which SMR biofeedback was hypothesised to be the treatment of choice. Comparisons of improvements obtained via appropriate feedback (n = 9) and inappropriate feedback (n = 9) revealed that sleep in the laboratory improved significantly (sleep efficiency, sleep-onset) for the appropriate feedback group relative to the inappropriate feedback group. Thus tailoring of treatment according to presenting characteristics may be valuable.

Also in 1978, Freedman, Hauri and others who had been involved in evaluations of biofeedback procedures reported collaboratively on their studies to date (Freedman et al, 1978). The pooled data from three separate, all-night studies of the effects of biofeedback and relaxation on insomnia failed to show pre–post treatment differences between experimental and control conditions. They concluded, therefore, that caution was warranted in the use of biofeedback and relaxation techniques. Besner (1978) also has highlighted limitations to biofeedback procedures. In her study 43 subjects with chronic sleep-onset insomnia were randomly assigned to EMG feedback, EEG-theta training, psychotherapy or control procedures. She found no differential treatment effects between the conditions. Rather, all groups demonstrated a reduction in sleep latency. Besner interpreted these results to indicate a large placebo effect and only a possible biofeedback effect. It was suggested that simply bringing an individual into the laboratory, attaching electrodes and providing instructions to relax were non-specific procedures which produced a change in sleep behaviour.

Coursey et al (1980) selected a sample of physician-referred chronic insomniacs for a study designed to compare relaxation associated with frontalis muscle EMG feedback and autogenic training. Six insomniacs were allocated to each of these groups and a control group of 10 patients received "electrosleep therapy", designed to be procedurally similar to biofeedback but without any known active relaxation component. The treatment protocol comprised six weeks of twice weekly individual sessions plus daily home practice. Sleep pattern was recorded on sleep logs throughout the treatment period and via all-night sleep EEG recording one week prior to and again one month after treatment. The particular merit of this study relates to the very stringent criteria which were applied to determine "meaningful improvement".

Coursey et al required that the subject reported a global subjective assessment of marked improvement, a 33% reduction in sleep latency according to sleep logs and a final sleep latency of less than 35 minutes; and on EEG assessment at follow-up a 25% reduction in sleep latency and an absolute value of 30 minutes or less. Thus Coursey et al sought to consider clinical improvement which was reliable, and not only statistical change. They elected to analyse their results in relation to success/failure in achieving these multiple criteria which revealed that three of the six EMG patients and two of the autogenic training patients improved significantly compared with none in the electrosleep group. The treatment effects for the two active therapies, therefore, were very similar. Taking the successful patients together as a group they observed significant decreases in sleep latency and significant increases in sleep efficiency from pre- to post-test, and successful patients also reported improved quality of sleep, more total sleep time and fewer awakenings than controls. Interestingly, an examination of the amount of time spent practising relaxation exercises at home revealed that successful EMG feedback patients had spent considerably more time practising than unsuccessful ones, although there was no such differentiation among autogenic patients.

Hauri (1981) allocated 48 insomniac subjects (mean age 41.3 years) randomly to frontalis EMG, EEG-theta, SMR biofeedback or no treatment conditions. Subjects received an average of 15 therapy sessions. No between treatment significant differences were found at post-treatment, although in the active treatment groups SOL was reduced by around 20 to 30 minutes on average and total sleep time was increased by 30 to 40 minutes (Table 17). Hauri reported a consistent finding that some patients improved very much while others not at all, regardless of treatment type. He hypothesised that this might be due to the subjects' learning of the treatment methods or to the appropriateness of the type of feedback to the presenting characteristics of the individual's insomnia. He reported some evidence in support of the latter hypothesis, that is people who were initially not highly aroused benefited less from relaxation-based feedback whereas those who were initially more highly aroused benefited most. (Assessment of arousal here comprised the Institute for Personality and Ability Testing (IPAT) Anxiety Scale and measures of frontalis tension.) It seems possible, therefore, that EMG biofeedback operates by treating anxiety and tension whereas SMR biofeedback may operate through neurologic mechanisms. Treatment gains were extended further in the SMR feedback group at nine month follow-up where average sleep latency was only 26 minutes. Some relapse had occurred in the other treatment groups.

Hauri et al (1982) conducted a replication of Hauri's original study but with some methodological and procedural refinements. Subjects were assigned to either theta or SMR biofeedback by the throw of dice although a matching procedure also was used to equate male/female ratios and to achieve similar age distribution in the two groups. All insomniacs first received some frontalis EMG biofeedback so that subsequent theta or SMR training could proceed smoothly and avoid EMG artefacts on the EEG channel. Patients then were switched to the appropriate feedback, either theta or SMR. In practice around six EMG sessions were required followed by around 26 EEG sessions. Total training, therefore, lasted around 13 weeks. Hauri et al reported both subjective and objective outcome data (Table 17).

According to sleep logs both biofeedback treatments led to improvements in patients' sleep. Interestingly, however, changes over baseline were considerably greater at follow-up than they had been at post-treatment for both sleep latency and total sleep time. Sleep laboratory evaluations revealed no significant improvements on any variable at either post-treatment or follow-up. However, Hauri et al, once again, found evidence of inter-subject variability in response to both treatments. They therefore re-tested their hypothesis that initial tension may be positively correlated with theta relaxation training and negatively correlated with SMR training. The great majority of correlations which were calculated supported this hypothesis. Hauri et al went on to re-analyse their data in terms of the subject's treatment by either "appropriate" or "inappropriate" feedback in terms of initial tension ratings. They reported significant improvement of sleep with appropriate feedback from intake to follow-up both for sleep efficiency and for sleep latency. However, inappropriate feedback was associated with statistically significant deterioration of total sleep time and sleep efficiency during training, although this effect had disappeared by the time of follow-up. Hauri et al concluded that the 14-cps SMR training may influence some basic neurological imbalance in the sleep–wake system of certain insomniacs, whereas EMG or theta training may benefit only tense insomniacs.

Nicassio, Boylan and McCabe (1982) reported on a recruited sample of 40 insomniacs who received either progressive relaxation, EMG biofeedback, a biofeedback placebo or no treatment. The two active treatments followed standard procedures and the biofeedback placebo subjects received non-contingent bogus feedback. For all subjects treatment spanned six weeks. These workers reported outcome in terms of sleep log estimates which confirmed the superiority of both progressive relaxation and EMG biofeedback over no-treatment control. The biofeedback placebo group also improved, and within group analyses revealed significant linear trends for all but the no treatment group. Absolute reduction in sleep latency was only around 15 minutes greater in the active treatments compared with placebo (Table 17). At six month follow-up placebo subjects had improved further and achieved average sleep latency of 34 minutes compared with 97 minutes at baseline. There is, therefore, very limited evidence from this study for the superiority of biofeedback or relaxation over the biofeedback placebo. In discussing their results Nicassio, Boylan and McCabe suggest that the treatments may have "fostered the ability of subjects to ward off extraneous, intrusive cognitive events". Certainly, this may have been more likely to be the case with this particular placebo than with the quasi-desensitisation placebo used in other studies since the latter concentrates on events leading up to bedtime and does not provide subjects with any response to make while actually in bed.

Vander Plate and Eno (1983) compared EMG biofeedback with a pseudo-feedback procedure where subjects received non-contingent tape-recorded feedback in a sample of volunteer undergraduates who reported some sleep disturbance. Both biofeedback and pseudo-feedback groups were found to improve significantly more than a self-monitoring control group in terms of sleep latency, but the EMG-trained group was not significantly different from the pseudo-feedback group. There were no significant treatment effects on other self-reported parameters. Using EMG measures, however, the biofeedback intervention was significantly better than the control procedures in reducing EMG levels across treatment. The authors took this to mean that the biofeedback subjects indeed did learn to reduce frontalis muscle tension whereas the pseudo-feedback subjects did not. Of course this again raises the suggestion that tension reduction per se may be neither necessary nor important. Consistent with this was the finding that baseline EMG level was not correlated significantly with pre-treatment sleep parameters whereas both state and trait anxiety were significantly correlated with sleep latency.

OVERVIEW OF RELAXATION-BASED TREATMENTS OF INSOMNIA

As has been the case with other clinically presenting conditions, relaxation therapy was in the vanguard of behavioural treatments of insomnia. Traditional desensitisation therapies, progressive relaxation training and variants of relaxation such as autogenic training, meditation and hypnosis have all been reported in the research literature. Table 17 presented some data from the most important of these studies and further controlled comparative investigations will be discussed in Chapter 9.

To summarise at the point, however, a number of conclusions may be drawn. Firstly, there is considerable evidence that relaxation treatments are more effective than no treatment and placebo treatments in reducing sleep-onset latency, and to a lesser extent, in effecting positive change in other sleep parameters. Secondly, a limited number of EEG studies provide corroborative evidence of results from self-report investigations. Thirdly, there is no convincing evidence of differential effectiveness across a wide range of relaxation-based treatments, including biofeedback methods. Finally, treatment effects are often statistically significant but clinically modest, with interpretation being limited by the large number of studies based upon non-clinic-presenting populations.

Chapter 7

Cognitive Treatments of Insomnia

There is now considerable evidence from both experimental and clinical studies that insomniacs experience particular difficulties in cognitive de-arousal (see Chapter 3, pp. 45–49). The indications are that the mind may remain alert even though the body may be relaxed physically. Consequently, the sleep period then becomes a focus of rehearsal, planning, rumination or frank worry for the insomniac. Indeed, even where treatments apparently deriving from other theoretical standpoints have proven effective in improving sleep pattern, some of the authors concerned have suggested that exclusion of or management of intrusive thinking may have been the principal mechanism of therapeutic change (e.g. Freedman and Papsdorf, 1976; Borkovec 1979; Zwart and Lisman, 1979).

This chapter is concerned with treatments of insomnia which are specifically cognitive in orientation. The treatment outcome literature here is smaller than that associated with the relaxation therapies (Chapter 6). However, research in this area is more recent and is ongoing compared with research on relaxation techniques which reached a peak during the 1970s and into the early years of the 1980s.

The procedure known as paradoxical intention has been the most widely studied cognitively based intervention. Thus it is logical to begin this chapter with an historical account of the development of this technique. Description of the application of paradox in clinical practice will be presented in association with a review of the research literature on its therapeutic effectiveness. The remaining part of Chapter 7 will introduce a number of other cognitive treatments which have been reported. Since much work remains to be done to evaluate both the cognitive model of insomnia and cognitively based therapies, the chapter will conclude with some suggestions for further study.

Consistent with the pattern set in Chapter 6 on relaxation-based therapies, the literature review on cognitive treatments in this chapter does not include those comparative outcome studies which have compared across diverse treatment strategies (e.g. cognitive treatment(s) versus behavioural treatment(s)). The reader, therefore, must read Chapter 7 in conjunction with Chapter 9 since the latter incorporates such comparative analyses and thereby identifies the advantages and shortcomings of the various therapeutic approaches which are available.

PARADOXICAL INTENTION

Some may dispute the inclusion of paradoxical intention in a chapter on cognitive therapies. Certainly, it was not born out of the cognitive-behavioural tradition. Nevertheless, paradoxical techniques have been increasingly adopted into routine clinical practice, and have been furnished with a learning theory rationale. Hopefully, it will become clear over the course of this chapter that a valid case can be made for regarding paradox as an intervention which has a primarily though not exclusively cognitive focus.

Therapists were using paradoxical techniques long before Viktor Frankl coined the phrase "paradoxical intention" (Frankl, 1955, 1960). In reviewing historical applications of paradox and related therapies Seltzer (1986) introduces early advocates of quasi-paradoxical approaches. Dubois (1908) recommended that patients approach their symptoms with a sense of humour, and Stekel (1920) described a method of treating impotence through the simultaneous prescription of intimate physical contact and the prohibition of sexual intercourse. Somewhat later, Dunlap (1930, 1942) employed "negative practice" to break undesirable habits. Patients were encouraged to repeat their problem behaviour in an effort to eliminate it. Other related techniques such as massed practice (often associated with the treatment of motor problems, e.g. tics) and stimulus satiation (e.g. chain smoking) similarly emphasise repetition rather than the attempted reduction or elimination of the symptomatic response. Although negative practice, massed practice and stimulus satiation may be justifiably regarded as different behavioural treatments, they are none the less readily confused and procedurally similar (Rimm and Masters, 1979). To the extent that avoidance behaviour is a contributory factor to the maintenance of, for example, fear responses, techniques such as flooding and response prevention which follow an extinction paradigm may also be regarded as paradoxical (Frankl, 1975).

Frankl's concern that patients took control of their symptoms stemmed from an existentialist philosophy. His logotherapeutic approach emphasised choice, volition and affirmative action and although symptom removal occurred, this was not regarded as an end in itself (Frankl, 1960, 1967). In fact logotherapy comprised two related techniques: paradoxical intention and dereflection. Whereas the former was concerned with increasing the frequency of responses which already were occurring too often, the latter involved attempting further to inhibit already infrequent responses. It is of course this latter response deficit which is the concern of the sleep-onset insomniac. Since both paradoxical intention and dereflection involve "prescribing the symptom" and differ procedurely only in the direction of change of frequency which the client desires, Ascher (1980) has suggested that the term paradoxical intention be employed to denote both the prescription intentionally to increase uncomfortably high frequency behaviours, and intentionally to decrease or inhibit uncomfortably low-frequency behaviours.

In recent years, Michael Ascher has been the foremost proponent of paradoxical intention, certainly within the behavioural context. He and his colleagues have presented a useful theoretical rationale for the operation of paradox across a wide range of clinically presenting conditions including urinary retention, impotence, agoraphobia and insomnia (Ascher, 1979; Ascher and Clifford, 1977; Ascher, 1981; Turner and Ascher, 1979a; Ascher and Turner, 1979).

With respect to insomnia the view is taken that, since sleeping cannot be placed fully under voluntary control, attempts to do so inhibit relaxation and sleep-onset through arousal of the autonomic nervous system. The insomniac's recognition of this aroused state causes anxiety both about the state per se and the failure to achieve sleep, but also about possible subsequent daytime consequences of failure to sleep. A vicious circle comprising self-monitoring, increased arousal, performance anxiety, efforts to sleep and performance failure is thus established. Paradoxical intention is presumed to work by obviating the performance anxiety which develops as the patient attempts directly to control sleep, which is essentially an involuntary physiological process. The patient's paradoxical intention is, therefore, to remain awake, and in the absence of effort to sleep to fall asleep naturally. The manner of presentation of both rationale and treatment instructions to insomniac clients will be dealt with shortly. However, it will be helpful first of all to present a brief summary of treatment outcome studies employing paradox to other clinically presenting conditions. This will serve to illustrate both the applicability of paradox and will demonstrate its cognitive-behavioural focus.

Strong (1984) reviewed the experimental evidence available at that time of the effectiveness of interventions which were explicitly paradoxical. Strong identified 12 controlled studies, seven of which were on clinical problems; one on agoraphobia, three on insomnia and three on depression. It should be noted, however, that each study in this last category was conducted on a volunteer college student population. The five remaining studies considered the impact of paradoxical intention upon procrastination amongst undergraduates. It will be helpful briefly to review the effectiveness of paradox across these studies.

Procrastination must be viewed as a sub-clinical problem, although, viewed as avoidance behaviour, it may be seen as an analogue state relative to anxiety and phobic reactions. The paradoxical directives for each study varied; however, all encouraged students to continue to procrastinate. In three of the five studies the paradoxical treatment resulted in significantly greater decreases in procrastination than did no treatment controls. However, the remaining two studies exhibited no significant benefits associated with paradox. Of greater interest, perhaps, are the results of studies on agoraphobia and depression. Ascher (1981) assigned 10 patients suffering from agoraphobia to either paradoxical treatment or a graded exposure programme. In the paradoxical condition clients were encouraged to experience intense anxiety and to court their feared disastrous consequences. It is clear that there was a strong cognitive element to this treatment since clients were required to confront their automatic negative thinking and to reality test the thoughts in order to demonstrate that the consequences would not occur. Ascher reported that clients receiving paradoxical treatment experienced rapid diminution of anxiety compared with the exposure treatment, where anxiety reduction was not significant. The three studies on "depression" (Beck and Strong, 1982; Feldman, Strong and Danser, 1982; Zodun, Gruszkos and Strong, 1983) compared "positive connotative interpretations" with "negative connotative interpretations" attributed to depressive symptoms. The former were paradoxical since they suggested that the depressive symptomatology evidenced positive personal characteristics within the individual and therefore should be maintained, whereas the latter evidenced negative characteristics such as irrational thinking and avoidance, and should be eliminated. Results from these studies indicated that both interpretations resulted in therapeutic change greater than an untreated control group; however, greater maintenance of change was achieved with the paradoxical condition. The remaining papers in Strong's review (Ascher and Turner, 1979; Ascher and Turner, 1980; Turner and Ascher, 1979a) were investigations of paradox with insomnia and will be discussed in detail later on in this chapter.

Selzter's (1986) book *Paradoxical strategies in psychotherapy* is the most comprehensive text available which reviews theory and treatment of paradox. In an appendix to his book, Seltzer provides a checklist of symptoms and problems treated paradoxically which runs to over six pages in length and comprises more than 200 references. Problems treated are as wide ranging as anorexia, marital conflict, psychosis and temper tantrums. The contrast between Strong's review of the literature and that of Seltzer is striking and reflects the narrow focus of those studies which are, as Strong puts it, "explicitly paradoxical" (and one might add clearly cognitive-behavioural), and those which could be regarded as containing at least a paradoxical component in terms of retrospective analysis. Mention was made earlier in this chapter that the roots of the procedure known as paradoxical intention lay in psychotherapeutic traditions. The reader is referred to Selzer's book, therefore, for background reading. A number of further studies falling within the cognitive-behavioural tradition do, however, merit brief consideration.

Paradoxical intention has been found useful when applied to various anxiety conditions. Both phobic and obsessional states have responded well to paradox (Gerz, 1966; Solyom et al, 1972; Milan and Kolko, 1984) and Last, Barlow and O'Brien (1983) reported positive results when using paradoxical intention with a patient complaining of generalised anxiety disorder. Like Ascher (1981), other researchers have investigated paradox in the treatment of agoraphobia (Mavissakalian et al, 1983; Michelson and Ascher, 1984). In an earlier study, Ascher (1979) applied paradox to five cases of psychogenic urinary retention, all of whom evidenced dramatic improvement. Treatment involved repeated practice in entering public toilet facilities and preparations to urinate, but with the intention not actually to urinate. In our own work with various client groups over the past years we have found paradox to be a useful component in cognitive-behavioural treatment of urinary urgency (Espie, 1985) and obsessive-compulsive disorder (Espie, 1986). Indeed, we have employed paradoxical techniques across a wide variety of psychological problems presenting at the primary care level (Espie and White, 1986a,b).

Treatment of insomnia with paradoxical intention

Before reviewing the literature on the effectiveness of paradox in treating insomnia, it may be helpful to describe the therapeutic rationale most commonly presented to insomniacs and the treatment instructions which are usually applied. First of all the rationale which we have presented to insomniacs in our own treatment studies is recorded in Table 18.

The text of Table 18 is written in a quite deliberately conversational style in an attempt accurately to communicate the manner in which paradox should be presented in the clinical setting, although of course it is bound to be more of a dialogue than this. Hopefully, the practitioner will find the rationale stimulating and useful. We have found that written material handed out to patients can be a helpful adjunct to the consulting room discussion and Table 18 may form the basis for such a handout. At times it may be helpful to be more explicit in the description of performance anxiety and even to use such jargon terms. This is probably a matter for clinical

Table 18 A suggested treatment rationale for paradoxical intention therapy as applied to insomnia

---

RATIONALE OF PARADOXICAL TREATMENT OF INSOMNIA

If you can't get to sleep it might seem reasonable to ask someone who can how she manages it. Then surely all you have to do is follow her example. The problem is you always get the same answer, something like ...

> I just fall asleep. . .it just happens . . . (shrug of shoulders) . . . it's easy. I just put the light out and close my eyes.

Not very helpful you think—but you would be wrong—the secret is right there. The good sleeper does precisely nothing to fall asleep.

Sleep is a natural process which happens involuntarily. The good sleeper doesn't make it happen and neither can you. In fact, the harder you try the worse your sleep problem is likely to get; you just get more aware of not getting over to sleep and probably more frustrated.

For the insomniac things get into a vicious circle. Instead of looking forward to bed as a time to relax and to enjoy a good sleep, apprehension often develops as bedtime approaches. Unpleasant memories of hours spent lying awake or tossing and turning can come to mind and there is the prospect that the same thing might happen again tonight. It can become like a self-fulfilling prophecy. You are so eager to fall asleep that you try too hard and all your efforts—turning this way and turning that way; thinking on these thoughts or on those thoughts—just seem to make you more alert. A fundamental problem is that your efforts to control the sleep process are part of the problem, not part of the solution. You actually snatch wakefulness out of the jaws of exhaustion. That really is frustrating!

Does this sound familiar? Well, I'm afraid there is nothing for it but to give up. Yes, that's right you must give up trying to fall asleep. You're useless at it! Instead you should try to stay awake. That's the only certain way for you to make sure that you stop interfering with your natural sleep. After all, if you're in your bed and it's dark and you're really tired then you're not going to be able to stay awake for very long. Staying awake will probably get you to sleep more quickly because it stops you worrying and it stops you trying. What's the point in worrying about still being awake when you're trying to stay awake anyway?

You're probably thinking, so I've to go ahead and be the worst insomniac I can be and just keep on staying awake. Then you would be quite right. A paradox isn't it?

---

judgement based upon the needs of the presenting individual. Equally, other examples of failures directly to control autonomic processes such as motor tics, blushing or penile erections may be provided for illustration and clarification of performance anxiety related problems.

It is noteworthy from Table 18 that one non-specific element of paradox has survived the transition into cognitive-behavioural practice, and that is the use of humour. Frankl recommended that paradoxical intention be presented in the most humorous manner feasible since, he believed, this helped clients detach themselves from their problems. Seltzer (1986) comments that this distancing enables clients "to experience a change of attitude, or new sense of freedom and self-determination" (p. 59). Ascher (1980) describes humour as "the positive, purposeful component of the treatment package" (p. 288). Administration of the humour, however, should not be premature and should not compromise the patient's trust that the therapist is actually taking the problem sufficiently seriously. Ascher's chapter contains an excellent discussion of therapist attitude during paradoxical treatment and provides instructive transcripts from actual interviews which evidence the skilled use of humour in appropriate ways.

It is important to consider for a moment how it is that humour may contribute towards attitude (cognitive) change. There are clear parallels between paradox and the rational therapies and other cognitively based approaches which emphasise rationalisation and de-catastrophising. Paradox disarms anxiety-laden cognitions which are overvalued by refusing to take them seriously enough to affect behaviour. The thought "I'm not getting over to sleep" rather than becoming anxiety-evoking and promoting of efforts to fall asleep becomes restated to, for example, "Well that's a good couple of hours of sleeplessness to my credit so far tonight ... maybe I'll break my record!" This is a form of de-catastrophising. Indeed such a cognitive process may be critical to the effectiveness of paradox. The patient's self-view as a hopeless insomniac with all the assumptions and beliefs associated with this perspective are challenged by the paradoxical approach when the patient is encouraged ostensibly to make matters worse. Paradox, therefore, challenges much of the neurotic and obsessive thinking which accompanies the presentation of insomnia.

However, there is also the issue of compliance. Paradoxical instructions require subjects to make a novel response to their problem, one which at first may appear counter-intuitive. Thus it seems fair to assume that compliance with paradoxical directives is more demanding of commitment to the therapeutic approach than other treatment approaches which may be less challenging. The use of paradox then may be a way of both testing commitment and of developing commitment. Indeed, Ascher (1988) has suggested that it may be appropriate to use paradox adjunctively with other psychological treatments. For example, an individual experiencing panic attacks may be requested to return to the next clinic appointment having experienced as many panic attacks as possible and to as high a level of stress as possible in order to help the clinician to evaluate the extent of the problem and to appreciate the full range of symptoms. Such a prescription may in itself have some therapeutic benefit, indeed may be sufficient; but if not, other cognitive-behavioural treatment might follow. The patient's readiness to co-operate with treatment certainly will have been tested and probably will have been enhanced.

To conclude this section, Table 19 summarises the procedural instructions which should be given to the insomniac once the treatment rationale has been accepted and understood. The table is self-explanatory; however, it should be noticed from these instructions that emphasis has been placed upon relatively passive attempts to remain awake. The goal should be to maintain wakefulness, that is to delay sleep-onset, rather than to promote high arousal levels. This is because some previous research work has suggested that some individuals may be too successful at remaining awake (Lacks et al, 1983a; Espie, 1985). Treatment is not intended to follow a sleep-deprivation model. Rather it is anticipated that, in circumstances conducive to sleep, but in the absence of anxiety and effort, the tired insomniac will fall asleep naturally.

Table 19   Procedural instructions for patients following a paradoxical intention programme for insomnia

---

(1) When you go to bed lie down in a comfortable position and put the light out.
(2) In the darkened room try to keep your eyes open rather than closing them. Each time they feel like closing tell yourself "it would be good to keep them open for another little while".
(3) As time goes by congratulate yourself on your success at remaining awake. Remind yourself that it is comfortable in bed and that relaxing is good even if you're not asleep.
(4) If you feel worried or irritable at not sleeping remind yourself "the plan is to remain awake so I'm doing fine".
(5) Try to stay awake for as long as you can.
(6) Do *not*, however, use active methods to stay awake such as reading or physical movement. The idea is to resist sleep-onset gently but persistently.

The effectiveness of paradoxical intention treatment of insomnia

Summary information on those studies which have investigated the effectiveness of paradox in treating insomnia is presented in Table 20. Those studies comparing paradox with other forms of intervention such as relaxation and stimulus control treatment are presented in Chapter 9.

Ascher and Efran (1978) provided the first case reports on the use of paradoxical intention with poor sleepers, although only three of their five subjects had a primary problem of sleep difficulty. Nevertheless, their demonstration of the effectiveness of paradox was impressive since these were patients who had failed previously to respond to a 10 week treatment period of more conventional treatments, i.e. relaxation and desensitisation.

Table 20 Treatment studies employing paradoxical intention

Authors	Sample	Total N	Age (mean years)	Duration (mean years)	Treatment(s)	SOL Pre (mean min.)	SOL Post (mean min.)	SOL F.up (mean min.)	F.up (month)
Ascher and Efran (1978)	P/R	5	30	9	Paradoxical intention	40[a]	10	"remained satisfied"	12
Relinger, Bornstein and Mungas (1978)	R	1	31	20	Paradoxical intention	64	10	10	12
Ascher and Turner (1979)	R	25	39	8	Paradoxical intention	62	29	NA	NA
					Desensitisation placebo	63	51	NA	NA
					No treatment	71	62	NA	NA
Relinger and Bornstein (1979)	R	4	19–63 (range)	23	Paradoxical intention	110	47	20	3
Ascher and Turner (1980)	R	40	37	9	Paradoxical intention (type A)	63	29	NA	NA
					Paradoxical intention (type B)	68	45	NA	NA
					Desensitisation placebo	57	44	NA	NA
					No treatment	64	60	NA	NA

Study	Key			Treatment				
Fogle and Dyal (1983)	R	35	41	12	Paradoxical intention (type A)	74%[b]	78%	NA	NA
					Paradoxical intention (giving up)	76%	82%	NA	NA
					Self-monitoring control	73%	80%	NA	NA
Ott, Levine and Ascher (1983)	R	56	NA	NA	Feedback (objective sleep monitoring device)	53	35	NA	NA
					Paradoxical intention (type B)	55	33	NA	NA
					Paradoxical intention + feedback	53	72	NA	NA
					No treatment	54	52	NA	NA
Espie and Lindsay (1985)	P	6	43	7	Paradoxical intention	3 patients rapidly improved; mean SOL reduction of 52 min. 3 patients experienced marked SOL exacerbation (2 withdrew from paradoxical treatment)			

Notes. [a]SOL value represents treatment score after "conventional programme" of therapy; [b]Data represent sleep efficiency scores.

Key   R = recruited subject; P = patient

This phase of treatment had led to minimal reductions in SOL and the clients continued to complain of sleep difficulties. Ascher and Efran then administered paradoxical intention treatment in one of two formats. For three of the clients the requirement "to try to remain awake" was posited in order that detailed descriptions of thoughts experienced just before falling asleep could be recorded. It was suggested that insufficient information regarding the sleep situation had led to previous failure and this information was now vital. They would have to remain awake to gather it. The remaining two clients were told that the relaxation component of their treatment had not been of sufficient duration to produce the levels of relaxation required for sleep-onset. They were instructed therefore to lengthen the number of steps in the relaxation practice and so the length of time to falling alseep was lengthened. They were asked to continue practising even if this meant resisting the urge to sleep. Both of these formats, therefore, involved placing the paradoxical instruction within a rational framework.

Ascher and Efran reported that all of the subjects were unable to achieve their respective goals because they had fallen asleep too quickly. The paradoxical phase of treatment had been in effect for only two weeks and mean post-treatment sleep latency was 10 minutes compared with 48 minutes at initial baseline and 40 minutes after the conventional treatment programme. Interestingly, for one subject, Ascher and Efran re-introduced the original programme (minus the paradoxical component) and demonstrated a reversal effect in sleep latency which was followed by improvement once again when paradox was re-administered. These workers reported only sleep latency measures although they stated in a footnote that a reduction in frequency of nighttime wakening was evident also and that improvements in ratings of sleep quality paralleled changes on sleep parameters. An informal one year follow-up by telephone indicated that all clients remained satisfied with their improvement.

Other early case study reports in support of paradox were presented by Relinger, Bornstein and Mungas (1978) and Relinger and Bornstein (1979). Relinger, Bornstein and Mungas employed time series analysis on a single case. They found that the paradoxical instruction produced and sustained substantial sleep latency reduction which was associated also with significant positive change in ratings of difficulty in falling asleep, restfulness of sleep and measures of daytime functioning. Again these treatment effects were achieved rapidly, after five, daily 30 minute treatment sessions, and were maintained at follow-up one year later. Final sleep latency was 10 minutes (Table 20). These workers employed a treatment rationale for paradox similar to the first of those outlined above in the Ascher and Efran study. The validity of this particular subject's sleep complaint must be, however, called into question since, in spite of a reported 20 year duration of insomnia, the individual had never sought professional help previously and had used only "over the counter" sleep preparations.

Relinger and Bornstein (1979), however, reported four cases for whom insomnia constituted a more substantial problem. These subjects were chronic insomniacs either self-referred or referred by hospital personnel. The experimental design involved a multiple baseline across subjects with experimental phases comprising baseline, a one week treatment and follow-up. Treatment consisted of five consecutive individually administered half-hour daily sessions as in their previous study. A demand instruction was also issued stating that "after this first week you will begin to experience dramatic improvement ... it is only after about 7 days and meticulous care on your part in following instructions that improvement will occur". Relinger and Bornstein presented graphical data which convincingly demonstrated the treatment effect during counterdemand instruction, replicated across subjects in the multiple baseline design, with maintenance of effects over follow-up at four, eight and twelve weeks. Combined mean scores indicated SOL reduction from 110 minutes at baseline to 47 minutes at post-treatment with a further reduction to 20 minutes at final follow-up. Significant effects were achieved also on number of awakenings, number of times on which difficulty returning to sleep was experienced, and ratings of difficulty in falling to sleep and restfulness upon awakening.

In concluding their study, Relinger and Bornstein made three suggestions concerning clinical management. Firstly, they suggested that subjects should be screened carefully to ascertain if their symptomatic insomnia was indeed maintained or exacerbated by anxiety. Secondly, they recommended that treatment by paradoxical intention should be individually tailored to eliminate that anxiety. Thirdly, they commented that paradoxical instructions do not eliminate original source causes of insomnia but act to remove maintaining factors, i.e. anticipatory anxiety. Therefore, they advocated that paradoxical treatment should be followed by lengthy follow-up to evaluate if the original problem was still evident and requiring further treatment.

Turner and Ascher (1979a) conducted an important comparative treatment outcome study comparing paradox with stimulus control and relaxation therapies. The results of this study had been very encouraging, indicating that paradox was significantly superior to placebo and no treatment and was equally effective to the other active interventions. The results of this study are presented in detail in Chapter 9 (pp. 183–185). However, relevant at this point is the controlled experimental investigation which was a partial replication of this study, comparing paradox with de-sensitisation placebo and no-treatment controls (Ascher and Turner, 1979).

Twenty-five subjects were recruited through media advertisement with an average age of 39 years, and a mean sleep latency of 65 minutes. Following a 10 day baseline self-monitoring period, eight subjects were randomly assigned to each of the paradoxical intention and placebo control groups, and nine subjects were randomly assigned to no treatment. Treatment comprised four, weekly sessions of approximately 30 to 45 minutes duration. Subjects in paradoxical treatment were advised not to engage in activity incompatible with sleep but to lie in bed in a darkened room with their eyes open for as long as possible. They were provided with a straightforward (unframed) rationale of this procedure and of the manner in which it was expected to operate with respect to their sleep difficulty. Ascher and Turner conducted multivariate analysis of variance upon four dependent variables from a daily sleep log. They reported a significant multivariate effect for group differences, with post hoc analysis indicating superiority of paradox over both control groups on measures of sleep-onset latency, number of wakenings during the night with difficulty returning to sleep, and rated difficulty encountered in attempting to fall asleep. No differences were observed on a rating scale measure of restedness after sleep. Mean values for the sleep latency variable at pre- and post-treatment are presented in Table 20, from which it is clear that SOL reduced by over 50% under paradoxical treatment with minimal change in the other conditions. Problematical awakenings fell from an average of two at baseline to 0.5 at post-test with paradoxical treatment. The controlled studies of Ascher and Turner, therefore, established paradox as a viable treatment for insomnia and confirmed some of the early promise provided by case study material.

Ascher and Turner next turned their attention to the instructional context in which paradox was administered. They designed a study to compare their own straightforward rationale of paradox (similar to that reported previously in Table 18) to the "reframing" procedure which had been employed in some of the earlier case study work (Ascher and Turner, 1980). They recognised the possible advantage of reframing which might provide less compliant subjects with a more comfortable framework within which to perform the paradoxical directive. Here, the explanation could be tailored to fit the specific frame of reference of the individual client while the primary goal of getting the client to remain awake would remain the same.

Ascher and Turner again recruited subjects and allocated them at random to conventional paradox which they described as "type A" administration, to the reframed "type B" paradoxical treatment, to quasi-desensitisation placebo and to no-treatment control. Their results indicated that type A paradoxical intention was superior to no-treatment control, type B paradoxical intention and placebo on measures of sleep latency, rated difficulty in falling asleep and ratings of morning restedness. In addition, type A paradox was superior to no treatment on rated difficulty in returning to sleep and in total sleep time. Table 20 presents sleep latency data across the four conditions. Thus, the performance anxiety-based rationale appeared preferable although Ascher and Turner did suggest that reframing may nonetheless be useful with subjects who can be described as refractory or resistant to treatment instructions. They also commented that with the reframing paradigm there may have been the implication that treatment proper would not begin until after initial data (on thoughts and feelings prior to sleep-onset) were collected. This factor may have influenced subjects' confidence in the treatment. Although Ascher and Turner had taken the precaution of including a treatment credibility assessment in their study; this was conducted at post-therapy and may well have been influenced by actual progress in treatment by that time. An assessment of credibility after delivery of the rationale would have been a stronger test of this non-specific factor.

Ott, Levine and Ascher (1983) took consideration of the administration of paradoxical intention a step further. Based upon their earlier view that reframing is most effective in cases where the new frame better fits the needs of the specific individual and/or when used with oppositional individuals, they designed an experiment to test the manipulation of paradoxical intention of the type B variety. Fifty-six subjects were randomly assigned to four experimental conditions. A "feedback group" completed a daily sleep log and used a "sleep monitoring unit" (Ott, Levine and Farley, 1982) to provide objective data on their untreated sleep pattern. This unit emitted a tone which subjects were instructed to re-trigger when the tone terminated. Data collected the next morning from a coded display provided an estimate of sleep-onset latency. A second group received paradoxical intention within the context of reframed instructions. Subjects were asked to remain awake and in the morning write down the most common thoughts which they had experienced in the previous sleep period. A third group had identical paradoxical instructions but were provided also with sleep monitoring units and were given instructions to de-code the data each morning. A fourth no treatment control group was included.

Ott, Levine and Ascher's results indicated that both feedback alone and paradoxical intention alone produced significant reductions in sleep latency between baseline and the first week of treatment compared with no significant change under no treatment. However, the combined paradoxical intention plus feedback group demonstrated a significant increase in SOL, rising from a baseline value of 53 minutes to 70 minutes after one week of treatment and 72 minutes at treatment week 2 in terms of self-reported sleep latency (Table 20). Comparable analyses using objective data from the sleep monitoring unit broadly confirmed this pattern of results. Ott, Levine and Ascher provided an interesting explanation for the exacerbation of sleep latency demonstrated in the combined treatment group. They suggested that since this was an experimental study, subjects may have been concerned to follow literally the experimental demand of remaining awake all night, particularly so with the addition of the requirement to submit objective sleep data confirming this wakefulness. Thus there is the implication that patients treated with paradoxical intention should understand that the paradoxical procedures should of themselves lead to reduce sleep latency, and demand characteristics should not operate against the communication of this (ultimate) intention.

In our own work we have obtained results which parallel those of other researchers, although our subjects have been physician-referred chronic insomniacs. We presented a series of six case studies which illustrated variability in therapeutic response to paradoxical intention (Espie and Lindsay, 1985). The subjects were within the age range 30 to 58 years and average sleep latency at baseline was greater then two hours. Paradoxical intention was administered following the conventional rationale. We found that three subjects responded promptly to paradoxical instructions even during a lengthy (four week) counterdemand period. These gains were maintained at follow-up of either three months or six months. Marked improvement was also evident in total sleep time in two of these subjects. However, the remaining three insomniacs responded unfavourably to paradoxical treatment. In two cases the exacerbation of sleep latency was such that paradox had to be withdrawn (after one week and three weeks respectively). Nevertheless, subsequent progressive relaxation treatment did produce substantial reductions in sleep latency. This appeared to indicate that these subjects were not simply poor treatment responders. Somehow paradox appeared to be unsuitable for them. The third subject in this group made an initially poor response to paradox, with sleep latency increasing by 60 to 100% during the first three weeks of paradox. However, during weeks 4 to 8 of active treatment sleep latency reduced below baseline levels.

We suggested that these variable outcomes may reflect the tendency of some individuals with performance anxiety to redirect their performance anxieties into trying to remain awake, that is an *active* avoidance of sleep, in order to achieve the therapist's criterion of success. This may be a mentally arousing process whereas, for the insomniac who benefits from paradox, more "passive" avoidance of performance effort may account for treatment gains. The subject responding well to paradox, therefore, may feel liberated from attempts directly to control the sleep process, whereas others may become more aroused in an effort to remain awake. Once again this evidence points to the cognitive basis of paradoxical treatments. Sleep-incompatible visualisation/imagery may be utilised by some patients to ensure that waking cognitions persist even when physically relaxed, thereby maintaining arousal levels and making it "too easy to remain awake". The subsequent success of relaxation training in our study, therefore, may be accounted for by the provision of physical relaxation in combination with distraction from such intrusive thoughts.

Fogle and Dyal (1983) conducted an interesting investigation which varied the instructions for paradox somewhat differently from the studies of Ascher and his colleagues. They allocated their sample of 35 subjects, with an average 12 year history of insomnia, to either conventional paradoxical intention or to an alternative version where individuals were told simply to "give up" trying to fall asleep. That is, no direct paradoxical instruction to stay awake was given. Fogle and Dyal argued that sleep efficiency was the best overall measure of outcome, and reported significant improvements on this variable for each of the experimental groups. In addition, they found that both paradoxical treatment groups improved on a self-report measure of sleep performance anxiety. In spite of the statistical changes which were demonstrated, however, the improvements in actual sleep parameters were relatively small and of limited clinical significance. Indeed, a self-monitoring control group achieved equivalent outcomes (Table 20) but without significant reduction in performance anxiety. The limited treatment effects may reflect the fact that both treatments were conducted as bibliotherapy. Fogle and Dyal's reporting of only sleep efficiency changes also obscures the locus of improvement. It is unclear whether improvements were due to changes in sleep latency, awakening frequency, total sleep time or to a combination of these factors. Nevertheless, the success of the giving up strategy in Fogle and Dyal's study again highlights the usefulness of a passive paradoxical response. The important common element in paradox may be to stop trying to sleep, in order to obviate performance anxiety, although in some cases to achieve this the direct paradox of attempting to remain awake may be necessary.

OTHER COGNITIVE STRATEGIES FOR TREATING INSOMNIA

This section comprises a literature review of cognitive interventions, other than paradox, for either sleep-onset or sleep-maintenance insomnia. The literature here is small and in some reports cognitive treatment was only a component of more broadly based treatment. Before commencing the review, however, it is important to reiterate that certain of the relaxation methods reported in Chapter 6, such as passive relaxation, imagery training and meditation, may reasonably claim a place in this section on cognitive strategies. Indeed, such attention-focusing techniques have been so categorised by both early and recent reviewers (e.g. Bootzin and Nicassio, 1978; Morin and Kwentus, 1988). Although the structure of this book favoured a comprehensive chapter on relaxation methods the reader should recognise the explicit cognitive element to these treatments as well as the implicit or hypothesised cognitive mechanisms associated with many interventions which may purport to operate via physiological or operant mechanisms.

Mitchell and White (1977) reported on a study which investigated various components of a "self-management" treatment of insomnia. Thirteen male college students and staff (mean age 23 years) with relatively brief histories of insomnia (mean 1.9 years) were randomly assigned to either incremental self-management (ISM), accelerated self-management (ASM) or delayed partial self-management (DPSM) treatments. In ISM there were three sequentially applied stages to treatment, namely progressive relaxation, mental relaxation and cognitive control. This last element comprised techniques such as thought-stopping, time out from worry and rational appraisal; all with the aim of increasing covert self-control. ASM was similar except that cognitive control was preceded by a combined relaxation phase. The DPSM group self-monitored only, for a duration equivalent to the 10 week treatment periods for ISM and ASM, thereafter receiving the cognitive control treatment alone.

The results of Mitchell and White's study indicated that the cognitive control strategies significantly enhanced the reductions in pre-sleep cognitive intrusion already achieved by relaxation methods. Cognitive control alone produced a 30% reduction in a measure of pre-sleep tension and a 48% reduction in intrusive cognitions. Sleep latency reduced from 81 to 39 minutes after both relaxation therapies were applied in ISM and a similar reduction (80 minutes to 33 minutes) was achieved in ASM. Cognitive control further reduced latencies to 19 and 14 minutes respectively in these groups. The DPSM group who received only cognitive treatment reduced their sleep latency to 47 minutes at post-training and to 31 minutes at four month follow-up (the latter being a 60% reduction from baseline values). All groups reported significant improvement in subjective sleep satisfaction at follow-up. Mitchell and White concluded that their cognitive control procedures were effective as a treatment for insomnia independent of the effects of the relaxation procedures. Clearly such an approach offered promise, although based upon a small sample of mild to moderate insomniacs.

In a further study Mitchell (1979) re-classified his mental relaxation technique as a cognitive control procedure. His argument for this re-classification arose from evidence from the first study that muscle relaxation was not associated with significant reduction in intrusive cognitions whereas mental relaxation reduced both tension and cognitive intrusion. He assigned at random 20 subjects who were older (mean age 37 years) and more clearly suffering from insomnia (mean duration of symptoms

6.3 years) to progressive relaxation, progressive relaxation plus cognitive control, a sleep education and time re-scheduling treatment or no-treatment control. All interventions covered an eight week period.

Mitchell found that the combined relaxation and cognitive control treatment was generally favoured compared with the relaxation alone condition in terms of effects upon measures of pre-sleep tension, intrusive thinking, sleep latency and sleep satisfaction. For example, the combined programme reduced sleep latency by 71% compared with 40% under progressive relaxation, with the latter being little better than the educative programme (37%). Mitchell also confirmed his previous findings that progressive relaxation affected tension levels but not pre-sleep cognitions. He tentatively concluded that intrusive thinking is a more therapeutically valid target than muscle tension, particularly where the treatment goal is to reduce both sleep latency and to improve daytime functioning. Unfortunately, it is not possible from Mitchell's studies to separate out the effects of the different components of cognitive treatment.

The remaining literature is confined to case study reports, and these have concentrated largely on sleep-maintenance insomnia. Five studies merit some consideration.

Coates and Thoresen (1979) presented an interesting single case study of a 58 year old woman who had a reported 33 year history of sleep-maintenance insomnia and associated daytime sleepiness and depression. Their study documented treatment over a five year period. In year one she participated in a drug evaluation study following which she was referred to Coates and Thoresen for treatment. After a one week baseline which comprised both sleep laboratory recording and the use of sleep logs, progressive relaxation training was instituted for a further three weeks. During the latter part of this relaxation phase, however, a more cognitive element was introduced in that she was encouraged to "focus her thoughts on a single pleasant image, and tell herself that she would consider her problems the following day". After the relaxation phase, the patient received a further seven treatment sessions over a 10 week period. These sessions were devoted to helping the patient solve additional problems preventing good sleep and comprised techniques such as time management, keeping a diary of positive thoughts and using cue-controlled relaxation. Follow-up evaluations were then conducted at annual intervals until four years after initial referral.

Coates and Thoresen evaluated treatment outcome in terms of various measures of intermittent wakening, total sleep time and sleep efficiency. Latency to sleep-onset was never problematic at any point across the experimental phases. They reported that self-management training (that is, both phases of training combined) was especially effective in improving sleep during the first third of the night. A reduction from 33 minutes to two minutes spent awake during this period was achieved, and arousal frequency was reduced by an average of 50% across the night. There was also a modest increase in sleep efficiency. Scores obtained during the final two years of follow-up were consistent with these post-treatment gains. Coates and Thoresen reported that their client felt as a result of treatment that she had the resources to manage her sleep pattern and they suggested that increasing skill and developing feelings of mastery may have been critical elements in treatment.

Thoresen et al (1981) presented a further three controlled case studies of sleep-maintenance insomniacs who were treated, at least in part, with cognitive techniques. These patients were physician-referred and had presented with insomniac complaints for 5, 10 and 14 years respectively. Sleep laboratory recordings were conducted at baseline, mid-treatment, post-treatment and at three and 12 month follow-up. Self-report sleep logs were also kept by the patients. Thoresen et al provided each subject with 13 hours of treatment which comprised progressive muscle relaxation, cognitive restructuring, mental relaxation and training in methods of problem-solving. These elements of treatment were sequentially applied. During cognitive restructuring, patients received education about sleep and sleep problems and were required to examine their belief system concerning sleep. Furthermore, patients practised identifying thoughts which interfered with sleep and were helped to encourage less irrational alternative thoughts which were trained up to be cued by simple behaviours (e.g. looking at a watch) when maladaptive thoughts occurred. The mental relaxation component involved training in the use of structured fantasies to reduce excessive worry at night. During the final problem-solving sessions each subject received further training in specific tactics to manage stress, to develop relaxation or to respond to feelings of depression.

Thoresen et al reported that Patient 1 showed considerable improvement over the treatment programme. The total number of arousals was reduced by 37% at post-treatment and by 53% at one year follow-up. Patient 2, who had a more severe sleep-maintenance problem, reduced minutes awake after sleep-onset from 89 minutes at baseline to 49 minutes at post-treatment, with a further reduction to 29 minutes at one year follow-up. Correspondingly, her overall sleep efficiency improved from 79% to 91%. Patient 3 did not demonstrate reductions in time awake after sleep-onset until the three month follow-up, making it impossible to attribute these changes to the treatment programme.

Similar to the results of Coates and Thoresen's (1979) study, therefore, the study by Thoresen et al is suggestive of the value of cognitive techniques in managing insomnia, but the lack of reported process measurement makes it impossible to identify the relative contributions of the different elements of treatment. In the latter study, however, the overall treatment strategy does appear to have been more cognitively orientated.

In 1984 Coates and Thoresen contributed a further two case studies to the literature. Both of these subjects were recruited by media advertisement. Subject 1 received Flurazepam 30 mg in the context of a double-blind protocol. Subject 2 was treated by means of a multi-component programme comprising one hour, weekly treatment sessions across 16 weeks. Treatment comprised progressive muscle relaxation, mental relaxation, cognitive restructuring, anger management and cue-controlled relaxation. Interestingly, in order to generate the necessary information on mood and self-talk, a miniature dictaphone was provided and the individual was required to set aside time at the end of the working day to answer three questions: what is on your mind right now?; how did your day go?; and what will the rest of the day be like? These data were later independently assessed for content and focus of content. The results of this study proved interesting.

Improvements in Subject 1's sleep were observed with Flurazepam; however, these effects reversed under the placebo and no drug conditions. When this subject benefited from Flurazepam, increases in positive self-statements were also identified. For Subject 2, the combined treatment programme was partially effective but perhaps less so than with the case reports reviewed above. Sleep efficiency increased under progressive relaxation and was maintained at a higher than baseline level throughout active treatment. Minutes awake after sleep-onset and arousal frequency, however, achieved their lowest levels during the assertiveness training phase when Subject 2 was taught alternative methods of managing anger. Similarly, positive statements about self and about others were at their highest during this phase of training. Although evidence arising from this study is extremely tentative, being based on only a single case, it does highlight the importance of identifying the *nature* of the patient's thought content and tailoring treatment accordingly. For example, incidental thoughts may be readily dismissed, whereas irrational worries may require to be rationalised, rational problems may require to be solved in practical ways, and frustration and hostility may require social skills training and training in appropriate assertive responses.

We have devised a cognitive treatment which we initially termed "worry control" (Espie and Lindsay, 1987). This approach comprises elements of cognitive restructuring and behavioural problem-solving. During the early evening, the patient is instructed to sit at a desk, with paper and pencil, and to jot down any current problems which might be liable to run through her mind during the night. Each problem is then examined in turn, and the patient must write down the next step of action which she intends to take towards its resolution. The patient is encouraged to be specific in doing this so that she can be clear in her mind that a decision has been made, thereby facilitating the restructuring process. This period of problem-solving is scheduled for 30 minutes each evening, usually after mealtimes, for example around 7.00 p.m. Such sessions must take place both temporally and situationally removed from bedtime and the bedroom environment (cf. stimulus control). If the patient is unable to fall asleep or awakes during the night she is instructed to remind herself that, for each problem, matters are "in hand". However, if a new difficulty occurs to her she has (mentally) to "refer" this on to the next day for action.

Our report of a single case treated by means of the cognitive control procedures indicated a substantial reduction in wake time after sleep-onset from a mean baseline score of 52 minutes to 14 minutes during cognitive control. This improvement was maintained at three and 12 month follow-up (Espie and Lindsay, 1987). The patient in this study did not appear to require training in any other anxiety management techniques such as relaxation exercises, and, similarly, extensive training in cognitive therapy was unnecessary. In fact, this subject had failed to respond to a previous treatment intervention comprising paradoxical instruction.

Levey et al (1991) reported a single case study of a 38 year old man with a 16 year history of sleep-onset and sleep-maintenance insomnia. These workers designed a four phase intervention. Phase One was a combination of sleep hygiene rules plus stimulus control instruction. Phase Two involved progressive muscular relaxation. Phase Three comprised the Espie and Lindsay technique of cognitive control described above, and Phase Four represented a novel technique which the authors referred to as "articulatory suppression". Here the subject was instructed to control intrusive thoughts by repeating the syllable "the" to himself, pacing it in a non-regular manner. This last technique, based upon the work of Baddeley (1986), stems from the intention to produce a repetitive stimulus which has minimum cognitive load and hence little capacity for arousal, but yet may be effective for blocking unwanted thoughts. In practice the technique is not dissimilar to folklore remedies such as counting sheep or from mantra repetition in meditation.

Analysis of variance of SOL data in Levey et al's case study revealed a non-significant trend towards improvement across the 9 week experimental period. Post hoc analysis, however, indicated that cognitive control treatment produced the lowest sleep latency scores of any phase. A significant main effect of weeks for number of awakenings was found and paired comparisons showed significant differences between baseline and each of Phases Two, Three and Four of treatment. It was observed post hoc, however, that the duration of the first awakening was at its lowest under articulatory suppression treatment. Levey et al tentatively suggest that the greater effectiveness of their articulatory suppression technique upon intermittent wakenings rather than sleep latency may be related to the fact that cognitive intrusions during the night are likely to be less coherent and may therefore be more susceptible to a simple blocking technique. Articulatory suppression may be useful if used at an early stage before the intrusive thoughts have become coherent and before they lead to increased physical arousal. Clearly, both cognitive control and articulatory suppression require more rigorous investigation but appear to offer initial promise.

OVERVIEW OF COGNITIVE TREATMENTS OF INSOMNIA

To summarise the literature on the various cognitive strategies introduced in this section is not an easy task. No one technique has been sufficiently evaluated such that it can be either rejected or accepted, and all of the supportive evidence which is available emanates from studies on small samples. Given the ascendency of the cognitive hyperarousal model it is to be expected that controlled treatment outcome studies will be forthcoming in the near future. In spite of the lack of firm evidence concerning cognitive interventions it is appropriate in the context of this book to provide some framework which will guide the practitioner in the appropriate selection of those cognitive strategies which have been forwarded. Inevitably, this framework is based in large measure upon the author's clinical experience but it is to be hoped that research workers will find the analysis stimulating since it raises questions to which answers have yet to be sought.

Table 21 presents an analysis of the various cognitive approaches which have been discussed in this chapter. It also incorporates sleep education (see Chapter 5, pp. 96–97) as an intervention since this has a largely cognitive/attitudinal focus. An attempt is made to contrast the techniques in terms of their focus of action upon cognitive processes, and suggestions are made concerning the nature of those processes most likely to respond to each approach.

Chapter 5 described the non-specific treatment of insomnia, one aspect of which is the presentation of information about sleep and patterns of sleep in relation to actual and perceived sleep requirements. In Chapter 4 (pp. 90–91) it was explained that this educative approach contributes towards the refinement of therapeutic goals upon which the patient and therapist can agree. Sleep education is, therefore, a didactic intervention which adds knowledge and is *corrective* of misunderstandings and misattributions. Shifts in perception or attitude are most clearly required where the patient's initial appraisal of the sleep problem and her desired outcomes of successful treatment are unrealistic (Table 21). Of course, as the name implies, elements of non-specific treatment should form part of the intervention with most insomniacs.

Table 21   A comparison of different cognitive treatments of insomnia with respect to proposed mechanisms of effect and possible indications for selection of treatment

Cognitive treatment strategy	Suggested mechanism of action upon thought processes	Thought content most likely to respond
Sleep education	Corrective	Misunderstanding of sleep processes and needs
Cognitive control	Pre-emptive	Rehearsal, planning, self-evaluative thoughts
Thought stopping; Articulatory suppression	Blocking	Repetitive but non-affect laden thoughts
Imagery training	Distraction	Agitated, unfocused, flitting thoughts; Tension
Cognitive restructuring	Appraisal	Intrusive, irrational but compelling thinking
Paradoxical intention	Enhancement	Rumination about sleeplessness, sleep loss and its consequences

The technique of cognitive control may be described as *pre-emptive* since it aims to preclude intrusive thinking from the nighttime period. The scheduling of specific sessions outwith the bedtime period appears to be most useful for individuals who *habitually* ponder the past day's events—weighing up the good and the bad, the successes and the failures, the completed and the unfinished. Such mental activity may or may not be affect-laden. Indeed, if it is so it may not be necessarily negative in its emotional effects. Some individuals look forward to and enjoy the opportunity to think things through at the end of the day. The process, however, is typically mentally arousing, whether negatively or positively. Forward planning (of the next day and of forthcoming events) is another aspect to this type of mental activity, and again the anticipations associated with this may vary between the exciting and the alarming, most usually falling somewhere in between. By providing the planned opportunity to round off the day past and to prepare for the next day, troublesome nighttime intrusions may be avoided. The process of self-appraisal and self-criticism which often accompanies such rehearsal and planning may also be removed from the bedtime period.

Thought-stopping and articulatory suppression are techniques which pay no respect to the nature of the thought content, either in terms of its importance to the individual or of its rationality. These techniques have one simple aim, that is to *block* thought intrusion and so to facilitate the development of sleep. There is reason, therefore, to suggest that such strategies may fail to provide an appropriate therapeutic solution for certain categories of mental event, and they may fail to block compelling and arousing thought material. However, as explained in Chapter 3, many insomniacs report that trivial and incidental thoughts do occur to keep them awake. These thoughts appear to be almost random and are not usually affect-laden. The problem here is one of *mental acuity* rather than active emotional processing. A blocking strategy may be very useful in these circumstances. Also, articulatory suppression and thought stopping may be appropriate early interventions for times when the insomniac's pattern of thinking is less well developed and less stimulating, e.g. soon after an arousal but before thought processes become cohesive and intrusive (cf. Levey et al, 1991).

Imagery training and other mental relaxation approaches rely upon visualisation and *distraction* from negative, preoccupying images and thoughts. To imagine a tranquil situation or to focus upon some aspect of a visualised object provides the insomniac with a consistent theme for selective attention. Imagery training appears then to be a competing response to rushing, fleeting thoughts which flit from topic to topic. Such poorly focused mental agitation is commonly reported by insomniacs and a relaxation strategy which involves mental focusing may be more effective than attempts to deal systematically with the actual thought content. Blocking and distraction techniques have similarities in that neither recognise any "need" actually to process and resolve the intrusive thought content.

Cognitive restructuring is a technique which inevitably imposes cognitive load (reasoning, appraisal, etc.) as the means by which dysfunctional thinking is reduced. The process of *appraisal* and rationalisation are themselves stimulating mentally. Thus, where possible, thought content which may predictably intrude should be dealt with earlier on in a waking environment and not near bedtime or in bed (cf. cognitive control). However, not all cognitive material is predictable and not all material responds to techniques such as blocking or distraction. It may be necessary, therefore, to provide some insomniacs with training in the use of re-structuring and/or self-statement techniques as a response to compelling anxieties, disappointments or self-evaluations which come to the fore during wakeful nighttime periods. It can be helpful to get such individuals to prepare in advance material for rehearsal which reflects evidence of successful anxiety management, achievement and skilled performance (self-statements) since it is more difficult to engage in successful rationalisation when tired and irritable than during ordinary waking life. It is often the case that people for whom cognitive re-structuring would be the most appropriate technique would benefit also from similar treatment for daytime presentations of psychological symptoms. The management of insomnia, therefore, may be seen as an extension of a broader therapeutic approach rather than a pragmatic response to sleeplessness per se.

Paradoxical intention is the only technique which does not explicitly aim to limit or reduce cognitive intrusion. At the least paradox encourages a "let it be" attitude. At the other extreme paradox *enhances* the cognitive response ... "Yes, I am still awake and what is more I shall stay awake for longer still." Paradox is most effectively applied where the insomniac grasps the subtlety of the paradoxical intention, i.e. she engages in relatively passive resistance to sleep and to the nurturance of wakefulness. A humouring mental attitude towards the sleep problem is required. On the other hand evidence of active inhibition of sleep is a contra-indication for paradox. The individual who self-monitors wakefulness and who feeds back this failure to sleep in a pernicious circle of worry, frustration and effort is a good candidate for paradox. Such an individual may also exhibit concern over the consequences to daytime functioning of inability to sleep. When the mental focus is not specifically upon the sleep process itself, paradox may appear less relevant to the insomniac, resulting in poorer compliance and reduced effectiveness.

Chapter 8

Stimulus Control Procedures in the Management of Insomnia

In Chapter 3 the concept of stimulus control was introduced in the context of discussion of various theoretical models of insomnia. It will be remembered that nervous system or physiological models were considered and these were seen to give rise to the relaxation-based treatments as described and evaluated in Chapter 6. Mental models were also presented, and associated cognitive strategies of treatment formed the focus for Chapter 7. Stimulus control procedures are best accommodated within a third theoretical viewpoint comprising environmental models of insomnia. Certainly, the principal treatment approach associated with situational influences upon sleep has been stimulus control therapy. This eighth chapter is devoted, therefore, to description of these procedures and to evaluation of their effectiveness in treating chronic insomnia. As for the previous two chapters on psychological treatments, the review of the treatment outcome research literature presented here should be read in conjunction with Chapter 9 where comparative outcome studies are reported.

STIMULUS CONTROL PROCEDURES

The concept of stimulus control has its roots in the research work of experimental psychologists. A discriminative stimulus is regarded as occurring in the context of a stimulus continuum and exhibits a typical generalisation gradient. Stimulus control may be defined as the extent to which an antecedent stimulus determines the probability of a conditioned response occurring. That is, stimulus control is measured as a change in response probability resulting from a change in stimulus value (Terrace, 1966). Mackintosh (1977) has expanded this definition helpfully, as follows:

> If a change in a particular stimulus is always followed by a change in the probability, amplitude, latency or rate of a particular response, we may say that this stimulus exercised some control over that response. The term stimulus control has come to be used as a convenient shorthand expression for describing such an observed relationship between changes in external stimuli and changes in recorded behaviour (p. 481).

As applied to insomnia, therefore, there are likely to be environmental stimuli which are discriminative of the desired reinforcement (sleep) and those that are discriminative of wakefulness (i.e. sleep-incompatible behaviours). For the good sleeper, lying down in bed and closing one's eyes exercises effective stimulus control over the sleep-onset response. Being in bed is associated with quickly falling asleep. For the poor sleeper, according to this model, difficulty in falling asleep may be due to inadequate stimulus control which results from either the absence of discriminative stimuli for sleep or the presence of stimuli which are discriminative of wakefulness.

Bootzin is credited with the introduction of stimulus control principles to the management of sleep disorders. In his 1972 paper, he reviewed first of all successful stimulus control treatments of other target behaviours such as over-eating, study problems and marital difficulties. He then went on to suggest that a stimulus control treatment might have potential as an intervention for insomnia since it was possible to differentiate those environmental stimuli which were compatible and those incompatible with the sleep response. He identified the aim of treatment as that of bringing sleeping under the stimulus control of the subject's bed and bedroom, and he established four rules as the basis for the development of a good sleeping habit (Nos. 1 to 4 in Table 22). Through the course of further treatment studies, Bootzin expanded these rules to include two other procedural elements (Nos. 5 and 6 in Table 22) (cf. Bootzin and Nicassio, 1978). This set of six behavioural instructions, therefore, has become known as stimulus control treatment. Each of these stimulus control rules will repay closer scrutiny.

(1) Lie down intending to sleep only when you feel sleepy

Feeling "sleepy tired" is perhaps the most important discriminative stimulus for sleep. It appears to be *sine qua non* to successful sleep-onset. Clearly, going to bed when alert and wide awake is likely to predict maintained wakefulness, especially in circumstances where the bed and bedroom environment are not operating as powerful external stimuli discriminative of a sleep response. Feeling "sleepy tired" refers of course to an internal state. Insomniacs may be particularly poor at monitoring this

Table 22   Stimulus control instructions for the treatment of insomnia

---

(1) Lie down intending to go to sleep only when you feel sleepy.
(2) Do not use your bed or bedroom for anything except sleep. When you go to bed put the light out and try to get to sleep. Do not read, watch television, eat, listen to the radio or worry in bed. Sexual activity is the only exception to this rule.
(3) If you do not fall asleep quickly (within about 10 minutes) get up and go into another room. Do something relaxing while there and go back to bed only when you feel sleepy again.
(4) If you still cannot fall asleep repeat step 3. Also if you waken out of your sleep and do not fall asleep quickly you should get out of bed as in step 3. (You may have to get up many times in the one night.)
(5) Set the alarm for the same time each morning and get up then regardless of how much sleep you have had. This will allow your body to acquire a consistent sleep rhythm.
(6) Do not nap during the daytime, even for short periods. This includes not napping in the evening.

---

internal state of sleep readiness and may (through negative experiences) lack confidence in their ability to predict the right time to go to bed. In these circumstances, patients may need guidance to help them identify those cues which evidence sleepy tiredness, e.g. lapses in concentration, yawning, eyes closing periodically, muscular relaxation and inertia. A sense of sleep readiness, therefore, should initiate preparation for bed and for sleeping.

By implication it should be clear that the insomniac should not respond to other, more arbitrary cues which have little predictive validity for sleep-onset. Typical examples of these are disinterest in the available selection of television programmes, general inactivity and having nothing purposeful to do, completion of tasks and duties which had been allocated for the evening, spouse and other family members deciding that it is time for them to go to bed, and it being "bedtime". The patient should be made aware of and discouraged from such habitual responses unless they happen to coincide with genuine sleep readiness. The reader may recall from Chapter 3 that in one of our own studies 34% of insomniacs acknowledged that they often did not feel tired when they retired to bed, and a further 29% stated that this was sometimes the case. Arbitrary decisions, therefore, appear to be made too readily. This first rule of stimulus control treatment seeks to rectify this.

Often patients find that they go to bed later when they follow the instruction to lie down intending to sleep only when sleepy tired. The practitioner, however, should avoid any explicit demand to the subject to try to stay up longer prior to retiring. The sleep pattern should be allowed to find its own equilibrium. The anchor point of a set rising time (rule 5) is important in this respect. Having warned the practitioner against influencing the decision concerning sleep readiness, our own experience nevertheless suggests that a "threshold time" may be appropriately agreed as part of the therapy contract (Espie and Shapiro, 1991). That is, the patient's response to her perceptions of sleep readiness should not be entirely open-ended. For example, it is not likely to be helpful for an individual to go to bed when sleepy tired at 9.00 p.m. The practitioner should do a rough calculation which relates the average sleep duration obtained by the subject during baseline recording to a suitable anchor time for rising each day. Subtracting the notional sleep duration from the anchor time will provide a notional sleep-onset time. The threshold time may be set no more than one hour earlier than this notional average. Thus and for example, an insomniac who obtains a mean of six hours sleep during baseline and who wishes to rise at 7.00 a.m. should have a threshold time for beginning to monitor sleep readiness of around 12.00 midnight. Subjective tiredness prior to the threshold should not precipitate retiral to bed and any tendencies to doze prior to that threshold time should be avoided (cf. rule 6).

To summarise, therefore, stimulus control will be improved when an individual becomes sensitive to her own pre-sleep state of de-arousal and sleep readiness. The cues associated with this state should become the predictors of preparation for sleep as long as the defined sleep period is imminent.

(2) Do not use your bed or bedroom for anything except sleep

The stimulus control model requires that all activities are categorised either as sleep-compatible or sleep-incompatible. This second instruction largely concerns the latter, that is, those activities which the individual may engage in while in bed or in the bedroom environment which require wakefulness, and which may maintain wakefulness. The most common examples of such sleep-incompatible behaviours are reading in bed, watching television or listening to radio programmes, speaking on the telephone, eating snacks and drinking, smoking and discussions with a bed partner. In relation to all of these activities the bed may be seen as a cue for being awake. Indeed, there is continuity between all such behaviours and other waking behaviours undertaken in waking environments. It is precisely the development of *discontinuity* between waking and sleeping environments which is regarded as critical in stimulus control treatment. The only exception to the rule is sexual activity. This is not precluded from the bedroom but the patient should be advised to follow the stimulus control instructions as above, once she intends to go to sleep.

The practitioner should be aware of potential motivational difficulties for patients in following the instruction to avoid using the bedroom for sleep-incompatible activities. Whereas it is true that sleep is rewarding, particularly for the insomniac, there appear to be many people who look forward to retiring to bed to read a book or to watch a television programme. Thus wakefulness is positively reinforced by a selected sleep-incompatible activity. Furthermore, the fact that lying awake in bed is an unpleasant and aversive experience may lead to a preference for activity rather than inactivity. The problem arises when the individual has made the decision to fall asleep but is unable to do so.

Nevertheless, the practitioner's task is to encourage the poor sleeper towards habit change which will reinforce rapid sleep-onset in bed. The combination of rules 1 and 2 directs the insomniac towards enjoying having her supper, reading a few chapters of her book and so on, in the living room, as part of a usual routine, but giving up these activities when sleepy tiredness becomes compelling.

Kazarian, Howe and Csapo (1979) have provided a useful assessment measure of sleep-incompatible behaviour. The Sleep Behaviour Self-Rating Scale provides ratings on a five-point scale of frequency of engagement in a number of targeted behaviours. Kazarian et al have reported satisfactory internal consistency and test/re-test reliability and also found that their scale reliably differentiated between insomniacs and non-insomniacs on the basis of latency to sleep-onset scores. The practitioner will find some form of checklist useful in interviewing the insomniac but should not be surprised to find that there are insomniacs who actually engage in relatively few overt sleep-incompatible behaviours in the bedroom. In our experience these individuals often lie awake thinking in a dark room. It is only the mind which is active. Some of the cognitive strategies outlined in the previous chapter will be helpful here.

The practitioner should recognise that sleep-incompatible activities per se are unlikely to account for the development of many sleep problems. It is not uncommon to find that insomniacs develop these habits *because* of their experience of being unable to fall asleep or stay asleep. They begin to take a magazine to bed as a coping response to occupy the mind after experiencing a period of being unable to fall asleep spontaneously. It seems, therefore, that for many individuals stimulus control does not offer an explanation of the aetiology of the insomnia. It may, nevertheless, contribute to the maintenance of a poor sleep habit as such responses are repeated and become established, automatic and potentially enjoyable.

There is also the problem for the stimulus control model that substantial numbers of *good* sleepers are in the habit of chatting in bed, making the occasional telephone call or writing the occasional letter. Certainly reading in bed is commonplace. It may be that for these individuals such activities are non-arousing, or even potentially de-arousing or soporific whereas for the insomniac they defer sleep and substitute wakefulness. A related possibility is that good sleepers have a better established pre-sleep routine. Lacks (1987) in her detailed discussion of stimulus control treatment of insomnia suggests that such routines signal that bedtime approaches. She suggests that patients should perform activities in a set order each night, for example locking the door, brushing teeth, setting the alarm, adopting a preferred sleep posture. This highlights an important point, that although discrete behaviours may have power to signal either sleepiness or wakefulness, sets of behaviours form routines which although more fluid may also lead the person towards rapid sleep-onset or away from it.

In summary of this second instruction, therefore, the practitioner should assist the patient in identifying those activities and routines which present in the bedroom and which may interfere with rapid sleep-onset. Such behaviours should be eliminated from this environment and replaced by a pre-sleep routine which facilitates de-arousal. Preferred waking activities should be scheduled into the evening routine in a waking environment but once in bed the light should go out and the individual should settle to go to sleep.

(3) If you do not fall asleep quickly get up and go into another room

An important goal of stimulus control treatment is to pair the bedroom environment with rapid sleep-onset. Thus Bootzin has recommended this "10 minute rule" which seeks to eliminate periods of continued wakefulness from the bedroom environment. If the individual is awake she should be in a waking environment and not lying in bed since the latter only serves to associate bed with a bad experience. The instruction, therefore, requires the subject to get out of bed and out of the bedroom if she has not fallen asleep within 10 minutes of retiring.

It should be noted that the 10 minute "limit" to wakefulness in bed is somewhat arbitrary. The point is that the insomniac must not learn to associate prolonged wakefulness but rather rapid sleep-onset with bed. In his first paper Bootzin in fact left this instruction deliberately vague by telling his subject to get up if he found himself "unable to fall asleep" (Bootzin, 1972). Bootzin was concerned to avoid clock-watching behaviour which might exacerbate the sleep-onset difficulty. In actual practice relatively few insomniacs adhere to this instruction literally and in our experience clock-watching has seldom been a problem. We have preferred, however, a 20 minute period for initial sleep latency (e.g. Espie et al, 1989). This has been because relatively few successfully treated insomniacs achieve post-treatment sleep latencies of 10 minutes. Such an early threshold time may also be unnecessarily strict when compared with the sleep pattern of good sleepers for whom a 10 minute sleep latency would not be regarded as problematic.

It is imperative, however, that the therapist creates an expectation within the patient that she is likely to be getting out of bed, perhaps on many occasions each night, especially in the early stages of treatment. This is a hard instruction to follow and patients may feel inclined to lie on in bed for too long before finally getting up. Simple tactics such as leaving the central heating system on, having a flask of tea in the living room, or leaving some books and magazines beside a comfortable chair are likely to make getting out of bed a less aversive experience and so foster compliance. It is important that the insomniac does *something* when she gets out of bed and goes into another room. Preferably the activity should be relaxing but a wide range of activities is suitable.

The patient should be encouraged to think of a period spent out of bed as simply a period of ordinary wakefulness. It is often helpful to get the patient to relate success in implementing treatment to the number of risings from bed, especially in the early stages of therapy. This is likely to facilitate compliance with an otherwise unpleasant and sometimes unacceptable or counter-intuitive instruction. The patient should be cautioned against the temptation to delay rising due to a mistaken rationalisation that "another minute or two" will see her safely asleep. Consistent with the earlier instructions the patient should be discouraged from returning to bed until the feeling of sleepiness returns (rule 1). Attempts to return to bed prematurely are unlikely to be fruitful. Once back in bed, however, the patient should have the light out and immediately settle down to sleep (rule 2).

(4) If you still cannot fall asleep repeat Rule 3

There is no guarantee that the insomniac will fall asleep quickly upon returning to bed after a period of wakefulness in another room. Indeed, it is likely that serial risings will be commonplace at first and such expectations should be expressed by the practitioner. This instruction, therefore, requires that the subject continue to follow the same stimulus control code of practice as before. That is, each instance of returning to bed marks the beginning of a *new* sleep latency period which, if it exceeds 10 minutes (or 20 minutes, depending upon the criterion adopted), should again signal rising from bed.

Similarly, where intermittent wakefulness with a difficulty in returning to sleep presents, the insomniac should be advised to get out of bed at these times also. The insomniac may expect, therefore, to be out of bed on many occasions both initially and later during the night and should be advised that this is unlikely to be a pleasant or restful experience. Persistence with the programme is essential in order to benefit.

(5) Set the alarm to rise at the same time each morning

As mentioned previously this rule and rule 6 (which refers to the avoidance of daytime napping) were not part of Bootzin's original instructions. The reader is also referred to the discussion on situational and temporal influences upon sleep in Chapter 3 of this book (pp. 51–53 and 53–55 respectively). Establishing a set time for rising and avoiding naps does not properly fit into the theoretical model of stimulus control. Nevertheless, as has been pointed out earlier in this chapter, these two rules have been elements of "stimulus control treatment" in the major treatment comparison studies. Interestingly, in her recent text book, Lacks includes these, along with the instruction not to go to bed until drowsy, as the first three instructions in a set of sleep hygiene rules (Lacks, 1987). In the present book it was decided to include rules 5 and 6 within the stimulus control framework partly for convenience and partly because it is not possible to separate out differing components in the majority of treatment outcome studies employing stimulus control.

The patient must select a time for waking and rising by alarm clock each morning and stick to this time throughout treatment. Clearly, careful thought must be given to selecting an appropriate time and this will vary from individual to individual. As a general rule it is better to err on the side of an earlier wakening time than one which is later. This is particularly so where the insomniac is known to have a relatively short sleep duration. Certainly, the waking time should be convenient for the individual's uptake of day to day activities. If there is an inevitable gap between waking time and the start up of the usual daily routine, this should not be left as a vacuum but the therapist should consider with the patient how this "extra" time may be put to best use.

It is important to stress that the waking time is also the rising time. The patient should be encouraged to get out of bed immediately rather than switching the alarm clock off and continuing to doze. This is a hard discipline, but the practitioner should remind the patient that the aim is to produce a strong biological sleep rhythm which has a reliable anchor point. If this point is not in fact an anchor, but rising time varies, then the sleep schedule is likely to remain less than optimal. We have always encouraged our patients to maintain the waking/rising time *seven* days per week, that is including weekends. Once a new sleep pattern has been established which proves satisfactory, it may be possible to allow a moderate degree of flexibility on this. Interestingly, however, a fair number of our successfully treated patients have found that they are quite happy to do without "a long lie" at weekends or to take only an extra 30 minutes or so.

Although it was made clear under rule 1 above, it is worth reiterating here, that there should be no set time for the insomniac to go to bed. The reason for this repetition is that the process of agreeing rising time can lead some patients also to fix in their minds a revised bedtime. Let us suppose that an individual now decides to rise at 6.30 a.m. instead of 7.30 a.m., that is one hour earlier. This should not be taken to imply that bedtime is likely to be earlier than before. Only rising time is anchored. The expectation is that the individual's natural sleep requirement will, over time, achieve its own equilibrium and will fall in behind this anchor point on a relatively stable night to night basis. It is, therefore, only after successful treatment that the insomniac will know with any reliability her approximate, appropriate bedtime hour.

(6) Do not nap during the daytime

Although it has been said that this is a temporal factor affecting sleep, it should be noted at the outset that most daytime or early evening naps are in fact taken within waking environments and thus the power of the bedroom as a discriminative stimulus for sleep is weakened. Aspects of both stimulus and temporal control are involved.

The insomniac, however, should be advised that napping at any time, whether in the bedroom or not, is likely to contribute to the maintenance of nighttime insomnia. There is, therefore, a total ban on all napping, even naps which are of short duration. Again, this may be a difficult instruction to follow, particularly for individuals who are in the habit of having a short sleep, say after an evening meal. Such naps are often highly valued and many individuals view them as a just reward after a hard day's work. For such individuals it may be helpful to suggest substituting some other pleasurable activity in place of the nap. For example, listening to music, doing a crossword, going for a short walk, having a nice bath or shower etc.

Daytime napping is more problematic amongst elderly people whose lifestyle is sedentary. Their day can be punctuated by frequent brief sleeps and, additively, a considerable period may be spent sleeping across what normally would be the waking day. The basic problem associated with this is usually lack of engagement in purposeful activities around the house, and the problem is especially common amongst those who are housebound or who seldom manage out.

Bootzin and Engle-Friedman (1987) have discussed the relationship between inactivity, napping and sleep disturbances in the elderly. Referring to the work of Webb (1975) they comment that sleep-onset latency is inversely related to the length of time since the individual last slept. Thus a morning nap has relatively little effect upon the subsequent night's sleep, whereas afternoon and evening naps prove more intrusive. Such naps contain more deep and less REM sleep and are associated with more light (stages 1 and 2) and REM sleep and with more frequent awakenings during the subsequent night. The reader will recall from Chapter 1 that the first cycle of sleep usually contains the greatest proportion of stages 3 and 4 (deep) sleep. It is probably this which explains why some relatively brief naps can feel very restorative. It is helpful to provide this rationale to the insomniac who habitually naps during the day, in order to achieve compliance with this instruction.

It should be noted, however, that many insomniacs report that they do not allow themselves to sleep outwith the sleep period. There appears to be a good lay understanding that naps should be avoided in order to promote a good night's sleep, and some insomniacs already will have corrected this aspect of their maladjusted sleep pattern prior to treatment.

It should be apparent that the above set of six stimulus control instructions represents a firmly behavioural and directive form of treatment. The rules are demanding of the insomniac, if properly applied. The practitioner also may find the instructions demanding to administer since they represent a hard code for patients who may present as emotionally distressed. Neverthless, stimulus control is the form of treatment which follows most logically from didactic, non-specific interventions such as those outlined in Chapter 5. As a treatment method stimulus control has been investigated quite thoroughly, and this research literature will be considered in the next section.

THE EFFECTIVENESS OF STIMULUS CONTROL TREATMENT OF INSOMNIA

Descriptive information from studies which have investigated stimulus control treatment for insomnia is presented in Table 23. The outcome literature on studies comparing diverse modalities of treatment will be described in Chapter 9.

Reference has been made already in this chapter to the pioneering case study paper of Bootzin (1972). Bootzin's successful treatment of a 25 year old man with a five year history of severe initial insomnia paved the way for more systematic study in later years. Bootzin presented the results of this single case in graphical format which demonstrated a dramatic reduction in the number of times which the subject had to get out of his bed as a result of treatment. Within three weeks of stimulus control treatment the subject did not require to get out of bed at all, compared with a typical four or five nightly risings at the outset. At follow-up around six weeks later, these gains were maintained with the subject getting up once during the night around once per week. Bootzin noted that the subject's spouse was able to confirm these findings.

Bootzin and Nicassio included an early study by Tokarz and Lawrence (1974) in their 1978 review paper. Tokarz and Lawrence compared the efficacy of the complete stimulus control procedure with two different constituent parts. These were a temporal control strategy, including only instructions aimed at regularising the sleeping pattern according to the constraints of time, and an alternative approach based solely upon improvement of the bed and bedroom environment's function as discriminative stimuli for falling asleep. Relaxation, placebo and no treatment control groups were included also. These workers found that all three active interventions resulted in highly significant reductions in sleep latency, from approximately 50 minutes at baseline to less than 10 minutes at post-treatment. All three active interventions achieved similar outcome and improvements were maintained at follow-up.

A study by Zwart and Lisman (1979) represented a more thorough attempt at a component analysis. Some detail of this study was presented earlier, in Chapter 3 (pp. 52–53). Zwart and Lisman recruited 47 undergraduate psychology students who reported that they usually took longer than 30 minutes to fall asleep and randomly assigned them within levels of severity to one of five treatment conditions (see Table 23 and earlier text for full details). Treatment comprised a once weekly 30 minute session for four weeks beyond baseline. All subjects were given the counterdemand instruction that improvement would not occur during the first three weeks of treatment. Zwart and Lisman's results indicated that those receiving stimulus control (i.e. the complete set of instructions) and those treated with countercontrol therapy (deliberate engagement in sleep incompatible activities in bed if unable to sleep) achieved shorter SOL scores, compared with non-contingent control (subjects required to rise a fixed number of times within 20 minutes of retiring) and waiting-list cases during the counterdemand period. However, after positive demand instructions were issued, the temporal control group became as effective as the stimulus control and countercontrol procedures (see Table 23). At follow-up one month later treatment gains were maintained and there were no significant differences amongst any of the treatment groups on any measure. Follow-up sleep latencies fell within the range 18 to 27 minutes across treatments (cf. waiting list SOL of 42 minutes), representing an approximate 50% reduction in sleep latency.

In 1975, Haynes, Price and Simons reported four single case experimental designs of subjects who had not benefited from prescriptions of hypnotic

Table 23 Treatment studies employing Stimulus Control and related treatments. Outcome data are sleep log ratings of sleep-onset latency (SOL; min.) unless otherwise stated.

Authors	Sample	Total N	Age (mean years)	Duration (mean years)	Treatment(s)		SOL Pre (mean min.)	SOL Post (mean min.)	SOL F.up (mean min.)	F.up (month)
Bootzin (1972)	S	1	25	5	Stimulus control		4/5	0 (risings from bed)	0	2
Tokarz and Lawrence (1974)	S	*	*	*	Stimulus control		51	6	7	*
					Temporal control		46	8	13	*
					Stimulus control without temporal control		56	7	11	*
					Relaxation placebo		49	47	NA	NA
					No treatment		45	56	NA	NA
Haynes, Price and Simons (1975)	R	4	22–71 (range)	3–25 (range)	Stimulus control (ABAB designs)		57	14	19	9
Turner and Ascher[a] (1979b)	P	6	47	15	Stimulus control	Group 1	90	25	NA	NA
						Group 2	80	77	NA	NA
Alperson and Biglan (1979)	R	29	37	NA	Stimulus control + relaxation (young)		59	29	25	2
					Stimulus control + relaxation (old)		52	47	49	2
					Countercontrol + active relaxation		73	53	37	2
					No treatment		54	79	39	2

Study					Treatment	>1 prolonged awakening)	0 (CD/PD)	0	3
Norton and DeLuca (1979)	P	1	22	6	Stimulus control + relaxation				
Zwart and Lisman (1979)	S	41	NA	NA	Stimulus control	46	26/26	25	1
					Non-contingent control	43	45/34	27	1
					Countercontrol	49	29/25	18	1
					Temporal control	41	31/19	23	1
					No treatment	46	45/39	42	1
Puder et al (1983)	R	16	67	15	Stimulus control	66	33	33	2
Lacks et al (1983b)	R	15	43	12	Stimulus control	60	25	29	3
					Desensitisation placebo	88	51 (WASO)	45	3
Spielman, Saskin and Thorpy (1987)	P	35	46	15	Sleep restriction therapy	48	19 (SOL)	31	7
						159	50 (WASO)	87	7
Lichstein (1988)[a]	P	1	59	30	Sleep compression	190	20 (SOL)	100	7 years
						75	10 (WASO)	25	7 years

Key. S = student; R = recruited subject; P = patient; CD = counterdemand; PD = positive demand; WASO = wake time after sleep-onset (min.)
Notes. [a]Data estimated from graphs.
*Original reports unobtainable. Data reported are from Bootzin and Nicassio (1978).

medication. Subjects varied widely in age (range 22–71 years), experience
of insomnia (range 3–25 years) and in severity of insomnia (SOL range 22–
94 minutes). For each subject an ABAB design was applied. Baseline sleep
monitoring over two weeks was followed by stimulus control treatment
which was maintained until stable improvement was demonstrated for
five consecutive days. A reversal phase was then included, followed by
re-introduction of the stimulus control package.

The first phase of stimulus control treatment was associated with
reductions in sleep latency in all subjects, although in one case initial
insomnia was minimal at the outset. Haynes, Price and Simons reported
that two subjects failed to demonstrate clear reversal trends when baseline
conditions were re-introduced; however, it is clear from the graphed
data presented in their paper that none of the reversals was impressive.
All failed to increase beyond the previous treatment phase, let alone
move substantially towards pre-treatment levels. An argument couched
in terms of maintained improvement during the reversal would have
been equally tenable from their data. Thus the re-introduction of stimulus
control treatment in the following phase was of little experimental value.
Nevertheless, the three individuals with significant sleep latency difficulties
did improve with stimulus control treatment and average SOL reduction
for the four subjects was around 40 minutes at post-treatment. Furthermore,
there were improvements for all four subjects in terms of other sleep
measures. All four had longer sleeps, three of the four had fewer wakenings
and all reported at least modest improvement in ratings of restedness after
sleep at post-treatment. A nine month telephone contact follow-up revealed
that the patterns of improvements obtained as a result of treatment were
generally maintained, suggesting that stimulus control therapy produced
some form of habit change.

Turner and Ascher (1979b) criticised the Haynes, Price and Simons
study on the grounds that ABAB designs are ill-advised with behavioural
procedures because of the possible "carry over" effects upon cessation of
treatment. Instead, these workers proposed the use of a multiple baseline
design (Hersen and Barlow, 1976) more adequately to test cause–effect
relationships.

Turner and Ascher's clients were six, self-referred out-patients with severe
initial insomnia. The subjects ranged in age from 32 to 61 years and had
an average duration of sleep disturbance of 15 years. In addition, five of
the subjects took regular sleep medication, and the sixth self-medicated
his sleep with alcohol. Clearly, therefore, Turner and Ascher's subjects
represented a considerable challenge to any behavioural therapeutic
programme. Unlike many other early studies these clients appeared
representative of the spontaneously presenting clinical population.

All of the subjects were required to complete a baseline of one week self-monitoring on a sleep log. Thereafter, three subjects were allocated to receive stimulus control therapy with the other three receiving a quasi-desensitisation placebo treatment (Steinmark and Borkovec, 1974). After four weeks, clients in this second group were transferred to active stimulus control therapy which the first group received throughout the eight week treatment phase. Turner and Ascher presented their results in graph format which demonstrated that stimulus control was rapidly effective in reducing sleep latency in both groups of subjects. The placebo therapy, by comparison, had little impact upon sleep latency. Interestingly, Turner and Ascher also tested the clinical significance of reductions in sleep latency by applying a 30 minutes SOL criterion. This showed that five of the six subjects achieved sleep latency of 30 minutes or less within four weeks of the institution of stimulus control treatment. Indeed, in two of these cases clinical improvement occurred in the first week. The only client who failed to reduce sleep latency to within 30 minutes did achieve a final post-treatment value of around 40 minutes which represented an overall reduction in sleep latency of greater than one hour on the average night. By means of the multiple baseline approach, therefore, Turner and Ascher were able to demonstrate the specific impact of stimulus control instructions upon sleep latency. Information from spouse/room-mate reliability checks evidenced marked agreement between the client's rating and the spouse/room-mate's rating of sleep latency. Turner and Ascher also reported that reductions in medication followed the introduction of stimulus control and that clients reported feeling more rested and less fatigued during the day as further outcomes of treatment.

Norton and De Luca (1979) reported on a case study of a 22 year old male with a six year history of both sleep-onset and sleep-maintenance insomnia. This subject had previously been treated unsuccessfully by hypnosis, counselling and relaxation training and his sleeplessness continued to interfere with his university work. The subject also complained of a number of other somatic symptoms, general irritability and tension. After a two week baseline period he was treated with sessions of abbreviated progressive relaxation. This was done because the authors recognised that the subject had not in fact learned how to relax from previous training periods. Norton and De Luca reported only summary data but stated that sleep latency fell from an average of more than 30 minutes at baseline to around 10 minutes after this relaxation training. Furthermore, total sleep time increased from 4.3 hours to an average of six hours per night.

However, the subject returned for additional therapy two months later, continuing to complain of tiredness and irritability and of intermittent awakening. Apparently he continued to fall asleep rapidly. A stimulus control procedure was then instituted along with the requirement to perform "a punishment activity" if he got out of bed because he was unable to sleep. This activity comprised filling out job application forms. After two sessions of this combined behavioural treatment the subject reported that he was no longer awakening during the night, and at follow-up three months after the termination of therapy average sleep was around seven hours with no wakenings. He also reported being less tense and less irritable.

Alperson and Biglan (1979) attempted to evaluate self-administered treatments for insomnia. Treatment was presented in the form of a manual with limited therapist contact. Twenty-two insomniacs recruited from a media advertisement and all under the age of 55 were randomly assigned to one of three interventions which followed a two week baseline period. One group received a manual comprising meditative relaxation along with stimulus control instructions. The manual for the second group comprised an alternative relaxation approach which involved back stretching exercises, along with behavioural instructions which prescribed activities to be conducted in bed (similar to Zwart and Lisman's countercontrol procedure). The third group self-monitored only both during baseline and the two week treatment period and thus formed an untreated control. Alperson and Biglan then added a final treatment group which comprised seven subjects who were over 55 years of age and who received the meditation and stimulus control package. This was to investigate the relationship between age and treatment outcome.

These workers found that the combined stimulus control and relaxation treatment, and the countercontrol and back stretching relaxation treatment were both significantly better than no treatment in reducing sleep latency, but were not significantly different from each other (Table 23). This result is similar to that of Zwart and Lisman using countercontrol. Mean reduction for the former was 30 minutes, however, compared with 20 minutes for the latter treatment manual. Furthermore, the older subjects responded significantly less well than the younger subjects. The greatest improvements in rated quality of sleep were also obtained with the stimulus control/relaxation treatment in the younger sample. This poor outcome with older persons has not been replicated in more recent studies of stimulus control treatment.

Puder et al (1983) provided a more comprehensive report of stimulus control treatment with older adults. These workers randomly assigned a final sample of 16 clients (mean age 67 years) to either immediate or delayed stimulus control treatment. The latter involved a 10 week waiting period. Data on sleep latency revealed considerable reductions for both groups once active intervention was applied and overall reductions of approximately 50% were maintained at two month follow-up. Therefore, Puder et al demonstrated that age alone may not be a sufficient factor to preclude treatment gain, even as in this case where therapy comprised only four, weekly small group sessions conducted by a clinical psychology student.

Lacks (1987) has devoted a section in her book to discussion of treatment issues with the older insomniac. She comments that another study conducted by their research group dispelled the notion that it would be unwise to mix younger and older adults in the same treatment groups (Davies et al, 1986). Lacks states that they have included individuals up to the age of 78 in a number of studies and found that although such older participants begin and end treatment with greater sleep disturbance, the degree of treatment response has not been related to the insomniac's age. Nevertheless, she advises that it may be helpful to extend treatment periods and to proceed more slowly in order to achieve optimum results with elderly clients. More time should be spent preparing such clients as part of a clarification and educational input and an additional treatment session may prove worthwhile.

It is noteworthy in passing that rescheduling treatments have proven effective also with sleep problems presenting in the *very young*. For example, Weissbluth (1982) reported on the case of a 9 month old baby girl whose disorganised sleep schedule was restructured successfully by instructing the parents to waken her at 7.00 a.m. every day, not permit her to nap after 11.00 a.m. and put her to bed in the evening whenever she appeared tired.

Lacks et al (1983b) conducted a small group comparison study comparing stimulus control with placebo treatment of sleep-maintenance insomnia. Fifteen volunteers were recruited through media announcements and letters to physicians. The mean age of the total sample was 43 years and average duration of insomnia was 11.7 years. At baseline, mean wake time after sleep onset (WASO) was 75 minutes. Sleep diaries revealed that these insomniacs did not suffer from sleep-onset difficulties since average SOL was only 11 minutes per night. Subjects were assigned either to a complete stimulus control programme or to quasi-desensitisation placebo procedures described in Chapter 6. Following a seven day baseline period four weeks of treatment were conducted in weekly small group sessions lasting 60 to 90 minutes. Follow-up was conducted at three months. Lacks et al reported outcome for three dependent measures. Firstly, WASO reduced from a pre-treatment value of 60 minutes to 25 minutes after stimulus control treatment (58%), compared with a reduction from 88 to 51 minutes in the placebo group (42%) (Table 23). Both of these reductions were significant and the two treatments did not differ from one another. Both treatments maintained these gains at follow-up. A similar pattern of results was obtained for the other measures of number of arousals during the night, and number of arousals which exceeded 10 minutes in duration, i.e. improvements were obtained under both treatments for both variables.

Lacks et al's study is one of very few which have considered specifically the impact of stimulus control procedures on sleep-maintenance difficulties. From this point of view the results appear encouraging. At final (three month) outcome, time awake during the night reduced by around 50%. Commenting on their finding that changes experienced by subjects under stimulus control were not significantly different from those experienced by the placebo group, Lacks et al have suggested that longer treatments may be required to achieve differential treatment effects for sleep-maintenance insomnia. Given the similarly equivalent follow-up data, however, this explanation appears to be unsupported. Both groups continued to improve. They also suggested that the quasi-desensitisation placebo may have an active ingredient when it comes to treating sleep-maintenance insomnia, particularly if the therapeutic instructions are followed during nighttime awakenings. This explanation appears more feasible since the mental rehearsal of pre-bedtime routines associated with visual imagery may preclude other, more intrusive thought processes, thereby facilitating a return to sleep.

It was recognised at an early stage in this chapter that the procedures known as stimulus control therapy in fact comprise elements of strict stimulus control (in the traditional behavioural sense) and elements of temporal harmonisation of the sleep–wake schedule. Before concluding this chapter, therefore, it may be appropriate to include description and discussion of a further behavioural technique which bears some relationship to the temporal management aspects of stimulus control.

Spielman, Saskin and Thorpy (1983, 1987) have recently introduced a technique known as Sleep Restriction Therapy. This intervention is based on the suggestion that insomniacs may spend excessive periods of time in bed. Clearly sleep efficiency reduces where the amount of time spent asleep falls short of the bedtime period, i.e. sleeplessness, insomnia. Also, however, an over-extended bedtime period will reduce sleep efficiency by facilitating wakefulness while in bed. It is proposed that this latter may be a maintaining factor in lengthy sleep latency, intermittent wakening and poor sleep efficiency although it may not have actually initiated the sleep disturbance. In a recent review paper Spielman lists excessive time in bed as one of a number of factors that perpetuate insomnia (Spielman, Caruso and Glovinsky, 1987). He comments that sleep restriction therapy, stimulus control instructions and sleep hygiene recommendations have all evolved from an appreciation that factors which perpetuate insomnia may operate long after precipitating factors have subsided.

Similar to the temporal control aspect of stimulus control therapy, sleep restriction therapy firstly involves the establishment of a wakening time each morning in accordance with daytime schedule needs. Average subjective total sleep time as recorded over one or two weeks of self-monitoring is then used to arrive at the amount of time which should be spent in bed. Retiring time at night may then be calculated and set to the nearest 15 minutes, such that time spent in bed equals this prescribed sleep period. The patient is encouraged to follow this revised sleep schedule. Retiring time may be altered only if greater than 90% sleep efficiency is achieved over a series of nights. Thus the term "sleep restriction" is appropriate for these procedures, although there is the expectation of increases in total sleep later in therapy, but without loss of sleep efficiency.

Spielman, Saskin and Thorpy (1987) conducted a treatment outcome study of sleep restriction on a sample of 35 subjects who had a mean age of 46 years and an average duration of insomnia of 15.4 years (Table 23). Half of the subjects presented with both sleep-onset and sleep-maintenance difficulties, with the majority of the remainder having sleep-maintenance problems alone. The authors reported that on the first night of treatment, subjects' time in bed was restricted to a level which was on average 140 minutes below the baseline mean value. Thus, in the early stages of treatment total sleep time reduced very considerably below baseline values. However, by the fourteenth day of treatment it had increased again to the pre-treatment level and thereafter steadily increased throughout treatment. During the final treatment week, total sleep was in fact 23 minutes greater than at baseline, although subjects were on average spending 86 minutes less in bed. Mean sleep efficiency increased, therefore, from 67 to 87%. There were dramatic reductions also in the amount of time spent awake during the night (from 159 minutes at baseline to 50 minutes at post-treatment). Interestingly, Spielman, Saskin and Thorpy also measured night to night variability and reported significant reductions from baseline to the end of treatment on most sleep parameters. Thus a further important clinical effect of the sleep restriction therapy was the stabilisation of sleep pattern across nights. A follow-up conducted 36 weeks after completion of treatment indicated that sleep improvements were maintained.

In discussing the success of their treatment approach, these workers have acknowledged the similarity between sleep restriction therapy and stimulus control in terms of initial sleep loss at the start of treatment. They suggest that this partial sleep deprivation may have consolidated sleep directly, produced daytime fatigue which dampened a chronic state of hyperarousal, or reduced maladaptive conditioning because less time was spent lying awake in bed. They regarded the clinical efficacy of their treatment as related to the reduction of nocturnal wakefulness, i.e. greater continuity of sleep which became reliable on a night to night basis. They commented, however, on practical difficulties with the procedures. Some patients found it difficult to stay awake until the scheduled bedtime. Also some subjects became concerned that their sleep pattern deteriorated at the start of treatment. In fact eight of their original cohort of 49 patients

(16%) withdrew because of discouragement and difficulty complying with the rigid schedule.

Lichstein has recognised that the problem of spending too long in bed relative to actual sleep requirement is particularly prevalent amongst the elderly. He regards such individuals as not truly insomniac but rather as "insomnoid" and recommends treatment aimed at reducing time spent in bed (Lichstein 1980, 1984, 1988). Lichstein's Sleep Compression Treatment is almost identical to sleep restriction therapy since it consists of advancing the time of entering bed in the evening and withdrawing the time of arising in the morning. The latter is similarly rigidly fixed to establish stable sleep routines and to raise the probability that sleepiness will present at bedtime on the following evening.

Lichstein (1988) presented a single case study of a 59 year old retired man with a very lengthy history of insomnia. Over the preceding 30 years he had regularly consumed barbiturates, tranquillisers or alcohol and had required lengthy spells of hospitalisation for de-toxification from sleep medications. Lichstein's first treatment approach was to use ocular relaxation, which involves tensing and relaxing the eyes in six positions. This procedure, however, failed to improve sleep efficiency beyond 50% and significant initial and sleep-maintenance difficulties remained. Stimulus control treatment was then initiated but produced only a weak trend towards improvement. Sleep efficiency achieved 60% and although sleep latency reduced on average across the treatment period it remained erratic and clinically problematic. The Sleep Compression Treatment was then applied for over eight months. The greatest part of the scheduling alteration occurred during the first three months when reductions averaged 15 minutes per week and led to the shortening of time in bed per night from eight hours to just four hours forty-five minutes. A further hour was taken off time in bed over the next five months. Interestingly, associated with these drastic reductions in time spent in bed were marked improvements in qualitative ratings. Quality of sleep improved by 50% and the initial problem of tossing and turning improved by over 100%. Changes in actual sleep parameters evidenced a final sleep latency of around 25 minutes and few intrusive awakenings. The patient continued to refrain from hypnotic medication at an extremely lengthy, seven year follow-up and most measures evidenced maintained improvement. However, by that time the client was obtaining approximately twice the amount of sleep as his post-treatment value for which there was no clear explanation.

Sleep restriction or sleep compression, therefore, appear to be effective methods for improving sleep efficiency and may be especially suitable for elderly insomniacs (Morin and Kwentus, 1988). However, it is somewhat misleading to consider sleep restriction as an alternative treatment to stimulus control. As was indicated earlier on in this chapter it has been our own practice in both clinical and research work to include temporal control strategies as part of the stimulus control package. Furthermore, in advising insomniacs to retire to bed when they feel sleepy, we have usually advised them of a "threshold time" prior to which they should fight off sleepiness but after which they should retire to bed. This threshold time has been calculated by means of a procedure very similar to that outlined by Spielman and his colleagues and Lichstein, i.e. by obtaining an approximation of sleep requirement from baseline data. The practitioner has to weigh up the potentially deleterious effects upon patient compliance of an overly rigid initial schedule against the fact that less conservative temporal control strategies appear effective in most cases. Further study would be welcome comparing the restriction/compression therapies with more conventional stimulus control treatments.

OVERVIEW OF STIMULUS CONTROL PROCEDURES

The treatment of insomnia using stimulus control instruction has been shown to be effective amongst both younger and older adults. Initial sleep latency, in particular, has demonstrated considerable reduction in most studies, and further comparative outcome reports (included in Chapter 9) also evidence that this improvement can be rapid after commencement of stimulus control treatment. Procedural similarities with sleep restriction/compression treatment, which has emerged in the literature more recently, continue to beg the question as to the critical therapeutic element in the stimulus control package. However, from the viewpoint of clinical practice the instructions are readily understood by patients and follow logically from the provision of educative information about sleep. Compliance can be enhanced by such supportive and didactic help.

Chapter 9

Comparative Outcome Studies Involving Relaxation, Paradox and Stimulus Control Treatments

Chapters 6 to 8 focused upon particular orientations towards the treatment of insomnia and considered the research literature pertinent to each orientation. Chapter 9 necessarily, therefore, draws together these alternative relaxation-based, cognitive and operant approaches. Consideration will be given here to those studies which have investigated the *relative* merits of the individual treatments. There has been evidence so far in favour of all treatments, but is one favoured over another, and in what circumstances? Consistent with the available literature, the following analysis will be based largely upon comparisons of the three most commonly applied psychological treatments—namely, progressive relaxation, paradoxical intention and stimulus control.

There are available to date 14 studies which have compared interventions across the above treatment modalities. Summary information is presented in Table 24. Inspection of the table reveals that whereas most studies included a waiting-list control group, less than half compared active treatments with a placebo intervention. Amongst the largest and best controlled studies have been those by Turner and Ascher (1979a), Lacks et al (1983a) and Espie et al (1989). These studies will be reported in greater detail here; however, all of the studies will be reviewed, starting with the earliest and progressing in chronological order.

The three earliest studies (Bootzin, 1975; Slama, 1975; Lawrence and Tokarz, 1976) were included in Bootzin and Nicassio's (1978) review paper. Unfortunately, not all of the original data are available and the source manuscripts are now unobtainable.

Bootzin (1975) randomly allocated a sample of 66 recruited subjects to either stimulus control, progressive relaxation, self-relaxation placebo or waiting-list control groups. Although self-reports of sleep latency suggest that these were severe initial insomniacs, they did not present through clinical channels, and the chronicity of the presenting problem is unstated. Inspection of the data on sleep latency in Table 24 indicates that stimulus control produced a mean SOL reduction of 67 minutes, compared with the active relaxation group where improvements of around 30 minutes were obtained. Bootzin and Nicassio (1978) reported that in absolute terms after treatment, 57% of those who received stimulus control averaged less than 25 minutes to fall asleep, as contrasted with only 29% of those who were trained in progressive relaxation. Importantly, however, 27% of the self-relaxation group and 22% of untreated insomniacs also achieved this criterion of improvement. Indeed, the post-treatment mean SOL score for stimulus control was a mere 10 minutes superior to the waiting-list procedure. In spite of the evident ambiguity of these results, Bootzin and Nicassio (1978) and Borkovec (1982) have cited Bootzin's study as evidence for the superior effectiveness of stimulus control treatment. Also, commenting on this study, Bootzin and Engle-Friedman (1987) referred to improvement in total sleep obtained after stimulus control treatment.

The study by Slama (1975) was conducted in Borkovec's laboratory using groups of undergraduate students who complained of significant sleep disturbance. It appears from baseline values that insomnia was relatively mild with mean sleep latency being less than 40 minutes. This could be regarded as constituting a sub-clinical sample according to some criteria (Espie et al, 1988). Slama, however, did include a counterdemand instruction to control for therapist-induced expectancy effects which revealed that both stimulus control and relaxation were superior to no treatment under conditions of negative demand. Stimulus control was also found to be superior to relaxation until positive demand instruction was instituted when subjects in both therapy conditions were sleeping similarly well. These improvements in sleep latency were maintained at an unspecified follow-up assessment.

Lawrence and Tokarz (1976) also recruited a student population although their subjects reported moderate sleep-onset problems. Subjects were randomly assigned to individual stimulus control, group stimulus control, where three clients were seen together, progressive relaxation training or desensitisation placebo. Both the individual and group stimulus control treatments were found to be highly effective in reducing mean SOL to less than 20 minutes. This improvement rate of greater than 75% was considerably higher than the approximate 30% improvement at post-treatment with relaxation. Unfortunately, the durability of these changes was not reported in this study. Nevertheless, taking these first three studies together, there is preliminary evidence consistent with a preference for stimulus control over progressive relaxation training, at least in terms of sleep-onset time.

Table 24 Treatment studies comparing outcome across different psychological therapies. Data presented represent sleep-onset (SOL; min.) unless otherwise indicated

Authors	Sample	Total N	Age (mean years)	Duration (mean years)	Treatment(s)	SOL Pre (mean min.)	SOL Post (mean min.)	SOL F.up (mean min.)	F.up (month)
Bootzin (1975)[a]	R	66	NA	NA	Stimulus control	96	29	NA	NA
					Progressive relaxation	105	76	NA	NA
					Relaxation placebo	81	63	NA	NA
					No treatment	63	39	NA	NA
Slama (1975)[a]	S	NA	NA	NA	Stimulus control	46	13	19	NA
					Progressive relaxation	36	16	18	NA
					No treatment	33	33	NA	NA
Lawrence and Tokarz (1976)[a]	S	NA	NA	NA	Stimulus control (individual)	65	8	NA	NA
					Stimulus control (group)	65	17	NA	NA
					Progressive relaxation	65	45	NA	NA
					Desensitisation placebo	65	66	NA	NA
Hughes and Hughes (1978)	R	36	34	NA	Stimulus control	57	28 ⎫		
					Progressive relaxation	55	40 ⎬	27	12
					EMG biofeedback	44	27 ⎬		
					Pseudo-EMG biofeedback	45	17 ⎭		
Turner and Ascher (1979a)	R	50	39	11	Stimulus control	64	21	NA	NA
					Progressive relaxation	63	28	NA	NA
					Paradoxical intention	63	29	NA	NA
					Desensitisation placebo	57	44	NA	NA
					No treatment	64	60	NA	NA
Lacks et al (1983a)	R	64	41	14			CD/PD		
					Stimulus control	75	34/28	23	3
					Progressive relaxation	61	49/48	33	3
					Paradoxical intention	63	53/60	34	3
					Desensitisation placebo	70	54/40	31	3

Study					Treatment				
Turner, Di Tomasso and Giles (1983)	P	40	31	NA	Stimulus control	70	64	NA	NA
					Progressive relaxation	48	59	NA	NA
					Stimulus control + progressive relax.	49	59	NA	NA
					No treatment	65		NA	NA
Ladouceur and Gros-Louis (1986)	R	25	42	10	Paradoxical intention		PI=SC>SI=NT (post-treatment)	PI=SC>SI=NT (2 months)	
					Stimulus control				
					Sleep information				
					No treatment				
Morin and Azrin (1987)[b,c]	R	21	57	12	Stimulus control	57	20	23	12
					Imagery training	52	46	26	12
					No treatment	63	50	NA	NA
Morin and Azrin (1988)[b]	R	27	67	19	Stimulus control	76	43	35	12
					Imagery training	73	57	59	12
					No treatment	67	71	NA	NA
Sanavio (1988)[c]	P	24	39	10	Frontalis biofeedback (High arousal)	62	25	15	12
					Frontalis biofeedback (Low arousal)	55	22	15	12
					Cognitive programme (High arousal)	62	30	12	12
					Cognitive programme (Low arousal)	60	30	12	12

Table 24 (*continued*)

Authors	Sample	Total N	Age (mean years)	Duration (mean years)	Treatment(s)	SOL Pre (mean min.)	SOL Post (mean min.)	SOL F.up (mean min.)	F.up (month)
Espie et al (1989)	P	70	45	12	Progressive relaxation	91	57	45	17
					Stimulus control	83	31	53	17
					Paradoxical intention	72	36	38	17
					Desensitisation placebo	85	64	NA	NA
					No treatment	85	97	NA	NA
Sanavio et al (1990)	R/P	40	40	12	EMG biofeedback	41	24	13	36
					Cognitive therapy	48	31	19	36
					Stimulus control + relaxation	44	28	16	36
					No treatment	49	50	NA	NA

Key. S = student; R = recruited subject; P = patient CD = counterdemand; PD = positive demand

Notes. [a]Data reproduced from Bootzin and Nicassio (1978).

[b]Data are wake time after sleep onset scores (WASO; min.).

[c]Data extrapolated from graph.

Hughes and Hughes (1978) recruited 36 volunteers (12 male, 24 female) through newspaper advertisements. The mean age of their sample was 34.2 years, and although no figures for chronicity of complaint are available, selection criteria specified a minimum of four months duration. Subjects were randomly assigned to one of four treatment groups, namely stimulus control, relaxation training, EMG biofeedback or pseudo-biofeedback. Subjects were also randomly assigned to one of three therapists who followed detailed treatment manuals for all conditions. Sleep measures were recorded on daily diaries for a two week baseline period, and for a further fortnight at post-treatment. Unfortunately, time in treatment appears to have varied considerably. Both biofeedback conditions comprised eight therapy sessions, compared with relaxation training which involved four sessions, and stimulus control which had only two sessions. Hughes and Hughes explained that these inconsistencies were due to "the complexity of the tasks". Stimulus control and progressive relaxation were along conventional lines, as was EMG biofeedback where subjects attended to actual frontalis muscle feedback through headphones attached to a myograph. The pseudo-biofeedback, however, listened to false feedback comprising a confederate's resting EMG activity.

Results from Hughes and Hughes' study indicated that all four groups improved significantly with no significant between group differences (see Table 24). Stimulus control did, however, produce this improvement very rapidly since there were only two treatment sessions. Interestingly, biofeedback had no effect upon EMG values. Indeed, even the lowest post-treatment EMG levels achieved were not typical of a state of low physiological arousal. It seems, therefore, that treatment outcome was for these subjects independent of a reduction in muscle tension. The reader is referred to the discussions on physiological processes in insomnia in Chapters 3 (p. 44) and 6 (p. 126) of this book where similar findings have been discussed. Also similar to other investigators, Hughes and Hughes suggested that a cognitively mediated process common to all treatments might explain the apparent equivalence in treatment outcome.

Follow-up data in the Hughes and Hughes study were rather unsatisfactory. Verbal estimates of sleep latency were available for only 12 cases out of the initial 36, and were summarised as a single 12 month follow-up cohort. Although treatment gains appeared to hold up well for this small sample it is impossible to differentiate between the treatments. Perhaps the most striking finding of the Hughes and Hughes study was the very rapid reduction in sleep latency achieved with stimulus control compared with the relatively labour intensive and longer relaxation-based treatments.

Turner and Ascher's (1979a) well controlled comparative study has been very influential. This study represented a creditable response to methodological and analytical shortcomings of previous comparative work. Turner and Ascher advised caution regarding the suggestion that stimulus control might be superior to relaxation and they designed a study which also brought the technique of paradoxical intention within the fold of systematic experimental appraisal. Five treatment conditions, therefore, were included, i.e. stimulus control, progressive relaxation, paradoxical intention, desensitisation placebo and waiting-list control. Twenty-five men and 25 women with an overall mean age of 39 years were selected from respondents to newspaper articles. It is noteworthy that Turner and Ascher were careful to exclude a number of other subjects whose sleep difficulties were regarded as sub-clinical or secondary to other complaints. Ten clients were randomly allocated to each of the experimental conditions where individual sessions of uniform length were conducted, once weekly for four weeks. Pre- and post-treatment measures were recorded on daily sleep diaries. Assessments of social acquiescence and therapy credibility were included also as part of the methodological controls. Treatments were found not to differ significantly on either of these measures. Unfortunately, the credibility assessment was completed at post-therapy and was not, therefore, a true reflection of perceived credibility of the therapeutic rationales, but rather was likely to have been contaminated by the subjects' actual treatment responses.

Turner and Ascher employed multivariate assessments for examining outcome, arguing that MANOVA provided a more conservative approach to significance testing, compared with numerous univariate analyses, by reducing the likelihood of Type 1 error. Their results revealed no significant between group differences at baseline, on any measure. However, post-treatment comparisons demonstrated significant differences between the treatment groups and the control groups, although there were no differences amongst the three active therapies. Discriminant weights for planned comparisons between active treatments and controls indicated that number of awakenings, sleep-onset latency and ratings of difficulty in falling asleep and of "restedness" after sleep contributed most to the significant between group difference. Total sleep time contributed little discriminant weight. Table 24 presents actual mean values at pre- and post-treatment for the variable sleep latency. These scores illustrate the similar effectiveness of the active treatments compared with control groups. Sleep latency was typically reduced from more than one hour to less than 30 minutes as a result of the four week treatment programme. SOL reductions appear, therefore, to have been of clinical benefit, being in the range 54% to 67%. The final mean values for all three active treatments would fail to meet criteria for inclusion as "insomniac" in most treatment studies.

An important feature of the Turner and Ascher study was the reporting of both quantitative and qualitative measures of outcome. In spite of the fact that subjective satisfaction with sleep may relate variously to actual sleep parameters and/or perceived sleep effects, the vast majority of studies has concentrated upon sleep pattern measurement only: indeed, principally upon sleep latency. Turner and Ascher's results may be interpreted as giving further support to the argument of equivalence across therapies, with the important addition of another treatment approach, namely paradox. They did not find that stimulus control was superior to the other treatments, even for reducing sleep latency; however, they did not report treatment process data, making it impossible to determine at what point in treatment significant therapeutic effects emerged. Turner and Ascher also did not provide any follow-up data, thus the persistence of treatment gains was not demonstrated. In spite of the excellent methodological control in the Turner and Ascher study, one shortcoming must be identified, the importance of which will become clear in Chapter 10 (pp. 208–213) where the effects of sleep medication are considered in detail. Turner and Ascher permitted the uncontrolled use of sleep medication across the experimental period. This is unsatisfactory because of the contaminating effects of varied usage upon sleep pattern. Indeed they cited drug intake as a useful dependent variable, with the inference that reduced intake was indicative of clinical improvement. Since both the addition and the removal of sleep medication may have effects upon sleep pattern (and perhaps perceived quality of sleep) this must be regarded as a possible contaminating factor in Turner and Ascher's results.

Lacks et al (1983a) completed a replication of Turner and Ascher's work in comparing the effectiveness of stimulus control, paradoxical intention and progressive relaxation with a credible placebo treatment. However, Lacks et al were interested also in the possibility of a severity (of insomnia) by type of treatment interaction. Their final sample comprised 64 participants (48 female, 16 male) who were solicited through media announcements and letters to potential referring physicians. On the basis of a seven day baseline sleep diary assessment, subjects were labelled as either mild (sleep latency 15 to 44 minutes), moderate (sleep latency 45 to 75 minutes) or severe insomniacs (sleep latency 76 to 152 minutes) and were randomly allocated, within severity blocks, to each of the treatments. Therapy was conducted in four, weekly, small group sessions, of approximately one hour duration. A counterdemand procedure was applied to the effect that improvement would not occur until the final (fourth) treatment week.

Lacks et al reported outcome data on the sleep-onset latency measure only. Mean values for this variable at baseline, counterdemand and positive demand are presented in Table 24. Under stimulus control treatment SOL reduced by around 40 minutes during counterdemand instruction, considerably more than for any other intervention. Indeed, statistical analyses confirmed significantly lower sleep latency scores for this group compared with the other three treatment groups which were not significantly different from one another. Similarly, during the positive demand phase no other treatment matched this level of success. In their paper, Lacks et al also presented in graphical form treatment process data on sleep latency. From this presentation it is clear that sleep latency under stimulus control was consistently lower at each assessment point after week one. The authors pointed out that, although all treatment groups continued to decrease their level of initial insomnia during follow-up, the major advantage of stimulus control was that higher levels of treatment success were accomplished very quickly.

As far as severity of insomnia was concerned, Lacks et al found that initial severity demonstrated a small, positive correlation with degree of improvement, suggesting that the improvement was proportional to initial severity. More importantly, however, they stressed that the opposite hypothesis, that degree of severity is inversely proportional to improvement, was strongly disconfirmed. This led them to conclude that, regardless of the severity of initial insomnia, the psychological treatment of choice is stimulus control.

Comparisons between the study of Turner and Ascher (1979a) and Lacks et al (1983a) prove interesting. Turner and Ascher had suggested that the three behavioural treatments were equally effective in statistical terms, although absolute sleep latency reduction had been greatest under stimulus control. Lacks et al found that the stimulus control programme was significantly superior to the other treatments and that these were equivalent in effects to desensitisation placebo. Commenting on paradoxical intention, Lacks et al reported that some of their patients had demonstrated increases in mean sleep latency after therapy, a finding similar to the results of one of our own previously quoted studies (Espie and Lindsay, 1985). Results from these two influential outcome studies, therefore, provided some confirmatory evidence of the effectiveness of stimulus control, at least in terms of a reduction in sleep latency. However, relaxation and paradox yielded conflicting results. It was partly with these considerations in mind that our own research group embarked upon a further replication study. Before presenting the results of our studies, however, it will be helpful to review some of the important methodological factors which also convinced us of the need for further systematic investigation of relaxation, stimulus control and paradoxical approaches.

Firstly, we have been concerned about the selection of subjects for research studies in insomnia. Reference to Tables 17, 20, 23 and 24 reveals that the great majority of reports on psychological treatments of insomnia have been largely on non-clinic presenting cases and are, therefore, subject to the criticisms commonly levelled against such research. Indeed, some studies could be justifiably regarded as analogue investigations. These of course have their place—being exploratory in nature, key issues may be identified and questions raised for further enquiry. However, the major issue of the generalisability of findings to the patient population remains questionable. Approximately half of the available behavioural treatment reports have been conducted on student populations, with most of the remainder being the product of recruitment efforts through media advertisements. Subjects also have been selected on the basis of ensured compliance. For example, individuals have often been excluded where they were unable or unwilling to pay a monetary deposit during the pre-treatment phase.

Of greatest importance, however, is the fact that most studies have given no indication as to whether or not selected subjects were actively seeking help for their insomnia at the time of selection. A few studies have utilised a combination of media announcements and physican referrals (e.g. Lacks et al, 1983a, b) and a few studies have employed referred clients only (e.g. Turner, Di Tomasso and Giles). These are, therefore, indicative of some awareness concerning the need more closely to approximate the clinical population. The greatest part of the literature is not, however, based upon clinic-presenting patients but populations which are self-selecting and arguably convenient and compliant.

The practising clinician cannot be satisfied until results are replicated in studies using unsolicited subjects. Killen and Coates (1979), for example, have made the point that "college students ... do not respond to treatments in the same way as do persons from the community", but this argument may also be extended by questioning the assumption that adults in the community equate readily with adults who present at the clinic requiring treatment. Coates and Thoresen (1980) refer to the modest outcomes often obtained when behavioural strategies are evaluated with older subjects, who have experienced insomnia for two years or more, who present themselves at clinics for treatment or who are referred by physicians. Our own research studies set out, therefore, to consider *only* the spontaneously presenting clinical population of insomniacs, thus completely obviating the critical problem of poor generalisability.

The decision to study the presenting clinical group immediately raises a second issue—concerning hypnotic drug use. Past research has generally excluded subjects currently taking hypnotic drugs. This of course has the major methodological advantage of eliminating a potentially confounding variable. The case for the inclusion of such subjects, however, merits consideration. It is known that a substantial proportion of out-patients attending sleep clinics make regular use of nighttime medication. The usage rate has been recorded as high as 82% in the study by Roth, Kramer and Lutz (1976). There is, therefore, the danger of selecting out of research studies a large proportion of the patient group. Furthermore, there appears to be sufficient understanding of hypnotic drug effects to make complete exclusion of such patients unnecessary. The rebound phenomenon is sufficiently documented to permit the presentation of reasonably accurate information regarding likely changes in sleep pattern subsequent to withdrawal. Supportive and educative input may enable patients to tolerate the initial few weeks more readily, and help to counteract the problem of misattribution which reinforces the patient's perception of herself as a poor sleeper. Chapter 10 provides a detailed review of the research literature on sleep medications. Suffice it to say at present that a systematic drug withdrawal programme is preferable to simply encouraging patients to discontinue medication, and to include them in the research study only if they are successful. Also, it is preferable to retain within the available population for research studies those subjects who are unable at first to cease hypnotic drugs. These are large numbers of such individuals and it could be argued that they are in *greatest* need of an alternative approach to management of their sleep disorder. Therefore, in our own research work we devised drug-management protocols which allowed either for a pre-treatment drug withdrawal period or a stabilised, habituated drug regime which was maintained throughout the experimental period (Espie, Lindsay and Brooks, 1988).

Thirdly, and apart from our concern to *select in* the clinic-presenting group, we were also concerned that measures of change should be clinically as well as statistically valid. For this reason we decided to incorporate measures of night to night variability in sleep (raw score variance) as well as mean values for sleep pattern variables. This reflects our own experience that however bad a sleep measure is, if it is largely predictable on a night to night basis (i.e. low variance), then it causes relatively little subjective distress and may not be reasonably regarded as insomniac. We also felt that treatment outcome should be appraised in terms of clinical change. Treatment gains ought to be substantial and final outcomes associated whenever possible with a return to levels of functioning within the normal range. The absence of follow-up or the availability of relatively short-term follow-up (to six months) in past research also has been a limiting factor. We sought, therefore, to extend follow-up periods very considerably. Long-term maintenance of treatment benefit is, alongside generalisability, the other quality feature of effective treatment which clinicians in routine clinical practice seek.

Finally, we have considered the fact that clinicians rarely apply a behavioural treatment in "pure" format. Clinicians find it sensible to tailor treatments of insomnia in relation to presenting characteristics of the sleeper and of the complaint. It is both a strength and a drawback that outcome reports hitherto have employed experimental designs requiring random assignment of subjects to discrete experimental conditions. The strengths of this approach are undeniable methodologically; however, there is a drawback in that routine practice is not accurately reflected. The practitioner finds it intuitively sensible to match treatment to presentation. Hence a cognitive approach is self-selecting for the patient who ruminates and plans in bed, and the insomniac who suffers from chronic muscular tension is likely to be trained in progressive relaxation methods. Furthermore, the practitioner thinks little of maximising efficiency and treatment benefit by combining elements of various treatment types. We attempted, therefore, a formal comparison of subjects treated at random with those for whom therapy programmes had been tailored, akin to clinical practice. Our research results have been published in two principal papers (Espie et al, 1989; Espie, Brooks and Lindsay, 1989).

Our subjects were a series of adult out-patients referred by primary care physicians and suffering from chronic sleep-onset insomnia. All subjects had a sleep latency of greater than 30 minutes on average per night and had experienced sleep disturbance for a minimum of one year. The final sample of 84 subjects (57 females, 27 males) had an average age of 46 years and a mean duration of insomnia of 11.8 years. Initial sleep latency was considerably higher than in most previous studies, averaging more than 80 minutes (see Table 24). Fourteen of the patients were allocated to a tailored therapy condition and comparisons between this group and randomly allocated groups will be presented shortly. The main comparative treatment outcome investigation, therefore, comprised 70 cases who were randomly allocated to either progressive relaxation, stimulus control, paradoxical intention, desensitisation placebo and no treatment (Espie et al, 1989). Fifty-nine of the 70 patients (84%) had made regular use of sleep medication and the average time since first prescription was almost 10 years. Referring physicians supervised cessation of hypnotics in 26 cases. The remaining 33 followed a formal withdrawal programme either before or after psychological treatment. Allocation to withdrawal protocol was largely pragmatic, withdrawing where possible at the outset ($n = 20$). But where patients were unable or unwilling to persevere with the standardised withdrawal regime, they were assigned to the maintenance design ($n = 13$). The use of alternative experimental models afforded flexibility and permitted the inclusion of "difficult cases" who otherwise would have been excluded. Illustrative examples of these protocols have been presented elsewhere (Espie, Lindsay and Brooks, 1988) (see also Chapter 10, p. 217 ff).

A self-report sleep log comprising items on both quantitative and qualitative aspects of sleep was completed throughout the experimental period which comprised two weeks of baseline monitoring and eight weeks of active treatment. The first four weeks of treatment operated under counterdemand instruction. A validity assessment was completed using the

Sleep Assessment Device (Kelley and Lichstein, 1980) which tape records responses to a fixed interval cue tone and provides an objective measure of sleep pattern. This assessment revealed highly significant correspondence between self-report and objective measurement for sleep latency and total sleep time ($r = 0.85$ and $r = 0.87$ respectively). The reader is referred back to Chapter 4 (pp. 72–73) on assessment for further information. Other rating scale assessments were included to measure symptomatic mood and to assess daytime functioning. These will be introduced as they become relevant to the discussion. Credibility evaluations, conducted for all the active treatments and the placebo, revealed uniformly high scores for credibility of treatment rationale and of therapist attitude and approach. The effects of the demand change (counterdemand to positive demand) were investigated by considering the simple effects of time within each of the treatment groups for each outcome variable. These investigations revealed that, where significant overall F ratios were obtained, univariate sub-effect F ratios almost always achieved significance firstly during counterdemand. It was appropriate, therefore, to consider the treatment period as one continuous series rather than as two identifiable phases of treatment. The non-significant effects of demand change in our studies contrast with previous work where placebo treatment has produced significant change in sleep pattern under positive expectancy. It may be, therefore, that demand characteristics are a more significant factor where insomnia is less severe.

Summary information on the effects of treatments upon sleep latency is provided in Table 24. Inspection of the table reveals that stimulus control and paradox produced final week sleep latency scores of 31 minutes and 36 minutes respectively, which compare favourably with the results of relaxation and placebo treatments where SOL was around one hour after the eight week treatment period. Untreated patients exhibited a slight increase in sleep latency. The percentage change scores presented in Table 25 indicate that for stimulus control this pre–post change represented a 62% reduction in time taken to fall asleep compared with 51% under paradox. It is interesting, however, to examine the treatment process data which are illustrated in Figure 8. Although the final outcomes for sleep latency were similar for these two effective treatments, it is clear that stimulus control produced an immediate and dramatic therapeutic effect at week 1 which was maintained thereafter, whereas the group treated by means of paradoxical intention did not improve significantly until week 4. This visual impression was indeed confirmed by statistical analyses of time within treatment group simple effects, whereas SOL change over time with relaxation appeared similar to the placebo effect.

Further descriptive information on the effects of treatment upon other sleep log measures is presented in Table 25. It can be seen that total sleep time increased by approximately 10% in all groups except waiting-

Table 25 Comparison across treatment conditions of percentage change scores (%) from baseline to post-treatment for a number of sleep log measures (from Espie et al, 1989, reproduced by permission of Pergamon Press PLC)

	Relaxation	Stimulus control	Paradoxical intention	Placebo	No treatment
SOL (mean; min.)	−36.6	−62.4	−50.6	−25.7	+14.2
SOL (SD; min.)	−25.2	−54.7	−70.4	−30.8	+18.5
Total sleep (mean; hr)	+10.7	+9.2	+11.8	+9.0	0.00
Total sleep (SD; hr)	−6.4	−8.5	−41.4	−23.6	+2.4
"Restedness after sleep" (0–4 rating)	+40.8	+18.1	+22.0	+18.9	−2.1
"Enjoyment of sleep" (0–4 rating)	+37.4	+19.4	+16.3	+24.7	+4.9

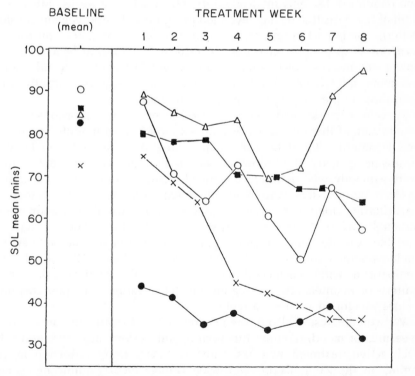

Figure 8 Mean sleep latency scores for each of the experimental groups across each week of the experimental period (data from Espie et al, 1989). Key: o Relaxation; • Stimulus Control; × Paradoxical Intention; ■ Placebo; △ No Treatment

list control; however, paradoxical intention reduced the variability in nightly sleep quite considerably. This is consistent with the finding that night to night variability in SOL also reduced dramatically with this treatment, suggesting that paradox is a good treatment for stabilising sleep pattern over time. Variability in sleep onset also reduced substantially with stimulus control but once again relaxation effects were similar to placebo intervention. Consideration of sleep quality variables, however, reveals a markedly different picture. A 41% improvement in ratings of "restedness" after sleep was achieved with relaxation, an improvement twice as large as any of the other treatment groups. Similarly, insomniacs' self-report of "sleep enjoyment" improved substantially with relaxation, whereas stimulus control and paradox achieved only modest positive changes. Indeed, sleep quality changes under placebo treatment were at least as great as with these latter treatments.

Detailed multivariate statistical analyses of our results are available elsewhere (Espie et al, 1989). Formal analyses supported the descriptive data. Stimulus control produced no measurable impact upon sleep quality and paradox did so only modestly during the final three weeks of treatment. Both of these treatments, however, led to significant improvements in sleep pattern. The impact of progressive relaxation was weak and inconsistent in terms of sleep pattern measures; nevertheless, significant benefit to sleep enjoyment and restedness after sleep was evident from the second week of treatment onwards. At no time did placebo subjects do significantly better than those in the waiting-list group on any measure.

We conducted detailed follow-up assessments on four occasions after the termination of therapy. These were at six weeks, three months, six months and 17 months. SOL data at the final follow-up are presented in Table 24. Assessments across the follow-up periods indicated that treatment effects were generally well maintained. Indeed, further improvements according to sleep log measures were frequently noted. Continued improvement was particularly evident with progressive relaxation across all follow-up points, although each of the treatments was associated with further gain on some variable. A modest but non-significant increase in sleep latency was evident under stimulus control at 17 month follow-up (Table 24). Paired T-test comparisons within each condition for each variable confirmed the general pattern of maintenance. No significant deterioration over post-treatment values was found for any variable.

We were interested also in the generalisation of treatment gains to other measures of mood, daytime functioning and performance. We found that each active treatment was associated with significant reduction in self-rating on the Zung Depression Scale (Zung, 1965). Significant changes in symptomatic anxiety (Zung Anxiety Scale; Zung, 1971) were obtained both with paradoxical intention and placebo, although the latter group averaged a score reduction of less than three points, which was similar to the non-significant effect for the relaxation group. Progressive relaxation, however, was found to be particularly effective in producing generalisation to daytime functioning in terms of reduced "worrying" and improvement in "coping with work" and "concentration" as measured by analogue rating scale scores. Stimulus control was the only group to exhibit significant improvement on the Sleep Behaviour Self-Rating Scale (Kazarian, Howe and Csapo, 1979). Analysis of the item scores for this rating scale revealed that significant alteration to pre-sleep bedtime routine was accounted for by patients no longer reading in bed and putting the light off immediately upon retiring.

To summarise, therefore, our studies indicated that stimulus control very quickly and effectively produced a more predictable pattern of rapid sleep-onset. However, the stimulus control instruction to refrain from going to bed until sleepy tired may be in itself a virtual guarantee of reduced sleep latency. Since patients generally go to bed later rather than earlier with this instruction, the period of time extending beyond usual bedtime (at baseline) is automatically excluded from treatment period estimates of sleep latency. Only modest increases in total sleep time emerged under stimulus control and did not become significant until the seventh week of therapy. The immediate effectiveness of stimulus control in terms of sleep latency appears then to be limited by latent impact upon length of sleep. Overall sleep pattern change, therefore, took longer to develop than the rapid changes in sleep latency implied. Furthermore, perceived quality of sleep did not improve significantly during stimulus control treatment with final week scores being similar to placebo outcome. This finding suggests that perception of sleep quality may be largely independent of sleep parameters per se. There are implications here for the matching of treatment to the nature of the patient's presenting complaint. If complaints are based upon lack of restedness and impairment of daytime functioning, for example, stimulus control may miss the mark, in spite of likely benefits to sleep pattern. The reader is referred back to Chapter 4 (pp. 87–92) where issues of assessment leading to the tailoring of treatment are discussed.

In contrast to stimulus control, relaxation produced significant improvements in sleep restedness and enjoyment of sleep and also displayed generalisation to daytime measures of concentration and general well-being. These improvements in sleep quality occurred in the context of relatively limited effects upon quantitative aspects of sleep. Three tentative suggestions can be made concerning relaxation's mechanism of effect upon sleep quality. Firstly, patients may become less concerned about their disordered sleep pattern and may learn to value a state of relaxation, even if not sleeping. Secondly, relaxation may enable subjects to "get more out of" the sleep obtained, either objectively e.g. a greater proportion of NREM stages 3 and 4 sleep (deep sleep) or subjectively (feeling more refreshed). Finally, relaxation may provide patients with a self-control skill which aids daytime functions and fosters a more positive evaluation of self and one's sleep pattern (cf. self-efficacy; Bandura, 1977).

Paradoxical intention patients achieved final sleep latency similar to stimulus control subjects although progress to that outcome was less straightforward. During the early weeks, stimulus control exhibited a superior response to paradox in terms of average sleep latency. Interestingly, inspection of individual scores for paradoxical intention subjects revealed that five of the 15 patients experienced increases in sleep latency of at least 33% during the first week of treatment. None of the stimulus control patients displayed this response. The potential for paradox to exacerbate sleep-onset problems has been discussed elsewhere (Espie and Lindsay, 1985; Lacks et al, 1983a; see also Chapter 7, p. 146). Paradox, however, was particularly effective in reducing standard deviation scores associated with weekly mean values, that is raw score variance. Significant effects on this variable in fact emerged prior to reduction in average sleep latency. In other words, night to night variability in the individual's sleep pattern reduced first, evidencing enhancement of stability in sleep latency as a prelude to sleep latency reduction per se. Paradox was not associated with consistent increases in sleep duration across treatment although a 12% gain was evident at post-treatment. Patients in this group reported greater restedness after sleep only towards the end of treatment but the magnitude of change in sleep quality was considerably less than with progressive relaxation.

In comparing the results of our study with the earlier studies of Turner and Ascher (1979a) and Lacks et al (1983a), four major points can be made. Firstly, our study provides firm evidence that psychological treatments can be applied effectively to clinical cases of chronic insomnia. Secondly, treatment gains have been shown to be durable even at very lengthy follow-up. Both of these points may encourage the practising clinician. (We have also considered treatment outcome against strictly clinical criteria and our results from these investigations will be presented shortly.) Thirdly, however, the three treatments may be best regarded as differentially effective, depending upon the feature(s) of presenting complaint which are regarded as of critical importance. Stimulus control appears to be effective in habit restructuring but patients will not necessarily become more contented with their sleep. Relaxation may be the treatment of choice for qualitative improvement where this is perceived by the patient to be more important than quantitative change. Paradox may offer some improvement in both spheres; however, it appears to have the unique capacity of producing, albeit temporary, exacerbation of sleep problems. Finally, the inclusion of a measurement of raw score variance alongside mean values as an outcome measure appears to have been justified since it provides a more full understanding of the processes underlying therapeutic change. We suggest that the combination of mean and deviation scores properly represents the information which is of subjective importance to the insomniac and of clinical importance to the practitioner.

It was mentioned at an earlier point that the methodological strength associated with random assignment to treatment leads to a situation where research studies have not accurately reflected the routine clinical practice of tailoring treatment to meet individual presenting requirements. A study by Turner, Di Tomasso and Giles (1983) has sounded a cautionary note with respect to combining treatments from different modalities (Table 24). Data previously collected from a no treatment control group, and stimulus control, and progressive relaxation conditions (within the Turner and Ascher (1979a) study) were contrasted with a new combined treatment condition where both stimulus control and relaxation elements were presented. Inspection of the outcome data reveal that stimulus control and progressive relaxation each produced a treatment response superior to both the combined therapy programme and waiting-list control (Table 24). The average reductions in sleep latency for the relaxation and stimulus control groups were, however, only 15 minutes and 21 minutes respectively. Turner, Di Tomasso and Giles also examined a number of other sleep parameters such as total sleep time, number of wakenings and ratings of restedness and difficulty in falling asleep, but found no significant changes.

Nevertheless, the failure of the combined "package" treatment remains interesting. It might reasonably be expected that such an approach would prove *more* powerful than either of the components alone, but conversely, Turner, Di Tomasso and Giles reported an 82% failure rate. They interpreted these results in terms of De la Pena's (1978) theory that treating insomniacs with an antagonistic, arousal-reducing procedure (relaxation) and an (arguably) arousal-increasing one (stimulus control) would lead to therapeutic failure. It should be noted that similar combination treatments in other studies have not replicated these results (see for example, Sanavio et al (1990) later in this chapter).

We have investigated the effectiveness of randomised treatment versus tailored treatment upon sleep-onset latency, both in terms of clinical and statistical significance of outcome (Espie, Brooks and Lindsay, 1989). In these analyses, "randomised therapy" comprised an amalgam of the relaxation, stimulus control and paradoxical intention groups which had been treated previously (n = 43; Espie et al, 1989). The desensitisation placebo (n = 14) and no treatment control (n = 13) groups were retained also for comparative analysis. A further 14 physician-referred chronic insomniacs were included, however, to form a "tailored therapy" group where treatment was designed based upon responses to a Sleep Disturbance

Questionnaire (see Chapter 3, p. 46 for details). This resulted in four subjects receiving progressive relaxation, four stimulus control, and six a cognitive intervention comprising either paradox or cognitive re-structuring (Beck and Emery, 1979). The experimental phases for the tailored group were identical to the randomised group and included eight weeks of active treatment. Credibility evaluations administered at the end of the first week of active therapy revealed no significant differences between randomised therapy, tailored therapy and placebo intervention.

Descriptive statistical analysis of outcome indicated that post-treatment improvement (baseline to final week) was considerably greater under randomised therapy (49%) than tailored treatment (35%) on the variable sleep latency. Placebo was associated with a 26% reduction in sleep latency whereas no-treatment subjects experienced a modest increase. With randomised therapy, process data revealed a gradual and steady reduction in sleep latency across the eight week period of intervention. Formal analysis revealed that significant reductions in sleep latency first emerged at week 1 with randomised therapy, with strong statistical effects emerging at week 3 which were maintained thereafter. By comparison, tailored therapy produced only modest improvement and the simple effects of time within treatment revealed that changes over baseline were statistically significant only during weeks 2 to 4. In summary of the statistical analyses, therefore, tailored therapy did not achieve superiority over randomised therapy, as might have been expected from clinical intuition. Indeed, both between and within group testing suggested that randomised therapy was associated with the more favourable outcome.

The assessment of clinically significant outcome was addressed in some detail in Chapter 4 and the reader is referred to that discussion at this point. To summarise, however, it has been recognised that statistical comparisons between experimental conditions, being based on average improvement scores, do not provide information on how individuals have responded to treatment. Furthermore, a statistically significant change may or may not be of clinical importance and thus may either over value or under value the therapeutic benefits which the patient has received from treatment. We decided, therefore, to apply three criteria to evaluate clinically significant change in sleep latency. The results of this analysis of clinical significance are presented in Table 26. This permits comparison of clinical outcome for the four experimental groups.

Firstly, it is evident that outcome both with no treatment and placebo treatment was considerably poorer than for the tailored and randomised groups on the more conservative indices of clinical change. Spontaneous remission was observed in only one untreated case and only two patients achieved a 50% SOL reduction or final sleep latency of 30 minutes or less after placebo treatment. Secondly, although around 30% of tailored

Table 26   Proportion of patients in each of the treatment conditions achieving sleep-onset latency (SOL; mean) reduction of clinical significance according to three criteria (from Espie, Brooks and Lindsay, 1989, reproduced by permission of Pergamon Press PLC)

Treatment group	n	Measures of clinical outcome		
		Absolute SOL reduction %	50% SOL reduction %	Final SOL <=30 min. %
No treatment	13	54	8	8
Placebo	14	78	14	14
Tailored treatment	14	71	50	43
Random treatment	43	84	47	37
Progressive relaxation	14	71	21	7
Paradoxical intention	15	80	47	40
Stimulus control	14	100	64	71

treatment patients achieved no sleep-onset latency reduction whatsoever, it is clear that where improvements did occur they were usually of clinical significance. In fact, eight of the 10 tailored therapy patients who demonstrated an absolute sleep latency reduction achieved one or both of the stricter criteria of outcome. Thirdly, comparisons of tailored and randomised therapy indicate that tailoring achieved the 30 minute and 50% reduction criteria in a slightly *greater* proportion of cases than randomised therapy. This result in particular contrasts markedly with the statistical analyses previously reported.

Table 26 also incorporates information on each of the psychological treatments which comprised randomised therapy. Stimulus control emerged as the most effective treatment according to all three criteria. Every patient improved and almost two-thirds reduced sleep latency by greater than half. Some 71% also achieved sleep latencies of 30 minutes or less at post-treatment. Notably, stimulus control was the only specific treatment to exceed tailored therapy in its clinical effects. Paradox was also quite effective on each measure. Almost half of the subjects reduced sleep latency by 50%, and 40% of subjects achieved the 30 minute cut-off. Progressive relaxation, however, compared very unfavourably. Only three patients halved baseline sleep-onset latency and only one achieved the 30 minute criterion. The effects of relaxation and placebo were clinically similar.

In summary, therefore, tailoring was at least as effective as randomised therapy using clinical outcomes. The problem with tailored therapy appears to be that a substantial proportion of patients may not improve at all. It is this effect which is likely to have contributed to the comparative ineffectiveness of the tailored therapy treatment in our statistical analyses. Clearly a discrepancy between statistical and clinical appraisal of outcome is a matter of concern. In this case the inter-subject variability in response to treatment appears to have had the effect of diluting the overall impact of tailoring in statistical terms. It may be helpful therefore, to consider individually those four subjects who were tailored therapy non-responders. It transpires that two of these patients had received progressive relaxation, one received paradox and the fourth received cognitive restructuring. In spite of the Sleep Disturbance Questionnaire predicting that these interventions would be appropriate, clearly they were not. The poor response to progressive relaxation in two cases may equate comfortably with the finding that this treatment is not clinically powerful in reducing sleep latency. Furthermore, the patient who presented with marked performance anxiety and who, consequently, was treated with paradox, actually experienced a 100% increase in sleep latency. Similarly, cognitive re-structuring appeared to have the effect of concentrating attention upon mentation while in bed and sleep latency increased with this case also.

A number of tentative comments can be made about the usefulness of a tailored approach to therapy. Firstly, it can be highly effective in clinical terms but will not necessarily be so simply because treatment can be matched to an *apparent* aetiological factor. Secondly, the power of tailored therapy is limited to the power of its component parts. To the extent that tailoring departs from the most effective form of intervention, it will be less advantageous in spite of its intuitive clinical appeal. For example, stimulus control emerged as the most effective of the randomised treatment programmes for reducing SOL in clinical terms whereas relaxation was ineffective in the vast majority of cases. Tailoring treatment should take account of the probability of benefit ensuing from the predicted intervention. As was stated in Chapter 4, the probability of benefit should be assessed in relation to the specific goals of therapy which have been agreed upon between the patient and therapist. Thirdly, mental anxiety emerged from the Sleep Disturbance Questionnaire as the most commonly ascribed reason for sleep disturbance. It is clear, therefore, that tailoring of treatment will often be aimed at the management of worries and thoughts. There is available a wide range of cognitively based interventions which may have differing modes of action (see Chapter 7; Table 21). The appropriate tailoring of specific cognitive treatments to presenting sleep-related cognitive dysfunctions has yet to be investigated.

Lacks and Powlishta (1989) have also presented an analysis of clinical significance of outcome following behavioural treatment for insomnia. They pooled for re-analysis data from a sample of 216 insomniacs who had participated in seven outcome studies of behaviour therapy for insomnia over a four year period. Two-thirds of their sample were female and the total sample had a mean age of 49 years and a mean duration of sleep disturbance of 13 years. A clinically significant response to treatment was defined according to a formula based upon recommendations made by Jacobsen,

Follette and Revenstorf (1984, 1986) and Christensen and Mendoza (1986). The non-distressed range for both sleep latency and wake time after sleep onset was operationalised as being within two standard deviations of the mean values of these variables amongst good sleepers (information taken from other studies). The actual cut off values were 25.0 minutes (SOL) and 30.7 minutes (WASO) respectively.

In overall terms Lacks and Powlishta reported that 23% of participants demonstrated resolution of their presenting problem after four weeks of treatment, and by short-term follow-up, 33% had achieved this status. By one year follow-up 32% could be regarded as good sleepers. Although, stimulus control achieved substantially greater proportions of clinically significant change at post-treatment, other treatments appeared to match this success rate at the time of follow-up.

Lacks and Powlishta also compared their formula for clinically significant improvement with other outcome criteria. Ninety-seven subjects from their initial sample were used for this comparative analysis. Some 32% of this sample had achieved their strict criterion for clinically significant improvement. This matches closely with 31% who were regarded as no longer having insomnia. However, statistically significant improvement was regarded as having been achieved in 49% of the sample. Some 63% had achieved a 50% decrease in complaint, and 76% took no sleep medication. In spite of the considerable range of improvement scores evidenced by these differing criteria, the results should be regarded as encouraging. It seems that the sleep patterns of *at least* one third of the insomniacs had returned to within the normal population range as a result of behavioural treatment and it may be that significant benefit was achieved for a further 20 to 30% of treated subjects.

Returning to Table 24 there are a number of other treatment outcome studies to consider which have compared across different treatment approaches. Ladouceur and Gros-Louis (1986) conducted a comparison of paradoxical intention, stimulus control, a sleep information only programme and no treatment on a small sample of 25 recruited insomniacs. These workers regarded their subjects as severe insomniacs since they had a minimum 60 minute sleep-onset latency, and as a group had a mean duration of insomnia of 9.5 years. Ladouceur and Gros-Louis, however, did not report detailed outcome data on their main dependent variable of sleep-onset latency, but only statistical effects which indicated that paradox and stimulus control groups were equally effective but significantly superior to sleep information and no treatment control. Similarly, at two month follow up only the two main treatment groups were significantly improved. Ladouceur and Gros-Louis included spouses' recordings of sleep latency which were in close agreement with the subjects' data ($r = 0.90$).

The results from this study, therefore, are not supportive of the superiority of stimulus control over paradox at *final outcome* and in this respect are similar to results obtained by Turner and Ascher (1979a) and Espie et al (1989). Since Ladouceur and Gros-Louis did not report process data, no information is available on the speed with which the treatments achieved their therapeutic effects. Before leaving this study one final point is worth noting. Subjects in the sleep information group were found to exhibit less motivation to continue therapy at the end of treatment, compared with the active treatment interventions. This suggests that whereas information may be a useful facilitator of active treatment it may not be a credible intervention per se when sleep disturbance is severe.

A study by Sanavio (1988) was introduced in the discussion of cognitive factors in insomnia in Chapter 3 (p. 48). Sanavio hypothesised that a cognitive programme of treatment would be more effective for subjects suffering from high cognitive arousal while waiting to fall asleep than for those suffering from low arousal. Sub-groups, therefore, were delineated on a measure of pre-sleep cognitive intrusion and the effectiveness of a cognitive programme, comprising elements of cognitive restructuring, paradoxical intention, thought stopping and positive imagery was compared with an EMG-biofeedback condition in which high and low arousal groups were also identified.

Twenty-four referred insomniacs participated in the study which comprised a one week baseline sleep monitoring period and two weeks of active treatment comprising six individual sessions. Sanavio reported treatment outcome in graphical form on the five variables sleep-onset latency, total sleep time, pre-sleep tension, pre-sleep cognitive intrusion and sleep quality. With respect to sleep latency, patients in both treatment conditions reduced average time required to fall asleep by 54%. Neither treatment type nor pre-sleep cognitive arousal difference affected reductions in latency. The treatments, therefore, appeared to be equally effective (see Table 24). Similarly, sleep time increased by an average of 52 minutes across the four conditions with no significant differences between groups. Pre-sleep tension decreased at post-therapy and a modest treatment by time interaction indicated that greater improvement on this measure was obtained by subjects receiving the biofeedback treatment. The hypothesised treatment by time interaction was found to be significant also for pre-sleep intrusions. The cognitive programme was more effective in reducing the frequency of cognitive intrusions, and larger decreases were obtained by insomniacs reporting higher cognitive intrusion at baseline. Both biofeedback and cognitive therapy were associated with significant improvements in sleep quality ratings. On this measure, however, subjects with more severe cognitive intrusions benefited more from biofeedback, whereas subjects with low pre-sleep intrusions benefited more in terms of sleep quality from the cognitive procedure.

Sanavio's analyses of follow-up data at 12 months indicated that treatment gains were maintained and indeed further extended; however, no evidence of differential treatment effects was found. Interestingly, eight of the 24 subjects had resumed taking sleeping pills either occasionally or regularly. A crude measure of clinical significance at follow-up was taken which revealed that seven subjects judged that they were "no longer insomniac" (29% of total group). A further 10 subjects reported "great improvement". Thus 17 of the 24 could be said to report substantial benefit (71%).

The improvement shown in both treatment groups goes against Sanavio's initial hypothesis that where cognitive intrusion is substantial the treatment of choice should be cognitive in focus. Sanavio suggested, therefore, that it may be appropriate to consider both treatments as promoting mastery of perceived pre-sleep arousal, but he did not offer any suggestions as to how this might have taken place. The report also fails to grapple with the rather surprising finding that the product-moment correlation coefficient between the measure of pre-sleep cognitions and self-reported SOL was found to be only 0.09. This result raises questions concerning the central importance of cognitive intrusion in the aetiology of sleep-onset insomnia. Alternatively, the validity of the measure of sleep latency and/or assessment of cognitive intrusion itself may be questioned. From a more clinical point of view, Sanavio's cognitive programme appears to have been very intensive, with no fewer than four cognitive techniques being introduced within the space of a two week period. It is not possible, therefore, to determine which of these elements were critical to treatment success, and indeed it seems unlikely that any of the elements could have been applied in an optimal fashion given the cursory treatment involved.

In a more recent study Sanavio and his colleagues added a third treatment approach (combined stimulus control and relaxation) and a no treatment control group to their earlier methodology (Sanavio et al, 1990). Forty insomniacs were assigned at random to one of the four experimental groups (see Table 24). All subjects also received general instruction on sleep patterns, needs and functions in the form of a sleep information videotape. The outcomes, after six sessions of treatment conducted over two weeks, were broadly indicative of equivalence in treatment effects. Biofeedback, cognitive therapy and stimulus control/relaxation all reduced SOL (by around 17 minutes on average) and wake time after sleep onset (by 29 minutes) whereas untreated subjects exhibited no change. Ratings of sleep quality and restedness demonstrated similar patterns. However, only cognitive therapy was associated with increased total sleep compared with no treatment.

Sanavio et al's impressive three year follow-up data are interesting. Further reductions in SOL and WASO were observed for all treatments and qualitative measures also evidenced long term maintenance. These results are particularly striking given the limited (six hours) interventions which were applied. Most notable perhaps is the reduction in WASO from 50–60 minutes at baseline to only 10–20 minutes, three years later. (Sleep-onset problems were only moderately severe at pre-treatment.) One suspects that Sanavio et al's total sample represented a mix of sleep-onset and sleep-maintenance insomniacs. If this were so, separate analyses of outcomes for these clinical sub-groups would have proven valuable.

Three studies have compared outcomes across treatment modalities amongst older insomniacs. Bootzin, Engle-Friedman and Hazlewood (1983) recruited 53 insomniacs, ages 47 to 76 years, from Senior Citizens' Clubs, and through media advertisement and physician referral. Twenty-two of the subjects complained primarily of sleep-onset insomnia and 31 of sleep-maintenance insomnia. Insomniacs were assigned randomly to one of three treatment groups or to a waiting-list control. The active treatments all comprised support and sleep hygiene information either alone or in combination with progressive relaxation or stimulus control instruction, and weekly treatment sessions were conducted for four weeks. Baseline to post-treatment improvements in sleep latency were greatest for the stimulus control group where a 35% reduction was achieved compared with 23% for sleep information alone and only 8% for the progressive relaxation group. However, adjusted sleep efficiency means were 77%, 79% and 60% for stimulus control, relaxation and sleep information respectively. These results largely reflected an almost 50% reduction in time spent awake for both stimulus control and relaxation compared with no change for the information only group. In spite of these differential treatment outcomes all three treatments were associated with some improvement. A two year follow-up was completed on these subjects whereby 42 of the original 53 subjects participated in a telephone interview and 21 of these completed sleep diaries for one week. Insomniacs who had received stimulus control reported that they continued to use components of this treatment more than did those receiving the other interventions. They also reported the greatest improvement in sleep latency according to sleep diaries. Again, however, Bootzin, Engle-Friedman and Hazlewood reported maintained effectiveness in all active treatment conditions with relatively few measures demonstrating differential effects.

In later discussion of their results Bootzin and Engle-Friedman (1987) comment that improvement obtained on a measure of intermittent arousal following behavioural treatment is quite impressive given the general tendency amongst elderly people for awakenings to increase. Thus, although some of the decreased sleep efficiency associated with age might be reasonably regarded as developmental, there is, nonetheless, the prospect of improving efficiency somewhat. It is noteworthy, however, that their final sleep efficiency means were all less than 80%, that is within the sleep disturbed range according to the usual criterion cut-off of 85%.

Morin and Azrin have reported two studies of behavioural and cognitive treatments of sleep-maintenance problems amongst older insomniacs (Morin and Azrin, 1987, 1988). Morin and Azrin (1987) investigated the comparative effectiveness of stimulus control and imagery training versus a no treatment control condition. Twenty-seven media recruits with an average age of 57 years were randomly assigned, within severity blocks, to each experimental condition. After completing a one week baseline, subjects attended four, weekly, one hour therapy sessions which were conducted in groups of between three and five persons. Stimulus control was along conventional lines and the imagery training treatment conformed to the attention-focusing procedures described by Woolfolk and McNulty (1983). Morin and Azrin presented graphed data on the frequency and duration of awakenings across the study period.

Stimulus control produced a 35% reduction in awakening frequency compared with 20% under imagery training and no change under waiting-list conditions. However, no significant between groups difference was obtained on this measure. With respect to duration of wakenings, stimulus control subjects reduced WASO significantly more than either of the other groups (Table 24). The 65% reduction associated with stimulus control was substantially greater than the 16% and 25% changes associated with imagery training and no treatment respectively. At 12 month follow-up a modest relapse in the stimulus control group and a continued improvement in the imagery training group produced an almost identical final outcome value for WASO of around 25 minutes in both treatment groups.

Morin and Azrin interpreted the results of their first study as suggesting that behavioural and cognitive procedures could afford substantial benefits in alleviating maintenance insomnia amongst older adults. Consistent with previous findings, on younger insomniacs with sleep latency difficulties, stimulus control produced a larger and quicker impact on wakening duration than did imagery training. The gradual post-treatment to follow-up improvement obtained with imagery training, however, led Morin and Azrin to suggest that both treatments might be efficiently combined to maximise sleep improvements.

Morin and Azrin's second study was similar in design (Morin and Azrin, 1988). A final sample of 17 women and 10 men with a mean age of 67 years was randomly assigned to treatment conditions identical to the earlier study. However, in addition to sleep diary measurement, a switch-activated clock was employed to record objectively duration of nighttime awakenings and latency to sleep-onset. Independent outcome ratings were obtained also from spouses and friends of the subjects in order to provide social and clinical validation of treatment outcome.

Results from this study indicated that duration of awakenings reduced under both active treatments, and a significant increase in total sleep time was obtained using stimulus control (mean increase approximately 65 minutes). Table 24 presents summary data on awakening duration which illustrates this improvement from pre- to post-treatment during stimulus control, and also illustrates the continued improvement evident through to 12 month follow-up of this group. It should be noted, however, that both post-treatment and 12 month follow-up scores were significantly lower than baseline values also for the imagery training group and the between group difference was non-significant.

Morin and Azrin also reported sleep-onset latency data. Under stimulus control, SOL reduced from a mean value of 56 minutes to 40 minutes at post-treatment and to 23 minutes at 12 month follow-up. Imagery training subjects reduced SOL from 38 minutes to 26 minutes after treatment and to 25 minutes at follow-up. However, waiting-list control subjects also exhibited a substantial reduction in sleep latency from 52 to 31 minutes across treatment. This apparently spontaneous improvement in sleep latency was in marked contrast to the absence of change in wakening duration in the waiting-list group.

Morin and Azrin pooled data from all three conditions to calculate the level of correspondence between sleep diary and mechanical device data. Average correlations of 0.91 for sleep latency and 0.81 for awakening duration were achieved, although the authors admitted that these data sets may not be regarded as truly independent since daily objective feedback may have enabled subjects to improve their own estimates. In terms of the ratings of significant others, statistical analysis revealed that stimulus control patients were perceived at post-treatment to have improved significantly over pre-treatment levels on ratings of severity, interference and noticeability of their sleep problem, whereas the imagery training and waiting-list subjects were not perceived as having improved. This finding was consistent with patients' own outcome ratings which indicated that stimulus control subjects were significantly more satisfied with progress in treatment than were subjects in the other groups.

AN OVERVIEW OF COMPARATIVE OUTCOME STUDIES

It is not any easy task to summarise the comparative benefits of the various psychological treatments for insomnia which have been studied. Some reports have indicated superior outcomes with stimulus control procedures, particularly in reducing sleep latency scores. Other, equally well controlled investigations have failed to demonstrate significant between group differences amongst active treatments, leading to the often stated conclusion that a common mechanism may account for treatment-induced changes. Most recent workers have agreed that this mechanism is likely to operate at the cognitive level.

What does seem to be clear is that failing to treat sleep complaints which are of clinical severity seldom leads to spontaneous remission and placebo interventions seldom work or have enduring effects in such cases. Drug management, as will become clear in Chapter 10, offers limited scope for therapeutic outcome amongst the chronic insomniac population. Cognitive and behavioural treatments, however, have now been widely and repeatedly investigated amongst severe, chronic populations, including the elderly, and none of these factors (severity, chronicity or age) appears to mitigate against treatment benefit. Furthermore, there is some evidence that treatment gains hold up well in the medium to long term, consistent with a habit restructuring/skill acquisition model.

Stimulus control procedures have often produced dramatic and rapid improvement in sleep parameters and have never been associated with deleterious effects. The practitioner, therefore, can feel quite confident that advice on environmental and temporal influences upon sleep will be helpful in most cases and possibly sufficient in some. A limiting factor, however, may be that stimulus control may offer less benefit to sleep quality than to sleep pattern disturbances. Stricter regimes, which have procedural similarities to stimulus control (such as sleep restriction therapy), have not been subject to the same level of rigorous study and should be treated with greater caution due to possible sleep deprivation effects in the early stages.

Relaxation methods vary widely but there is no substantial evidence to support a preference for one particular mode of relaxation-based treatment. Rather, procedures as widely varying as meditation, progressive relaxation and frontalis EMG-biofeedback have tended to evidence functional equivalence and similarity in outcome. Proportionate reductions in sleep variables such as sleep latency and intermittent wakefulness have been found to be less with relaxation treatment than with stimulus control, and sometimes have been little different from placebo. However, relaxation may offer more generalised benefits in the form of a practical skill to counteract tension and anxiety over the 24-hour period. This may be valued highly by some insomniacs whose daytime functioning is less than optimal. If stimulus control can be reliably associated with quantitative changes in sleep pattern, relaxation can be counted on to effect some change in qualitative aspects of functioning. The fact of the matter is that people like relaxation exercises.

Paradoxical intention is a relative newcomer to the treatment literature. Reports of the effectiveness of paradox have been much less equivocal than for say stimulus control treatment. Paradox can be very effective, if not immediately so, and many insomniacs relate readily to its performance anxiety based rationale. It is perhaps the de-catastrophising therapy par excellence. Significant improvements in both sleep pattern and sleep quality have been reported with paradox. However, caution appears warranted since several studies have revealed the potential for exacerbation of sleep problems with paradoxical treatment. It seems probable that this could be resolved by careful matching of treatment to patient characteristics and careful monitoring of the patient's implementation of paradoxical procedures. These areas require further research evaluation.

There is, of course, a wider range of cognitive techniques from which the practitioner may select (see Chapter 7). Few of these have been studied in detail although preliminary reports have been generally supportive.

In conclusion, the practitioner is reminded that effective intervention must stem from a shared understanding between patient and therapist of the goals of treatment. The contractual stage in therapy remains crucial (cf. Chapter 4, p. 88). The information on treatment techniques and their effectiveness, presented in Chapters 5 to 9, should help to guide the practitioner in selecting appropriate therapeutic responses to address agreed therapeutic goals.

Chapter 10

Practical Management of the Hypnotic-dependent Insomniac

It is typical of the psychological literature to find that outcome research generally has compared one psychological treatment with another or several others, rather than comparing psychological treatments with pharmacological treatments. Thus, cognitive treatments have been compared with behavioural treatments, or one cognitive intervention has been compared with another cognitive intervention. For example, it is only relatively recently that controlled research has considered the comparative effectiveness of psychological therapies against minor tanquillisers in the treatment of generalised anxiety disorders (Lindsay et al, 1987; Power et al, 1990) after many previous investigations of cognitive-behavioural treatments per se. The scenario is much the same when it comes to research on insomnia. Pharmacological studies have been abundant, and Chapters 6 to 8 in this book evidence a considerable volume of psychological investigation over the past 20 years. However, the seemingly obvious comparisons have seldom been made, making it difficult to answer the question—would this psychological treatment be more effective for this patient than a prescription for hypnotic drugs? It is appropriate, therefore, to include a section on pharmacological management within a book which is concerned largely with the cognitive-behavioural treatment of insomnia.

The psychological practitioner ought to be familiar with the effects of drugs upon sleep and with the recognised indications and contra-indications for the use of such drugs. Most insomniacs referred for psychological treatment have made use of sleeping pills and are continuing to take such medication at the time of referral. The task very often, therefore, is that of substituting an effective cognitive or behavioural treatment for drug treatment rather than simply providing psychological treatment itself.

This chapter has two principal aims: firstly, to provide a comprehensive review of the effects of hypnotic drugs upon sleep and to present guidelines for appropriate clinical administration of such drugs; and secondly, to guide the practitioner on the clinical management of the hypnotic-using insomniac, particularly where such medication is taken habitually. Although the psychological therapist will not have been responsible for the prescription of the drug, often he is closely involved with any programme of withdrawal and replacement with alternative management.

HYPNOTIC DRUGS—EFFECTS, USES AND SHORTCOMINGS

Sedative-hypnotics, at first barbiturates and more recently the benzo-diazepine drugs, have been the medical treatment of choice for insomnia. It is beyond the scope of this book to explain in detail the effects of sleeping pills upon sleep but the following information has been drawn from review papers.

Hartmann (1978) reported on more than 150 pharmacological studies covering 10 barbiturate and 25 non-barbiturate sleep medications. He concluded that when used with insomniacs at the usual clinical doses, these drugs do generally reduce sleep latency and increase sleep time. However, they also produce clear distortions of the normal sleep pattern. The most striking distortion effect, consistently found, has been that of REM sleep suppression, although several drugs have been reported to be free from this phenomenon at low doses (Kales et al, 1970). Hartmann also referred to the common finding that sleeping pills suppress stage 4 sleep, that is the deepest portion of NREM sleep.

For many years now the restrictions placed upon the prescription of barbiturate drugs have led to a focusing of attention upon the benzo-diazepine group. These drugs are usually, but somewhat arbitrarily, divided into two sub-groups on the basis of their anxiolytic versus sedative effects. The practitioner will find the review paper by Hayward, Wardle and Higgitt (1989) a useful resource for comparing and contrasting anxiolytic and hypnotic benzodiazepine drugs. Greenblatt et al (1982) have highlighted the incorrect assumption that hypnotics and anxiolytics have important neuropharmacological differences, and have stated that drug effects are entirely dose-related. That is, at low doses benzodiazepines act as anti-anxiety agents and at high doses as sleeping pills. These workers also reviewed the available range of medications and came to the conclusion that although benzodiazepines are clearly superior to other classes of hypnotic agents, in terms of safety and possibly also in efficacy, clinically meaningful differences among the various benzodiazepines are often subtle. It should be noted that other pharmacotherapy of insomnia, apart from benzodiazepines and barbiturates, has been investigated. Sedative antidepressants and non-benzodiazepine hypnotics such as zopiclone may be indicated at times (e.g. Mendelson, 1987; Wheatley, 1986). In the remainder of this chapter, however, the term "hypnotic" should be taken to be synonymous with benzodiazepine hypnotic.

Although EEG studies have demonstrated that hypnotic drugs reduce sleep latency and increase total sleep time, the key question remains—do hypnotics turn insomniacs into good sleepers? This most important issue was addressed by Adam (1984) who reported on some of the work undertaken by a research group in Edinburgh. These workers found that poor sleepers indeed reported qualitative improvement in their sleep, which was maintained for a few months of continued use (Adam and Oswald, 1982; Oswald et al, 1982). Unfortunately, however, it has been known for some time that hypnotic drugs become ineffective in longer-term administration and often render their users, not only persistingly poor sleepers, but also drug-dependent (Kales et al, 1974b). The prevailing opinion and advice offered to medical practitioners, therefore, is to administer sleep medication only as a short-term course of therapy, to evaluate carefully factors of aetiological significance in the development of the sleep problem, and to exercise care in the withdrawal of sleeping pills, paying due attention to likely withdrawal effects (Institute of Medicine, 1979; Lader, 1986; Council on Scientific Affairs, 1981; Kales et al, 1983b; Kales and Kales, 1987; Rogers, 1987). The drawbacks of using sleep medication for any extended period require further consideration since chronic insomnia (the most common sleep complaint referred for psychological appraisal and management) is frequently associated with a history of drug use. There appear to be five main areas of concern.

Firstly, Hartmann (1978) has made the simple but important observation that pressure of work upon the general medical practitioner often facilitates prescription as a fortuitous *expedient*, thereby undermining the exploration of potential aetiological factors. He states the obvious but nevertheless critically important point that patients with sleep problems are far more likely to have a sleeping pill prescribed if their physician has only 10 minutes to spend with them than if he or she has 30 or 40 minutes. It is often within the context of restricted consultation time, or alternatively, through the ready availability of sleeping tablets to medical and surgical patients in hospital, that patients are first introduced to benzodiazepines. There would appear, therefore, to be some disharmony between the attested applicability of medications for sleep and much routine medical practice.

A second reason for caution stems from evidence that *tolerance* develops to hypnotic drugs. Indeed it can develop very rapidly. Tolerance has been found to occur with most hypnotics with a diminution of effect over a period of two to six weeks of nightly administration (Kales et al, 1974b, 1975). Such habituation proves less problematic when medication is used only occasionally, but after regular use the drugs tend not to have a substantial potentiating effect upon sleep. They do, however, continue to suppress REM sleep and stage 4 sleep, and percentage REM is likely to be reduced relative to total sleep time (Kales et al, 1975). Thus, within a short period of time, the benzodiazepine may have little beneficial effect upon sleep and the benzodiazepine-using insomniac may continue to complain of insomnia. It is due to these relatively short periods of effectiveness that many chronic insomniacs have been on a wide variety of hypnotics. For persistent cases of sleep disorder, therefore, there is evident danger of the development of a vicious circle involving prescription and regular nightly use, followed by an increased dosage requirement, followed in turn by the substitute prescription of an alternative sleeping tablet. Particular care should be exercised in the provision of benzodiazepines to elderly poor sleepers (Cook, 1986). Elderly people are known to be much more sensitive to the effects of benzodiazepines, requiring smaller doses to achieve hypnotic effects.

Thirdly, it has been known for some time that certain hypnotics produce "carry over" effects, including morning drowsiness, nausea and headache (Oswald, 1968). These are caused by drug accumulation during chronic use, determined primarily by the elimination half-life and metabolic clearance rate of the drug (Greenblatt and Koch-Weser, 1975). If a drug's half-life is short there will be minimal accumulation, and conversely if the half-life is long, some portion of the prior dose will remain in the body when the next is given. Long half-life implies, therefore, that the medication will continue to promote drowsiness and fatigue during the day. For example, triazolam has a short elimination half-life (2–4 hours) and temazepam has an intermediate one (10–15 hours). Flurazepam's duration of action, however, is much longer because one of its active metabolites has an elimination half-life of 47–100 hours (Kales and Kales, 1987). Triazolam being rapidly eliminated may produce early wakening, whereas temazepam has longer action and may lead to morning sleepiness. Flurazepam's carry-over effects are greater still and daytime sleepiness may be even more intrusive.

Clearly, in as far as an hypnotic is given to improve sleep, and thereby improves subsequent daytime functioning, the impairment of such functioning proves to be a serious shortcoming. Dement, Seidel and Carskadon (1982) have commented on the exhibition of micro-sleeps, involuntary sleep, and interruption to on-going behaviour and performance as part of the carry-over phenomenon. More vividly, they comment that individuals are simply more likely to fall asleep while driving a car, or while listening to a lecture, etc. O'Hanlon and Volkerts (1986) have conducted systematic studies of hypnotics and driving performance. They concluded that drugs such as nitrazepam and flurazepam "possess a real potential for adversely affecting driving safety". Reports by Hindmarch (1984) and Hindmarch and Ott (1984) amongst many others have also identified impairments in psychomotor performance, reaction time and arousal levels consequent upon regular drug use.

Fourthly, Kales et al (1983b) have reviewed extensively the literature on *withdrawal* from hypnotic drugs. They have pointed out that physicians are generally concerned with issues of efficacy and with side effects during administration, but neglect to give due attention to possible changes which can follow drug withdrawal. Since sedative-hypnotics are basically Central Nervous System depressants, they are capable of producing dependence and a withdrawal syndrome. Alcohol also should be included in discussion of these matters since it too is a CNS depressant, and a commonly self-prescribed hypnotic agent. (Evidence from Pokorny (1978) substantiates the similarity in effects of alcohol and prescribed medications.) A withdrawal syndrome may include nausea, excitation, agitation, insomnia and nightmares and, of course, with more severe reactions (especially from barbiturates and alcohol), gross behavioural and perceptual disturbances may be found. In addition to this general abstinence syndrome, drug withdrawal insomnia may present, consisting of severe difficulty in initiating sleep, and thereafter during sleep, a fragmentation and disruption of sleep pattern associated with marked increase in REM sleep above baseline levels. The term *"rebound insomnia"* appears appropriately descriptive of the type of withdrawal sleep disturbance identified with benzodiazepine drugs (Kales, Scharf and Kales, 1978).

Rebound effects occur particularly with the short elimination half-life drugs and in some instances are observable after a single nighttime dose (Kales et al, 1983b). Lader and Lawson (1987) have recently critically reviewed the research literature on rebound effects. They summarise the evidence by first of all concurring with Kales and associates that rebound insomnia is most clearly established after the withdrawal of short-acting benzodiazepines (midazolam, triazolam, brotizolam). In those cases rebound effects may be severe but tend to be short-lived. Lader and Lawson further state that withdrawal of intermediate-acting hypnotics (loprazolam, lormetazepam, temazepam) may lead also to discernible rebound but this may be delayed for two or more nights, be less severe but more pro-longed. This also applies to the longer acting benzodiazepines nitrazepam and flunitrazepam, whereas the very long acting compounds flurazepam and quazepam demonstrate rebound insomnia on a more sporadic basis.

Increased frequency of REM periods is also related to a number of other sleep disturbances including intense dreams and nightmares and frequent arousals. With the very short acting drugs earlier morning wakening also may present. The clinical problem posed by these withdrawal phenomena, therefore, may be considerable. The challenges associated with ceasing hypnotic medication, however, may be even greater still since rebound effects are not necessarily short-lived (see above). Withdrawal effects have been observed in some cases to endure up to five weeks after total drug withdrawal (Oswald and Priest, 1965; Nicholson, 1980). This perhaps explains why many insomniacs fail to persevere with abstinence programmes. Furthermore, rebound effects are not restricted to effects upon sleep pattern but have been associated with increased daytime anxiety levels (Kales, Scharf and Kales, 1978; Kales et al, 1983b) and even with anti-social behaviour (Salzman, 1974; Oswald, 1982).

To summarise so far it seems that limiting factors to the use of hypnotics in cases of chronic insomnia include the expediency of prescription as against more detailed appraisal of aetiological and maintaining factors, the development of tolerance after regular use, the risk of daytime carry-over effects impairing performance, and drug-withdrawal problems, which, rather paradoxically, include significant sleep disruption. Although such problems have been well documented, Kales et al (1979) have demonstrated the lack of sufficient knowledge amongst many physicians concerning drug-related effects. In their study Kales et al found that a large number did not recognise that insomnia could be produced by abrupt withdrawal of hypnotics, and 42% of physicians did not know that most hypnotics lose their effects after several weeks of nightly use.

Finally, there are also psychological factors implicated in the protracted use of sleeping pills. Ribordy and Denney (1977), in their consideration of behavioural treatments as an alternative to pharmacological therapy, stressed the importance of *attributional effects* during drug use. They suggested that the insomniac taking sleep medication is likely to attribute the sleep which she does get to the drug and to attribute to herself little capacity for falling asleep. Correspondingly, the removal of the drug not only introduces physical rebound effects, but also gives rise to apprehension concerning ability to fall asleep on one's own. These apprehensions are then largely confirmed by the withdrawal syndrome itself. In the absence of the drug the patient is forced to rely on self-control methods of initiating and maintaining sleep precisely at a time when sleep pattern may be further (and unavoidably) disrupted. Unless the insomniac clearly understands withdrawal phenomena the whole experience is likely to reinforce self-perceptions of being "insomniac" and "out of control". There is also evidence to suggest that overestimation of time asleep (perhaps due to reduced recollection of wakefulness) during drugged nights, followed by heightened awareness of sleep deficits upon drug withdrawal, may be responsible for difficulties in coming off sleeping pills (Schneider-

Helmert, 1988). The combination, therefore, of possible misperceptions and misattributions may produce marked psychological dependence. (The reader is referred also to the discussion of attribution and efficacy in Chapter 2, pp. 34–37.)

It is clear then that there are a number of serious shortcomings (practical, physical and psychological) associated with pharmacological treatment for chronic insomnia. However, researchers concur in advising of the potential benefits of selective use of hypnotics in cases of transient insomnia. They recommend that although medication may represent an effective coping strategy it should be administered within the context of strengthening other adaptive coping mechanisms (Dement, Seidel and Carskadon, 1984; Kales and Kales, 1984). Similarly, Oswald (1979) has reiterated an earlier view (Clift, 1972) that patients should be educated into regarding any hypnotic drug as a temporary expedient, in order to minimise long-term usage. According to Dement, Seidel and Carskadon the major issue is whether or not a course of hypnotic therapy could induce a remission. Kales and Kales have proposed that the primary goal of using hypnotic drugs in the treatment of chronic insomnia is to alleviate the symptom of sleeplessness so that psychotherapy can proceed effectively.

For cases of severe and long-standing sleep disturbance, therefore, the regular use of medication is likely to offer an incomplete therapeutic approach and may represent poor clinical practice because of the likelihood of ultimate ineffectiveness and the possible deleterious consequences both of prolonged use and of drug withdrawal. The use of hypnotics in order to induce a remission, or their intermittent use which avoids habituation to the drug, however, may be acceptable. To conclude this section it may be helpful to reproduce some of the agreed statements arising from the NIMH Consensus Conference on the use of medication to promote sleep.

> Insomnia is a symptom or condition of heterogeneous origin. It signals the need for careful and systematic diagnostic inquiry. Primary medical, psychiatric, and other causes of insomnia should be identified and treated accordingly. Treatment of insomnia should start with the assessment and necessary correction of sleep hygiene and habits. Psychotherapeutic treatment, behavioural approaches and pharmacotherapy, alone or in combination, should be considered in the formulation of a comprehensive treatment plan. When pharmacotherapy is indicated, benzodiazepines are preferable. Patients should receive the smallest effective dose for the shortest clinically necessary period of time. The choice of a specific drug should be based upon its pharmacological properties in conjunction with the particular clinical situation and needs of the patient. Physicians should educate and monitor patients in order to evaluate and reduce the risks of dependence, side-effects and possible withdrawal difficulties. (Consensus Conference, 1984)

SUBSTITUTION OF PSYCHOLOGICAL TREATMENT FOR DRUG TREATMENT

Having considered the effects upon sleep of hypnotic drugs and the indications and contra-indications for pharmacological therapy, it is necessary now to consider appropriate practical management of the hypnotic-using patient who presents at the clinic.

It is of course good practice on the occasion of each new referral (for any problem) for the practitioner to address the question—"Why has this particular individual been referred to me at this particular time?" In pursuing these reasons for referral not only is important descriptive information brought to light, but also information on motivational state. Considering this question may be especially important, however, when it comes to attempts to achieve the two related goals of eliminating the use of a drug and substituting an alternative psychological treatment. Clearly, active participation in *both* elements of the therapeutic endeavour will be critical. Although each presenting case is unique and should be assessed individually, it may be helpful to characterise some of the common background factors precipitating referral for alternative treatment of insomnia.

Presentation type A

This insomniac may have presented to the General Practitioner before but never have received a prescription of sleep medication. This may be due to the individual's own desire to avoid using drugs or to the reluctance of the physician to prescribe. In these circumstances some general advice may have been offered, but an agreement is likely to have been reached between the patient and physician that more specialised non-pharmacological treatment is indicated. Although such subjects are likely to be younger, there are insomniacs who have experienced problems with sleep for many years without recourse to sleeping pills. Amongst this group there will be those who feel they have already tried every self-control technique available. Their scepticism, however, may not preclude the thought that they have nothing to lose by coming along to an appointment.

Presentation type B

A second type of referred subject has some similarities to the individual in the type A presentation. This insomniac will have prescribed medication available but makes sensible and only occasional use of that medication. This individual is likely to recognise, and may have experienced, some of the problems associated with hypnotic drugs and may as a rule prefer self-control methods in the management of personal problems. Alternatively, this individual may suffer periodic bouts of insomnia and may use medication only at these times. It is not uncommon for insomniacs who make occasional use of sleep medication to seek adjunctive treatment which will supplement their own management of their sleep pattern. They may hope to obviate the need to take sleep medication at all.

Some subjects in this group, therefore, will welcome referral for assessment with a view to psychological treatment, although there will be some who will regard referral as evidence of distrust, or of a change in prescription policy on their physician's part. It is worth noting that many individuals draw great comfort from knowing that they have medication available in the house should they ever need it. This knowledge and availability may be more important than the actual consumption of medication, which may be very rare. Where referral for alternative treatment is seen to threaten this flexibility the practitioner may expect to find some resistance.

Presentation type C

With growing public awareness of the limitations of benzodiazepine drugs, of their ultimate ineffectiveness in treating chronic insomnia, and of some of the problems inherent in both consumption and withdrawal of these drugs, drug-using insomniacs may become concerned and themselves request referral to be made. For these people, drug withdrawal per se may be the most valued outcome. Perhaps the majority of such individuals will be treated successfully by the primary care physician since motivation towards withdrawal of drugs for them is high, making it more likely that they would put up with potentially unpleasant withdrawal effects. However, a significant number are referred on. Some will have failed in their drug withdrawal programme and will feel frustrated and disappointed. Others will be disappointed that in spite of successful withdrawal, a poor sleep pattern continues to present and there is the temptation to resume medication. They may recognise the need for an alternative approach to be taken. Still others, will have resumed medication and may have found it to be once again quite effective owing to dishabituation having occurred during the abstinent period.

Presentation type D

There is a fourth group, however, who are commonly referred for assessment and potential psychological management. For this group, the motivation behind referral stems from the physician's own changing perception of what is appropriate prescribing practice. This may or may not be accepted or understood by the patient herself. With the guidelines now available to medical practitioners (as described above) it is hardly surprising that the issuing of repeat prescriptions of benzodiazepine hypnotics has become less common. Thus, the physician may take a decision regarding an individual case, no longer to issue the prescription. Sometimes this happens as part of a "policy" adopted by the physician or the group practice, thus making it easier for him to justify and sustain a change in prescribing tablets.

Another common juncture is when the hypnotic-using insomniac returns to the physician's surgery continuing to complain of insomnia. Pharmacological treatment would require either an increase in dosage of the same drug or substitution of an alternative. The physician then decides that enough is enough. Many of the individuals described within this category of referral will be ambivalent about attending for alternative treatment. Some may have been quite happy to continue to take sleep medication. Some may have been unsympathetically withdrawn from their hypnotic drugs and have experienced severe withdrawal symptoms. Others may fear the prospect of withdrawal because of past unpleasant and unsuccessful experiences. Of course there will be those who recognise the importance of seeking an alternative approach but some of these will fear that it may not work for them.

The author accepts that the above descriptions, in so far as they are cohesive at all, owe that cohesiveness more to clinical caricature than to any scientific analysis of presenting features. Nonetheless, to go back to the original point, background motivational factors concerning the referral of drug-using insomniacs play a central role in establishing what is about to be a new therapeutic contract (cf. Chapter 4, p. 88). Therefore, if these presentations serve as a prompt to the practitioner carefully to consider motivational factors their purpose will have been served.

The remainder of this chapter is devoted to description and illustration of two protocols for withdrawal of hypnotic drugs and the substitution of alternative psychological treatment. The information to be presented is based upon an earlier paper but with greater detail provided on treatment processes (Espie, Lindsay and Brooks, 1988). It is suggested that the models are applicable both in clinical work and in research study. With respect to the latter, the protocols may enable the inclusion, within treatment outcome research studies, of drug-using subjects who might otherwise be excluded on the grounds of methodological rigour. It is argued that the protocols offer a clinically and methodologically valid approach since decisions to shift from one treatment (or experimental) phase to another are based upon the exhibition of stable scores on a target variable.

Model A: A protocol for pre-treatment drug withdrawal

Where motivation and patient compliance permit it is preferable to follow a systematic drug withdrawal programme before offering any formal cognitive-behavioural treatment. There are a number of reasons for this preference. Firstly, withdrawal of medication may be in itself a sufficient treatment of insomnia. Support, information and general advice may be necessary but the re-emergence of a strong natural sleep pattern without further "treatment" is a desirable outcome. Secondly, the simultaneous combination of drug withdrawal and psychological intervention may lead to considerable confusion in the interpretation of the patient's progress. It would not be possible to determine critical factors either in success or failure using this approach. For example, it is not reasonable to expect a behavioural treatment to obviate far less overturn drug withdrawal effects. The presentation of an exacerbated sleep problem (upon withdrawal) may lead, therefore, to an undermining of the subject's confidence in using the behavioural treatment. Conversely, if a good outcome is achieved through simultaneous drug withdrawal and behavioural treatment it may not be possible to determine which ingredients were critical to this success. Such information is of great importance given the possible relapse either to drug-taking and/or to disordered sleep.

The prior administration of a drug-withdrawal programme, therefore, is preferable. This does not mean, however, that the insomniac should be simply discouraged to discontinue medication. A structured, prescriptive programme must be devised on an individual basis. Where the therapist is not a qualified medical practitioner, any withdrawal programme should be agreed with the responsible physician. However, the aim should be to progress towards a total withdrawal period as quickly as is possible without compromising the patient's compliance to maintain withdrawal, and without increasing unduly the level of withdrawal effects experienced by the subject. It is generally recommended that a gradual reduction of medication is appropriate, i.e. at the rate of one therapeutic dose per week of withdrawal (Kales et al, 1974b).

Both prior to and during withdrawal the insomniac should complete a daily sleep log to permit the monitoring of sleep pattern changes associated with the withdrawal programme, and regular review meetings with the therapist should be held to discuss progress, to make decisions about the next stage in planned reduction, and importantly also to provide the support and information which will be necessary to achieve the goal of total and sustained withdrawal. These features of the withdrawal programme along with the later substitution of the psychological treatment are illustrated in the case study presented below. It may be useful, however, at this point to provide more detail on the nature of the support and information which is required as part of the drug-withdrawal programme.

The early part of this chapter provided descriptive information on the effects of drugs upon sleep and on the effects of drug withdrawal upon sleep structure and sleep pattern. This information should be incorporated into a didactic package which aims to provide accurate information, to foster accurate attributions and to reinforce drug-withdrawal behaviours. The range of information central to a successful drug withdrawal programme is outlined in Table 27. It is recommended that this information is presented

Table 27   Information for hypnotic-using insomnia patients who are contemplating following a drug withdrawal programme

---

What hypnotic drugs (sleeping pills) do to your sleep
(1) They depress the Central Nervous System to promote sleep.
(2) Sleep with drugs is not natural sleep.
(3) The deepest part of sleep (called stage 4 sleep) and REM (rapid eye movement) sleep are both suppressed.
(4) Some drugs cause continued drowsiness during the morning.
(5) Regular use of drugs leads to the body becoming accustomed to the drug (drug tolerance) and they can stop working after a matter of weeks.

What happens when you stop
(1) Stopping taking sleeping pills can be hard. There may be withdrawal effects.
(2) These effects can lead to restlessness and a less satisfying sleep. It may take much longer to fall asleep.
(3) Since REM sleep was suppressed while taking drugs, stopping can lead to an increase in REM sleep with vivid dreams, even nightmares.
(4) Withdrawal, therefore, causes insomnia (called "rebound insomnia"). This is often associated also with heightened daytime agitation and anxiety.
(5) Withdrawal effects can last for quite a few weeks. This can be discouraging.

Will you make it without them?
(1) Withdrawal effects are temporary. A natural sleep pattern will develop.
(2) A structured withdrawal programme with support and advice helps a good deal.
(3) Tailoring the programme to suit your needs and careful monitoring of your progress ensures that withdrawal effects are kept to a minimum.
(4) Psychological treatments can be very effective for sleep problems.
(5) The longer term gains by far outweigh the shorter term problems.

---

to the patient along with general sleep information, outlined as part of the non-specific treatment of insomnia in Chapter 5.

Inspection of Table 27 reveals that the information to be imparted is very straightforward and does not seek falsely to reassure. In our own experience, in fact, we have found it more helpful to emphasise to the patient the potential problems which can be experienced and to paint a picture of the worst scenario, rather than to err on the side of optimism. There are two reasons for this. Firstly, this is an extremely good test of motivation and of the individual's ability to sustain motivation over the necessary period of time; and secondly, individuals are more likely to be able to report success even with average withdrawal profiles (relative to expectations). This may be considered an application of the principles of paradox (cf. Chapter 7). The following extract from a consultation is illustrative.

Patient: Remember last time you said it could take me two or three times as long to fall asleep once I'd stopped taking these pills.

Therapist: Yes, I think that's right. That's about the usual. How did you get on?

Patient: Well, last week it varied a bit, but it took me around 85 minutes to fall asleep. That's just about 30 minutes more.

Therapist: So how do you feel about that?

Patient: Well that's good, isn't it?

Therapist: Yes. I'm really pleased you're working so hard at this, but don't be surprised if it does get worse. Lots of people find the second week is pretty tough.

The therapist must ensure that the main criterion for success or failure (from both the patient's and therapist's point of view) during the withdrawal programme is compliance with the withdrawal programme and not changes in the sleep pattern parameters per se. Following the withdrawal programme represents 100% and the patient should be praised with direct reference to that attainment alone. Changes in sleep variables at this stage should be attributed directly to the withdrawal phenomenon and not to personal (in)effectiveness. These data should be looked over carefully with the patient in order to provide accurate feedback, but efforts should be made to ensure that the patient does not feel responsible for either positive or negative change. It is particularly important that patients do not feel that exacerbated sleep problems (actually withdrawal insomnia) represent a re-emergence of sleep problems which had been successfully controlled by the medication. We have found it useful to graph data from sleep logs in order to summarise changes in sleep pattern across the withdrawal period. This can help to demonstrate to the patient the nature of the withdrawal effects and, subsequently, the development of stability in sleep pattern which emerges, often after four to five weeks of total withdrawal. Such visual presentations can help to reinforce the appropriateness of following the drug withdrawal protocol.

It will be helpful at this point to refer to a case illustration.

A case example of pre-treatment drug withdrawal

C. was a 53 year old female referred by her General Practitioner for help with chronic sleep-onset insomnia. C. complained of significant sleep disturbance since around the age of 30 and she had a 20 year history of regular use of sleep medication, at first barbiturates. At the time of presentation she was taking Temazepam 80 mg nightly and appeared to be habituated at this level. Her pre-withdrawal baseline sleep latency averaged around 60 minutes and she obtained approximately five and a half hours sleep per night (see Figure 9).

In spite of the very lengthy history and her dependence upon hypnotic drugs, C. was highly motivated to come off all medication and wanted to begin to do so immediately. Information and advice were presented to C. as described in Table 27. She remained committed to the drug withdrawal programme. Therefore, after a one week baseline sleep log recording period, drug withdrawal commenced and was conducted over a five week period. During this time C. had regular sessions with the therapist who offered support and encouragement. Inspection of Figure 9 indicates that, during the first two weeks of withdrawal, sleep latency increased dramatically and thereafter evidenced considerable variability for a number of further weeks.

At post-withdrawal, significant sleep disturbance persisted. It was felt that relaxation therapy might be of benefit. Thus, a second baseline phase was instituted until C.'s sleep pattern appeared to have stabilised over two consecutive weeks. Reference to Figure 9 reveals that this in fact took place during the eighth and ninth weeks after the commencement of the withdrawal programme. Progressive relaxation training was instituted for four weeks under counterdemand instruction to control for expectancy effects (Steinmark and Borkovec, 1974). By the end of the counterdemand phase sleep latency had reduced to 22 minutes. These improvements were generally maintained during a further four weeks of relaxation training under positive demand conditions. C. remained drug free and sleeping well with a sleep latency of 17 minutes at 12 month follow-up.

C. was one of five cases presented to illustrate the pre-treatment drug withdrawal protocol in an earlier report (Espie, Lindsay and Brooks, 1988). In that paper grouped data were presented, because the overall pattern of results was fairly similar for all the individuals concerned. To summarise

221

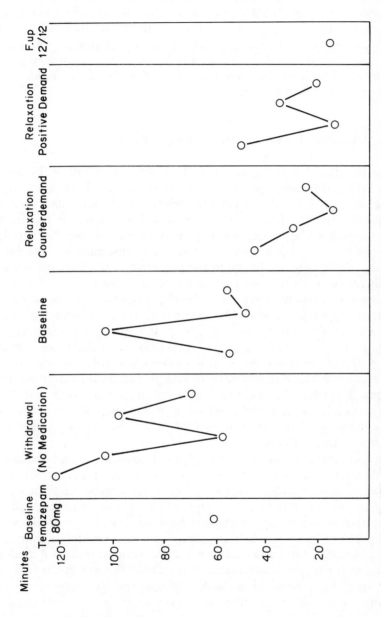

Figure 9   A case example (C.) illustrating the pre-treatment drug-withdrawal protocol. Data are weekly mean sleep latency scores (min)

these data, rebound effects upon sleep latency were observed, particularly in the early weeks after drug withdrawal, but thereafter there was a return to near baseline levels. Significant sleep disturbance, however, did remain and the institution of psychological therapy (various methods) led to substantial reduction in sleep latencies for all subjects. Follow-ups within the range 10–15 months for these five patients revealed that in four cases treatment gains were maintained without resumption of medication; however, in one case hypnotic medication had been resumed.

Model B: A protocol for post-treatment drug withdrawal

For some patients drug tolerance will have developed but withdrawal cannot be achieved without the immediate provision of an alternative, active treatment strategy (i.e. other than the supportive/didactic intervention described in Chapter 5). If the therapist were to insist upon pre-treatment drug withdrawal in these cases, there is every likelihood that they would default from the clinic but continue to suffer from insomnia and continue to present a therapeutic challenge to the physician. The physician would be left, therefore, with the prospect either of increasing drug dosage or substituting an alternative hypnotic, thereby perpetuating the problem of long-term hypnotic dependence. Insomniacs such as these represent the hard core of the clinic-presenting group. It is particularly important, therefore, to test out whether or not psychological treatments can be effective with such severe cases who have been generally excluded from research studies, because of problems in withdrawal from medication. We have found, however, that exclusion may be unnecessary and that it is possible to include such individuals for research purposes, and also to achieve some good clinical outcomes. There is an alternative protocol for post-treatment drug withdrawal.

This model requires that medication is held constant at an habituated level while pre-treatment baselines are recorded and sleep pattern stability over time is demonstrated. A psychological treatment may then be instituted to promote therapeutic change which can be measured against the stable baseline values. Assuming that demonstrable change is achieved, this therapeutic outcome will help promote the confidence of the insomniac and help restructure hitherto negative beliefs concerning ability to develop self-control over sleep. The psychological treatment, thereafter, can be used to help "wean" the patient off medication at the prescribed rate.

Of course, rebound effects may be expected still to present and the didactic approach (Table 27) is likely to be required with these cases also. This post-treatment withdrawal protocol represents a methodologically and clinically valid procedure since the effects of hypnotics can be justifiably considered as constant if taken at the same dosage after habituation. Drug intake, therefore, essentially becomes a controlled variable; the control being demonstrated by baseline stability. Treatment effects can then be attributed to the psychological intervention per se and the hypnotic drugs can be eliminated by means of a structured withdrawal programme. With the continued application of the psychological treatment, however, sleep pattern may be expected to return to acceptable levels by the end of the entire programme.

Once again an illustrative case study may be helpful.

A case example of post-treatment drug withdrawal

D. was a 51 year old male referred by his General Practitioner with an eight year history of severe initial insomnia. During this entire period D. had taken one of a number of sleep preparations. At the time of referral his medication was Triazolam 0.25 mg plus Chlorazepate 15 mgm nightly. He reported considerable distress at his unsatisfactory sleep pattern which he felt interfered greatly with work performance. D. had experienced severe rebound insomnia during previous attempts at drug withdrawal and had been unable to sustain withdrawal for more than a few nights. It should be noted that Triazolam is a particularly short-acting hypnotic. Drugs with short elimination half-life generally produce more severe rebound effects (see earlier in this chapter, p. 211).

D. completed a sleep log during a two week baseline period. Figure 10 presents sleep latency data for all phases of the withdrawal and treatment programme. D.'s medicated sleep latency at baseline was approximately 75 minutes. He was instructed to continue to take his medication as prescribed while a stimulus control treatment programme was instituted. It was stressed that he must not miss out any sleeping pills even if he felt his sleep pattern was improving. He was assured that drug withdrawal would be dealt with at a later point in the programme. Inspection of Figure 10 reveals that stimulus control treatment produced a reduction in D.'s sleep latency under counterdemand conditions although he appeared to sleep better during some weeks than others. By the end of the complete eight week treatment programme he was falling asleep very quickly (sleep latency approximately 15 minutes). He was of course still on medication at this stage.

Prior to the withdrawal phase, D. was instructed on the likely effects of the withdrawal programme, and told that it may take a number of weeks before his sleep pattern again began to improve. However, there was now reason to believe that he had an effective alternative treatment and that once the withdrawal effects were over he should be able to sleep reasonably well relying only on self-management strategies. As can be seen from Figure 10,

224

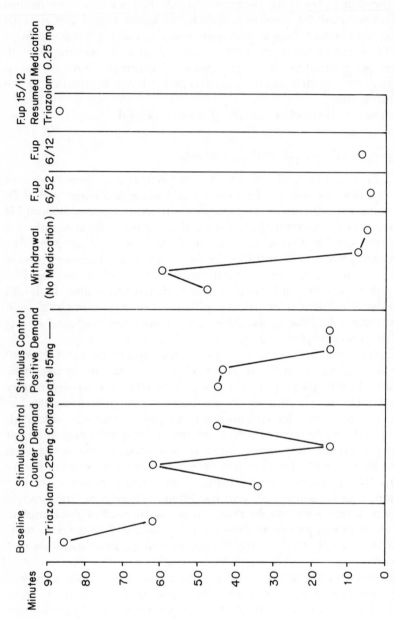

Figure 10 A case example (D.) illustrating the post-treatment drug-withdrawal protocol. Data are weekly mean sleep latency scores (min)

D. did experience marked sleep latency increases beyond post-treatment levels during the first two weeks of withdrawal. During the third and fourth week without medication, however, withdrawal effects had ceased and he had no significant sleep latency difficulties. Encouraging results were obtained at both six week and six month follow-up where no deterioration had occurred (SOL approximately five minutes). A long-term (15 months) follow-up, however, revealed that D. had resumed medication around one year after the termination of contact and once again was at an habituated level on Triazolam, and was displaying significant initial insomnia.

Case D., like case C. above, was drawn from our grouped data study (Espie, Lindsay and Brooks, 1988). Interestingly, three of the five subjects allocated to the post-treatment withdrawal protocol in that study were observed to have resumed medication at the long-term follow-up, which represents a much greater failure rate than with the pre-treatment withdrawal programme. A number of tentative comments may be proffered based upon our experience of pre- and post-treatment drug withdrawal programmes.

Firstly, it may be expected that subjects unable initially to stop hypnotics will present with lengthier sleep latency difficulties and may feel less able, because of this, to cope with the further exacerbation of sleep problems caused by rebound effects. Secondly, although a figure of around five weeks for drug withdrawal is suggested, this may be at best an approximate one. The length of withdrawal period necessary should be determined for the individual by monitoring sleep pattern and identifying the point at which stability re-emerges. Thirdly, the prevalence of relapse from psychological treatment back to pharmacological treatment perhaps indicates the need for a regular monitoring procedure, long after the formal programme of withdrawal and alternative treatment has been discontinued. This could be regarded as a form of booster therapy to remind the individual of the principles and practice of psychological treatments. Fourthly, it may be necessary to rehearse the importance of avoiding use of medications even on a one off basis lest drug-taking once again becomes habitual.

The practitioner should be aware that many insomniacs retain a supply of hypnotic drugs, "just in case" they should be needed at some point in the future. Patients certainly should be discouraged from this practice since such availability provides an expedient solution should a sleep problem re-emerge. Although insomniacs will have learned from experience that benzodiazepines tend to become less effective in the long term after persistent use, they also know that a sleeping pill can produce a very dramatic and immediate result on a given night. Such immediate benefits are not always available through psychological techniques, and these techniques also require greater commitment and application. In the situation, therefore, where sleep pattern has been satisfactory for some time and psychological techniques have not been regularly practised, the ingestion of a sleeping tablet may prove the more attractive option to help the individual cope with a period of stress and poor sleep.

AN OVERVIEW OF PRACTICAL MANAGEMENT OF THE DRUG-USING INSOMNIAC

This chapter was included in this book in order to provide the clinician with a systematic structure within which to approach the clinical management of the insomniac who is a regular user of hypnotic drugs. To summarise, it is always necessary to obtain some baseline measures of sleep pattern while the individual is still on medication so that subsequent drug withdrawal and treatment intervention phases can be reasonably evaluated against presenting characteristics. A decision has to be made on how best to achieve withdrawal of medication, and on how to provide the insomniac with the help necessary to sustain that withdrawal and to achieve a satisfactory sleep pattern when drug free. Motivation and compliance are major factors here. Whenever possible the option of choice should be the immediate withdrawal of sleep medication at the recommended reduction of one therapeutic dose per week, or otherwise as recommended by the responsible physician. Both prior to and during drug withdrawal the insomniac will require information on what to expect and interpretation of what is actually happening. This didactic intervention may be usefully presented within a paradoxical framework. For some individuals drug withdrawal may be a sufficient "treatment" since sleep disturbance can be primarily drug-induced. Some patients, however, will find it impossible to withdraw from medication without the provision of an active therapeutic intervention to substitute for drugs. In these cases, demonstrable change in sleep pattern may be achieved by the application of a psychological treatment while drug intake remains constant. Post-treatment withdrawal may then be implemented in such cases. Finally, it should be noted that treatment outcome for severe cases of insomnia, particularly where there has been long-term use of hypnotics, cannot be satisfactorily measured at the termination of therapy or even six months later. A significant proportion of people may relapse even after one year or longer. Regular contact and booster therapy should be provided to foster maintenance of treatment gains and to ensure appropriate adaptation to and coping with transient periods of poor sleep. These, it should be emphasised, are part of normal experience.

References

Adam, K. (1980a). Sleep as a restorative process and a theory to explain why. *Progress in Brain Research*, **53**, 289–305.

Adam, K. (1980b). Dietary habit and sleep after bedtime food or drinks. *Sleep*, **3**, 47–58.

Adam, K. (1984). Are poor sleepers changed into good sleepers by hypnotic drugs? *Psychopharmacology Suppl.*, **1**, 44–55.

Adam, K. and Oswald, I. (1977). Sleep is for tissue restoration. *Journal of the Royal College of Physicians*, **11**, 376–388.

Adam, K. and Oswald, I. (1979). One gram of L-tryptophan fails to alter the time taken to fall asleep. *Neuropharmacology*, **18 (12)**, 1025–1027.

Adam, K. and Oswald, I. (1982). A comparison of the effects of chlormezanone and nitrazepam on sleep. *British Journal of Clinical Pharmacology*, **14**, 57–65.

Agnew, H. W. and Webb, W. B. (1972). Measurement of sleep-onset by EEG criteria. *American Journal of EEG Technology*, **12**, 127–134.

Agnew, H. W., Webb, W. B. and Williams, R. L. (1967). Comparison of stage four and 1-REM sleep deprivation. *Perceptual and Motor Skills*, **24**, 851–858.

Alperson, J. and Biglan, A. (1979). Self-administered treatment of sleep-onset insomnia and the importance of age. *Behaviour Therapy*, **10**, 347–356.

American Psychiatric Association (1987). *Diagnostic and statistical manual of mental disorders (DSM III-R)*. Washington, DC: American Psychiatric Association.

Ancoli-Israel, S., Kripke, D. F., Mason, W. and Messin, S. (1981). Comparisons of home sleep recordings and polysomnograms in older adults with sleep disorder. *Sleep*, **4**, 283–291.

Ascher, L. M. (1979). Paradoxical intention in the treatment of urinary retention. *Behaviour Research and Therapy*, **17**, 267–270.

Ascher, L. M. (1980). Paradoxical intention. In A. Goldstein and E. B. Foa (eds). *Handbook of behavioural interventions*. New York: Wiley.

Ascher, L. M. (1981). Employing paradoxical intention in the treatment of agoraphobia. *Behaviour Research and Therapy*, **19**, 533–542.

Ascher, L. M. (1988). Paradoxical intention. Paper presented at the World Congress of Behaviour Therapy, University of Edinburgh, Scotland.

Ascher, L. M. and Clifford, R. E. (1977). Behaviour considerations in the treatment of sexual dysfunction. In M. Hersen, R. M. Eisler, and P. M. Miller, (eds). *Progress in behaviour modification* (Volume 3). New York: Academic Press.

Ascher L. M. and Efran, J. (1978). The use of paradoxical intention in cases of delayed sleep-onset insomnia. *Journal of Consulting and Clinical Psychology*, **46**, 547–550.

Ascher, L. M. and Turner, R. M. (1979). Paradoxical intention and insomnia: An experimental investigation. *Behaviour Research and Therapy*, **17**, 408–411.

Ascher, L. M. and Turner, R. M. (1980). A comparison of two methods for the administration of paradoxical intention. *Behaviour Research and Therapy*, **18**, 121–126.

Aschoff, J. (1965). Circadian rhythms in man. *Science*, **148**, 1427–1432.

Aserinsky, E. and Kleitman, N. (1953). Regularly occurring periods of eye motility and concomitant phenomena during sleep. *Science*, **118**, 273–274.

Association of Sleep Disorders Centers (1979). Diagnostic classification of sleep and arousal disorders (first edition). *Sleep*, **2**, 21–57.

Baddeley, A. D. (1986). Working memory. Oxford Psychological Series No. 11. Oxford: Clarendon Press.

Baekeland, F. and Hoy, P. (1971). Reported versus recorded sleep characteristics. *Archives of General Psychiatry*, **24**, 548–551.

Baekeland, F. and Lasky, R. (1966). Exercise and sleep patterns in college athletes. *Perceptual and Motor Skills*, **23**, 1203–1207.

Bandura, A. (1977). Self-efficacy: Toward a unifying theory of behaviour change. *Psychological Review*, **84**, 192–215.

Bandura, A. (1986). *Social foundations of thought and action: A social cognitive theory*. Englewood Cliffs, N. J.: Prentice-Hall.

Bandura, A. (1989). Self-efficacy mechanism in physiological activation and health promoting behaviour. In J. Madden, S. Matthysse and J. Barchas (eds). *Adaptation, learning and affect*. New York: Raven Press.

Barlow, D. H. (1981). On the relation of clinical research to clinical practice: Current issues, new directions. *Journal of Consulting and Clinical Psychology*, **49**, 147–155.

Beck, A. T. (1976). *Cognitive therapy and the emotional disorders*. New York: International Universities Press.

Beck, A. T. and Emery, G. (1979). Cognitive therapy of anxiety and phobic disorder. Unpublished treatment manual. Philadelphia, Pa.: Center for Cognitive Therapy.

Beck, A. T. Ward, C. H., Mendelson, M., Mock, J. and Erbaugh, J. (1961). An inventory for measuring depression. *Archives of General Psychiatry*, **4**, 561–571.

Beck, J. T. and Strong, S. R. (1982). Stimulating therapeutic change with interpretations: A comparison of positive and negative connotation. *Journal of Counselling Psychology*, **29**, 551–559.

Benson, H., Beary, J. F. and Carrol, M. D. (1974). The relaxation response. *Psychiatry*, **37**, 37–46.

Bergin, A. and Strupp, H. (1972). *Changing frontiers in the science of psychotherapy*. Chicago: Aldine-Atherton.

Bernstein, D. A. and Borkovec, T. D. (1973). *Progressive relaxation training: A manual for the helping professions*. Champaign, Ill.: Research Press.

Besner, H. F. (1978). Biofeedback—possible placebo in treating chronic-onset insomnia. *Biofeedback and Self-Regulation*, **3**, 208.

Beutler, L. E., Thornby, J. I. and Karacan, I. (1978). Psychological variables in the diagnosis of insomnia. In I. Karacan and R. L. Williams (eds). *Sleep disorders: Diagnosis and treatment*. New York: Wiley.

Billiard, M., Besset, A. and Passouant, P. (1981). The place of sleep disorder centers in the evaluation and treatment of chronic insomniacs. *International Journal of Neurology*, **15**, 56–61.

Birrell, P. C. (1983). Behavioural, subjective and electroencephalographic indices of sleep-onset latency and sleep duration. *Journal of Behavioural Assessment*, **5**, 179–190.

Bixler, E. O., Kales, A., Soldatos, C. R. Kales, J. D. and Healey, S. (1979). Prevalence of sleep disorders in the Los Angeles Metropolitan Area. *American Journal of Psychiatry*, **136**, 1257–1262.

Bohlin, G. (1971). Monotonous stimulation, sleep-onset and habituation of the orienting reaction. *Electroencephalography and Clinical Neurophysiology*, **31**, 593–601.

Bohlin, G. (1972). Susceptibility to sleep during a habituation procedure as related to individual differences. *Journal of Experimental Research on Personality*, **6**, 248–254.

Bohlin, G. (1973). Interaction of arousal and habituation in the development of sleep during monotonous stimulation. *Biological Psychology*, **1**, 99–114.

Bolton, S. and Null, G. (1981). Caffeine: Psychological effects, use and abuse. *Journal of Orthomolecular Psychiatry*, **10**, 202–211.

Bonnet, M. H. and Rosa, R. R. (1987). Sleep and performance in young adults and older normals and insomniacs during acute sleep loss and recovery. *Biological Psychology*, **25**, 153–172.

Bootzin, R. R. (1972). Stimulus control treatment for insomnia. *Proceedings of the American Psychological Association*, **7**, 395–396.

Bootzin, R. R. (1975). A comparison of stimulus control instructions and progressive relaxation training in the treatment of sleep-onset insomnia. Unpublished manuscript, North Western University, USA.

Bootzin, R. R. and Engle-Friedman, M. (1981). The assessment of insomnia. *Behavioral Assessment*, **3**, 107–126.

Bootzin, R. R. and Engle-Friedman, M. (1987). Sleep disturbances. In B. A. Edelstein and L. L. Cartensen (eds). *Handbook of clinical gerontology*. New York: Pergamon Press.

Bootzin, R. R., Engle-Friedman, M. and Hazlewood, L. (1983). Insomnia. In P. M. Lewinsohn and L. Teri (eds). *Clinical geropsychology: New directions in assessment and treatment*. New York: Pergamon Press.

Bootzin, R. R., Herman, C. and Nicassio, P. M. (1976). The power of suggestion: Another examination of misattribution and insomnia. *Journal of Personality and Social Psychology*, **34**, 673–679.

Bootzin, R. R. and Nicassio, P. M. (1978). Behavioural treatments for insomnia. In M. Hersen, R. M. Eisler and P. M. Miller (eds). *Progress in behaviour modification* (Volume 6). New York: Academic Press.

Borkovec, T.D. (1979). Pseudo-(experiential) insomnia and idiopathic (objective) insomnia: Theoretical and therapeutic issues. *Advances in Behaviour Research and Therapy*, **2**, 27–55.

Borkovec, T. D. (1982). Insomnia. *Journal of Consulting and Clinical Psychology*, **50**, 880–895.

Borkovec, T. D. and Fowles, D. (1973). Controlled investigation of the effects of progressive relaxation and hypnotic relaxation on insomnia. *Journal of Abnormal Psychology*, **82**, 153–158.

Borkovec, T. D., Grayson, J. B., O'Brien, G. T. and Weerts, T. C. (1979). Relaxation treatment of pseudoinsomnia and idiopathic insomnia: An electroencephalographic evaluation. *Journal of Applied Behavioural Analysis*, **12**, 37–54.

Borkovec, T. D. and Hennings, B. L. (1978). The role of physiological attention-focusing in the relaxation treatment of sleep disturbance, general tension and specific stress reaction. *Behaviour Research and Therapy*, **16**, 7–20.

Borkovec, T. D., Kaloupek, D. and Slama, K. (1975). The facilitative effect of muscle tension release in the relaxation treatment of sleep disturbance. *Behaviour Therapy*, 6, 301–309.

Borkovec, T. D., Lane, T. W. and Van Oot, P. A. (1981). Phenomenology of sleep among insomniacs and good sleepers: Wakefulness experience when cortically asleep. *Journal of Abnormal Psychology*, 90, 607–609.

Borkovec, T. D. and Nau, S. D. (1972). Credibility of analogue therapy rationales. *Journal of Behaviour Therapy and Experimental Psychiatry*, 3, 257–260.

Borkovec, T. D. and Sides, J. K. (1979). Critical procedural variables related to the physiological effects of progressive relaxation: A review. *Behaviour Research and Therapy*, 17, 119–125.

Borkovec, T. D., Steinmark, S. W. and Nau, S. D. (1973). Relaxation training and single item desensitisation in the group treatment of insomnia. *Journal of Behaviour Therapy and Experimental Psychiatry*, 4, 401–410.

Borkovec, T. D. and Weerts, T. (1976). Effects of progressive relaxation on sleep disturbance: An electroencephalographic evaluation. *Psychosomatic Medicine*, 38, 173–180.

Boyle, G. J. (1985). Self-report measures of depression: Some psychometric considerations. *British Journal of Clinical Psychology*, 24, 45–59.

Brezinova, V. and Oswald, I. (1972). Sleep after a bedtime beverage. *British Medical Journal*, 431–433.

Brezinova, V., Oswald, I. and Loudon, J. (1975). Two types of insomnia: Too much waking and not enough sleep. *British Journal of Psychiatry*, 126, 439–445.

Brockner, J. and Swap, W. C. (1983). Resolving the relationships between placebos, misattribution and insomnia: An individual-differences perspective. *Journal of Personality and Social Psychology*, 45, 32–42.

Browman, C. and Tepas, D. (1976). The effects of pre-sleep activity on all-night sleep. *Psychophysiology*, 13, 536–540.

Budzynski, T. H. (1973). Biofeedback procedures in the clinic. *Seminars in Psychiatry*, 5, 537–547.

Buysse, D. J., Reynolds, C. F., Monk, T. H., Berman, S. R. and Kupfer, D. J. (1989). The Pittsburgh Sleep Quality Index: A new instrument for psychiatric practice and research. *Psychiatry Research*, 28, 193–213.

Campbell, S. S. and Webb, W. B. (1981). The perception of wakefulness within sleep. *Sleep*, 4, 177–183.

Carr-Kaffashan, L. and Woolfolk, R. L. (1979). Active and placebo effects in the treatment of moderate and severe insomnia. *Journal of Consulting and Clinical Psychology*, 47, 1072–1080.

Carskadon, M. A. and Dement, W. C. (1981). Cumulative effects of sleep restriction on daytime sleepiness. *Psychophysiology*, 18, 107–113.

Carskadon, M. A. and Dement, W. C. (1982). The Multiple Sleep Latency Test: What does it measure? *Sleep*, 5 (Suppl. 2), 67–72.

Carskadon, M. A., Dement, W. C., Mitler, M. M., Guilleminault, C., Zarcone, V. P. and Spiegel, R. (1976). Self-reports versus sleep laboratory findings in 122 drug-free subjects with complaints of chronic insomnia. *American Journal of Psychiatry*, 133, 1382–1388.

Carskadon, M. A., Mitler, M. M., Billiard, M., Phillips, R. and Dement, W. C. (1975). A comparison of insomniacs and normals: Total sleep time and sleep latency. *Sleep Research*, 4, 211.

Christensen, L. and Mendoza, J. L. (1986). A method of assessing change in a single subject: An alteration of the RC Index. *Behaviour Therapy*, 17, 305–308.

Cirignotta, F., Mondini, S., Zucconi, M., Lenzi, P. L. and Lugaresi, E. (1985).

Insomnia: An epidemiological survey. *Clinical Neuropharmacology*, **8 (Suppl. 1)**, 49–54.

Clift, A. D. (1972). Factors leading to dependence on hypnotic drugs. *British Medical Journal*, **3**, 614.

Coates, T. J., Killen, J. D., George, J., Marchini, E., Silverman S. and Thoresen, C. E. (1982b). Estimating sleep parameters: A multitrait-multimethod analysis. *Journal of Consulting and Clinical Psychology*, **50**, 345–352.

Coates, T. J., Killen, J. D., Marchini, E., Silverman, S., Hamilton, S. and Thoresen, C. E. (1982a). Discriminating good sleepers from insomniacs using all-night polysomnograms conducted at home. *Journal of Nervous and Mental Disease*, **170**, 224–230.

Coates, T. J., Strossen, R. J., Rosekind, M. R. and Thoresen, C. E. (1978). Obtaining reliable all-night sleep recording data: How many nights are needed? *Sleep Research*, **7**, 285.

Coates, T. J. and Thoresen, C. E. (1979). Treating arousals during sleep using behavioural self-management. *Journal of Consulting and Clinical Psychology*, **47**, 603–605.

Coates, T. J. and Thoresen, C. E. (1980). Treating sleep disorders: Some answers, a few suggestions and many questions. In S. Turner, H. E. Adams and K. Calhoun (eds). *Handbook of clinical behaviour therapy*. New York: Wiley.

Coates, T. J. and Thoresen, C. E. (1984). Assessing daytime thoughts and behaviour associated with good and poor sleep: Two exploratory case studies. *Behavioural Assessment*, **6**, 153–167.

Coleman, M., Roffwarg, H. and Kennedy, S. (1982). Sleep–wake disorders based on a polysomnographic diagnosis—a national cooperative study. *Journal of the American Medical Association*, **247**, 997–1003.

Consensus Conference (1984). Drugs and insomnia: The use of medication to promote sleep. *Journal of the American Medical Association*, **251**, 2410–2414.

Cook, P. J. (1986). Benzodiazepine hypnotics in the elderly. *Acta Psychiatrica Scandinavica*, **74**, 149–158.

Cooper, J. R. (1977). *Sedative-hypnotic drugs: Risks and benefits*. Rockville, Md.: National Institute of Drug Abuse.

Coren, S. (1988). Prediction of insomnia from arousability predisposition scores: Scale development and cross-validation. *Behaviour Research and Therapy*, **26**, 415–420.

Council on Scientific Affairs (1981). Hypnotic drugs and treatment of insomnia. *Journal of the American Medical Association*, **245**, 749–750.

Coursey, R. D., Buchsbaum, M. and Frankel, B. L. (1975). Personality measures and evoked responses in chronic insomniacs. *Journal of Abnormal Psychology*, **84**, 239–250.

Coursey, R. D., Frankel, B. L., Gaarder, K. R. and Mott, D. E. (1980). A comparison of relaxation techniques with electrosleep therapy for chronic, sleep-onset insomnia: A sleep-EEG study. *Biofeedback and Self-Regulation*, **5**, 57–73.

Craske, M. G. and Barlow, D. H. (1989). Nocturnal panic. *Journal of Nervous and Mental Disease*, **177**, 160–167.

Czeisler, C. A., Weitzman, E. D., Moore-Ede, M. C., Zimmerman, J. C. and Knauer, R. S. (1980). Human sleep: Its duration and organisation depend on its circadian phase. *Science*, **210**, 1264–1267.

Davidson, R. J. and Schwartz, G. E. (1976). The psychobiology of relaxation and related states: A multiprocess theory. In D. I. Mostofsky (ed.). *Behaviour control and modification of physiological activity*. Englewood-Cliffs, N.J.: Prentice-Hall.

Davies, R., Lacks, P., Storandt, M. and Bertelson, A. D. (1986). Countercontrol treatment of sleep maintenance insomnia in relation to age. *Psychology and Aging*, **1**, 233–238.

Davison, G. C., Tsujimoto, R. N. and Glaros, A. G. (1973). Attribution and the importance of behaviour change in falling asleep. *Journal of Abnormal Psychology*, **82**, 124–133.

De la Pena, A. (1978). Toward a psychophipidogic conceptualisation of insomnia. In I. Karacan and R. L. Williams (eds). *Sleep disorders: Diagnosis and treatment*. New York: Wiley.

Dement, W. C. (1960). The effect of dream deprivation. *Science*, **131**, 1705–1707.

Dement, W. C. (1986). Normal sleep, disturbed sleep, transient and persistent insomnia. *Acta Psychiatrica Scandinavica*, **74**, 41–46.

Dement, W. C. and Kleitman, N. (1957). The relation of eye movements during sleep to dream activity: An objective method for the study of dreaming. *Journal of Experimental Psychology*, **53**, 339–346.

Dement, W. C., Miles, L. E. and Carskadon, M. A. (1982). "White paper" on sleep on aging. *Journal of the American Geriatric Society*, **30**, 25–50.

Dement, W. C., Seidel, W. and Carskadon, M. A. (1982). Daytime alertness, insomnia and benzodiazepines. *Sleep*, **5** (Suppl. 1), 28–45.

Dement, W. C., Seidel, W. and Carskadon, M. A. (1984). Issues in the diagnosis and treatment of insomnia. *Psychopharmacology Suppl.*, **1**, 12–43.

Dewan, E. M. (1970). The programming "p" hypothesis for REM sleep. In E. Hartmann (ed.). *Sleep and dreaming*. International Psychiatry Clinic Series (Volume 7). Boston: Little, Brown.

Dubois, P. (1908). *Psychic treatment of nervous disorders*. New York: Funk and Wagnalls.

Dunlap, K. (1930). Repetition in the breaking of habits. *Science Monthly*, **30**, 66–70.

Dunlap, K. (1942). The technique of negative practice. *American Journal of Psychology*, **55**, 270–273.

Dunnell, K. and Cartwright, A. (1972). *Medicine takers, prescribers and hoarders*. London: Routledge and Kegan Paul.

Edinger, J. D. and Stout, A. L. (1985). Efficacy of an outpatient treatment program for insomnia: A preliminary report. *Professional Psychology: Research and Practice*, **16**, 905–909.

Edinger, J. D., Stout, A. L. and Hoelscher, T. J. (1988). Cluster analysis of insomniacs' MMPI profiles: Relation of subtypes to sleep history and treatment outcome. *Psychosomatic Medicine*, **50**, 77–87.

Engle-Friedman, M. (1985). *An evaluation of behavioral treatments for insomnia in the older adult*. Unpublished Ph. D. dissertation. Evanston, III.: North Western University.

Erwin, C. W. and Zung, W. W. K. (1970). Behavioural and EEG criteria of sleep in humans. *Archives of General Psychiatry*, **23**, 375–377.

Espie, C. A. (1985). Treatment of excessive urinary urgency and frequency by retention control training and desensitisation: Three case studies. *Behaviour Research and Therapy*, **23**, 205–210.

Espie, C. A. (1986). The group treatment of obsessive-compulsive ritualisers: Behavioural management of identified patterns of relapse. *Behavioural Psychotherapy*, **14**, 21–33.

Espie, C. A. (1989). What does "successful treatment" mean for the insomniac? Paper presented at the British Psychological Society Annual Conference, St Andrews, Scotland.

Espie, C. A., Brooks, D. N. and Lindsay, W. R. (1989). An evaluation of tailored psychological treatment of insomnia. *Journal of Behaviour Therapy and Experimental Psychiatry*, **20**, 143–153.

Espie, C. A. and Lindsay, W. R. (1985). Paradoxical intention in the treatment of chronic insomnia: Six case studies illustrating variability in therapeutic response. *Behaviour Research and Therapy*, **23**, 703–709.

Espie, C. A. and Lindsay, W. R. (1987). Cognitive strategies for the management of severe sleep-maintenance insomnia: A preliminary investigation. *Behavioural Psychotherapy*, **15**, 388–395.

Espie, C. A., Lindsay, W. R. and Brooks, D. N. (1988). Substituting behavioural treatment for drugs in the treatment of insomnia: An exploratory study. *Journal of Behaviour Therapy and Experimental Psychiatry*, **19**, 51–56.

Espie, C. A., Lindsay, W. R., Brooks, D. N., Hood, E. M. and Turvey, T. (1989). A controlled comparative investigation of psychological treatments for chronic sleep-onset insomnia. *Behaviour Research and Therapy*, **27**, 79–88.

Espie, C. A., Lindsay, W. R. and Espie, L. C. (1989). Use of the Sleep Assessment Device (Kelley and Lichstein, 1980) to validate insomniacs' self-report of sleep pattern. *Journal of Psychopathology and Behavioural Assessment*, **11**, 71–79.

Espie, C. A., Lindsay, W. R. and Hood, E. M. (1987). Analysing the sleep data of insomniac patients: Sleep pattern variability before and after stimulus control treatment. Unpublished manuscript.

Espie, C. A., Monk, E., Hood, E. M. and Lindsay, W. R. (1988). Establishing clinical criteria for the treatment of chronic insomnia: A comparison of insomniac and control populations. *Health Bulletin*, **46/6**, 318–326.

Espie, C. A. and Shapiro, C. (1991). The practical management of insomnia— behavioural and cognitive techniques. *British Medical Journal* (in press).

Espie, C. A. and White, J. (1986a). Clinical psychology and general practice: A four year review. *Health Bulletin*, **44/5**, 266–273.

Espie, C. A. and White J. (1986b). The effectiveness of psychological intervention in primary care: A comparative analysis of outcome ratings. *Journal of the Royal College of General Practitioners*, **36**, 310–312.

Evans, D. R. and Bond, I. K. (1969). Reciprocal inhibition therapy and classical conditioning in the treatment of insomnia. *Behaviour Research and Therapy*, **7**, 323–325.

Evans, F. J. (1977). Subjective characteristics of sleep efficiency. *Journal of Abnormal Psychology*, **86**, 561–564.

Feinstein, B., Sterman, M. B. and Macdonald, L. R. (1974). Effects of sensorimotor rhythm biofeedback training on sleep. *Sleep Research*, **3**, 134.

Feldman, D. A., Strong, S. R. and Danser, D. B. (1982). A comparison of paradoxical and non-paradoxical interpretations and directives. *Journal of Counselling Psychology*, **29**, 572–579.

Fletcher, D. J. (1986). Coping with insomnia: Helping patients manage sleeplessness without drugs. *Postgraduate Medicine*, **79 (2)**, 265–274.

Fogle, D. O. and Dyal, J. A. (1983). Paradoxical giving up and the reduction of sleep performance anxiety in chronic insomniacs. *Psychotherapy: Theory, Research and Practice*, **20**, 21–30.

Frankel, B. L., Buchbinder, R., Coursey, R. D. and Snyder, F. (1973). Sleep pattern and psychological test characteristics of chronic primary insomniacs. *Sleep Research*, **2**, 149.

Frankel, B. L., Coursey, R. D., Buchbinder, R. and Snyder, F. (1976). Recorded and reported sleep in primary chronic insomnia. *Archives of General Psychiatry*, **33**, 615–623.

Frankel, B. L., Patten, B. M. and Gillin, J. C. (1974). Restless legs syndrome: Sleep-electroencephalographic and neurologic findings. *Journal of the American Medical Association*, **230**, 1302–1303.

Frankl, V. E. (1955). *The doctor and the soul: From psychotherapy to logotherapy*. New York: Knopf.

Frankl, V. E. (1960). Paradoxical intention: A logotherapeutic technique. *American Journal of Psychotherapy*, **14**, 520–535.

Frankl V. E. (1967). Logotherapy. *Israel Annals of Psychiatry and Related Disciplines*, **5**, 142–155.

Frankl, V. E. (1975). Paradoxical intention and dereflection. *Psychotherapy: Theory, Research and Practice*, **12**, 236–237.

Franklin, J. (1981). The measurement of sleep-onset latency in insomnia. *Behaviour Research and Therapy*, **19**, 547–549.

Freed, A. (1976). Prescribing of tranquillisers and barbiturates by general practitioners. *British Medical Journal*, 1232.

Freedman, R. (1976). Psychological and physiological characteristics of sleep-onset insomnia. *Sleep Research*, **1**, 253–277.

Freedman, R. (1987). Chronic insomniacs: Replication of Monroe's findings. *Psychophysiology*, **24**, 721–722.

Freedman, R., Hauri, P., Coursey, R. and Frankel, B. L. (1978). Behavioural treatment of insomnia: A collaborative study. *Biofeedback and Self-Regulation*, **3**, 208.

Freedman, R. and Papsdorf, J. (1976). Biofeedback and progressive relaxation treatment of sleep-onset insomnia: A controlled all-night investigation. *Biofeedback and Self-Regulation*, **1**, 253–271.

Freedman, R. and Sattler, H. I. (1982). Physiological and psychological factors in sleep-onset insomnia. *Journal of Abnormal Psychology*, **91**, 380–389.

Galliard, J. M. (1978). Chronic primary insomnia: Possible physiopathological involvement of slow-wave sleep deficiency. *Sleep*, **1**, 133–147.

Ganguli, R., Reynolds, C. F. and Kupfer, D. J. (1987). EEG sleep in young, never-medicated schizophrenic patients: A comparison with delusional and non-delusional depressives and with healthy controls. *Archives of General Psychiatry*, **44**, 36–45.

Geer, H. J. and Katkin, E. S. (1966). Treatment of insomnia using a variant of desensitisation: A case report. *Journal of Abnormal Psychology*, **71**, 161–164.

Gering, R. C. and Mahrer, A. R. (1972). Difficulty falling asleep. *Psychological Reports*, **30**, 523–528.

Gershman, L. and Clouser, R. A. (1974). Treating insomnia with relaxation and desensitisation in a group setting by an automated approach. *Journal of Behaviour Therapy and Experimental Psychiatry*, **5**, 31–35.

Gerz, H. O. (1966). Experience with the logotherapeutic technique of paradoxical intention in the treatment of phobic and obsessive-compulsive patients. *American Journal of Psychiatry*, **123**, 548–553.

Gierz, M., Campbell, S. S. and Gillin, J.C. (1987). Sleep disturbances in various nonaffective psychiatric disorders. *Psychiatric Clinics of North America*, **10**, 565–581.

Gillin, J. C., Duncan, W. C., Murphy, D. L., Post, R. M., Wehr, T.A., Goodwin, F. K., Wyatt, R. J. and Bunney, W. E. (1981). Age-related changes in sleep in depressed and normal subjects. *Psychiatry Research*, **4**, 73–78.

Gillin, J. C., Duncan, W. C., Pettigrew, K. D., Frankel, B. L. and Snyder, F. (1979). Successful separation of depressed, normal and insomniac subjects by EEG sleep data. *Archives of General Psychiatry*, **36**, 85–90.

Glenville, M., Broughton, R., Wing, A. M. and Wilkinson, R. T. (1978). Effects of sleep deprivation on short duration performance measures compared to the Wilkinson Vigilance Task. *Sleep*, **1**, 169–176.

Goldberg, D. (1978). *Manual of the General Health Questionnaire*. Windsor: NFER Publishing.

Golden, R. N. and James, S. P. (1988). Insomnia: Clinical assessment and management of the patient who can't sleep. *Postgraduate Medicine*, **83 (4)**, 251–258.

Good, R. (1975). Frontalis muscle tension and sleep latency. *Psychophysiology*, **12**, 465–467.

Goodman, W. and Gilman, A. (1969). *The pharmacological basis of therapeutics*. New York: MacMillan.

Graham, K., Wright, G., Toman, W. and Mark, C. (1975). Relaxation and hypnosis in the treatment of insomnia. *American Journal of Clinical Hypnosis*, **18**, 39–42.

Greenblatt, D. J., Divoll, M., Abernethy, D. R. and Schader, R. I. (1982). Benzodiazepine hypnotics: Kinetic and therapeutic options. *Sleep*, **5** (Suppl. 1), 518–527.

Greenblatt, D. J. and Koch-Weser, J. (1975). Clinical pharmacokinetics. *New England Medical Journal*, **293**, 702–705, 964–970.

Griffiths, A. N., Tedeschi, G. and Richens, A. (1986). The effects of repeated doses of temazepam and nitrazepam on several measures of human performance. *Acta Psychiatrica Scandinavica*, **74**, 119–126.

Gross, R. T. and Borkovec, T. D. (1982). The effects of a cognitive intrusion manipulation on the sleep-onset latency of good sleepers. *Behaviour Therapy*, **13**, 112–116.

Guilleminault, C. (1987). Obstructive sleep apnea syndrome: A review. *Psychiatric Clinics of North America*, **10**, 607–621.

Guilleminault, C. and Dement, W. C. (1977). Sleep apnoea syndromes and related disorders. In R. L. Williams and I. Karacan (eds). *Sleep disorders: Diagnosis and treatment*. New York: Wiley.

Guilleminault, C. and Dement. W. C. (1978). *Sleep apnoea syndromes*. New York: Allan R. Bliss Inc.

Hammond, E. C. (1964). Some preliminary findings on physical complaints from a prospective study of 1,064,004 men and women. *American Journal of Public Health*, **54**, 11–23.

Hartmann, E. L. (1978). *The sleeping pill*. Newhaven: Yale University Press.

Hartmann, E., Cravens, J. and List, S. (1974). Hypnotic effects of L-tryptophan. *Archives of General Psychiatry*, **31**, 394–397.

Hartmann, E., Spinweber, C. and Ware, J. C. (1983). Effect of amino acids on quantified sleepiness. *Nutrition and Behaviour*, **1**, 179–183.

Hathaway, S. R. and McKinlay, J. C. (1942). A multiphasic personality schedule (Minnesota): III The measurement of symptomatic depression. *Journal of Psychology*, **4**, 73–84.

Hauri, P. (1975). Psychology of sleep disorders: Their diagnosis and treatment. Paper presented at the 83rd Annual Convention of the American Psychological Association, Chicago.

Hauri, P. (1978). Biofeedback techniques in the treatment of chronic insomnia. In R. L. Williams and I. Karacan (eds). *Sleep disorders: diagnosis and treatment*. New York: Wiley.

Hauri, P. (1981). Treating psychophysiological insomnia with biofeedback. *Archives of General Psychiatry*, **38**, 752–758.

Hauri, P. (1982). *The sleep disorders*. Kalamazoo, Mich.: Upjohn.

Hauri, P. and Olmstead, E. (1983). What is the moment of sleep-onset for insomniacs? *Sleep*, **6**, 10–15.

Hauri, P., Percy, L., Hellekson, C., Hartmann, E. L. and Russ, D. (1982). The treatment of psychophysiologic insomnia with biofeedback: A replication study. *Biofeedback and Self-Regulation*, **7**, 223–235.

Haynes, S. N., Adams, A. and Franzen, M. (1981). The effects of pre-sleep stress on sleep-onset insomnia. *Journal of Abnormal Psychology*, **90**, 601–606.

Haynes, S. N., Adams, A. E., West, S., Kamens, L. and Safranek, R. (1982). The stimulus control paradigm in sleep-onset insomnia: A multimethod assessment. *Journal of Psychosomatic Research*, **26**, 333–339.

Haynes, S. N., Fitzgerald, S. G., Shute, G. E. and Hall, M. (1985). The utility and validity of daytime naps in the assessment of sleep-onset insomnia. *Journal of Behavioural Medicine*, **8**, 237–247.

Haynes, S. N., Follingstad, D. R. and McGowan, W. T. (1974). Insomnia: Sleep patterns and anxiety levels. *Journal of Psychosomatic Research*, **18**, 69–74.

Haynes, S. N., Price, M. G. and Simons, J. B. (1975). Stimulus control treatment for insomnia. *Journal of Behaviour Therapy and Experimental Psychiatry*, **6**, 279–282.

Haynes, S. N., Sides, H. and Lockwood, G. (1977). Relaxation instructions and frontalis muscle electromyographic feedback intervention with sleep-onset insomnia. *Behaviour Therapy*, **8**, 644–652.

Haynes, S. N., Woodward, S., Moran, R. and Alexander, D. (1974). Relaxation treatment of insomnia. *Behaviour Therapy*, **5**, 555–558.

Hayward, P., Wardle, J. and Higgitt, A. (1989). Benzodiazepine research: Current findings and practical consequences. *British Journal of Clinical Psychology*, **28**, 307–327.

Healey, E. S., Kales, A., Monroe, L. J., Bixler, E. O., Chamberlain, K. and Soldatos, C. R. (1981). Onset of insomnia: Role of life-stress events. *Psychosomatic Medicine*, **43**, 439–451.

Heffler, D. and Lisman, S. A. (1978). Attribution and insomnia: A replication failure. *Psychological Record*, **28**, 123–128.

Hersen, M. and Barlow, D. H. (1976). *Single case experimental designs*. New York: Pergamon Press.

Hicks, R. A. and Pellegrini, R. J. (1977). Anxiety levels of short and long sleepers. *Psychological Reports*, **41**, 569–570.

Hindmarch, I. (1984). Psychological performance models as indicators of the effects of hypnotic drugs on sleep. *Psychopharmacology Suppl.*, **1**, 58–68.

Hindmarch, I. and Ott, H. (1984). Sleep, benzodiazepines and performance: Issues and comments. *Psychopharmacology Suppl.*, **1**, 194–202.

Hinkle, J. and Lutker, E. (1972). Insomnia: A new approach. *Psychotherapy: Theory, Research and Practice*, **9**, 236–237.

Hoch, C. C., Reynolds, C. F., Kupfer, D. J., Berman, S. R., Houck, P. R. and Stack, J. A. (1987). Empirical note: Self-report versus recorded sleep in healthy seniors. *Psychophysiology*, **24**, 293–299.

Hoddes, E., Dement, W. C. and Zarcone, V. (1972). The history and use of the Stanford Sleepiness Scale. *Psychophysiology*, **9**, 150.

Hoddes, E., Zarcone, V., Smythe, H., Phillips, R. and Dement, W. C. (1973). Quantification of sleepiness: A new approach. *Psychophysiology*, **10**, 431–436.

Holborn, S. W., Hiebert, D. E. and Bell, C. L. (1987). Computer-interfaced operant measurement in treating insomnia. *Journal of Behaviour Therapy and Experimental Psychiatry*, **18**, 365–372.

Horne, J. A. (1983). Human sleep and tissue restoration: Some qualifications and doubts. *Clinical Science*, **65**, 569–578.

Horne, J. A. (1988). *Why we sleep: Functions of sleep in humans and other animals*. London and New York: Oxford University Press.

Horne, J. A. and Porter, J. M. (1976). Time of day effects with standardised exercise upon sleep. *Electroencephalography and Clinical Neurophysiology*, **40**, 178–184.

Hugdahl, K. (1981). The three systems model of fear and emotion—a critical examination. *Behaviour Research and Therapy*, **19**, 75–85.

Hughes, R. C. and Hughes, H. H. (1978). Insomnia: Effects of EMG biofeedback, relaxation and stimulus control. *Behavioural Engineering*, **5**, 67–72.

Institute of Medicine (1979). *Report of a study: Sleeping pills, insomnia and medical practice*. Washington, DC: National Academy of Sciences.

Jacobs, E. A., Reynolds, C. F., Kupfer, D. J., Lovin, P. A. and Ehrenpreis, A. B. (1988). The role of polysomnography in the differential diagnosis of chronic insomnia. *American Journal of Psychiatry*, **145**, 346–349.

Jacobsen, N. S., Follette, W. C. and Revenstorf, D. (1984). Psychotherapy outcome research: Methods for reporting variability and evaluating clinical significance. *Behaviour Therapy*, **15**, 336–352.

Jacobsen, N. S., Follette, W. C. and Revenstorf, D. (1986). Toward a standard definition of clinically significant change. *Behaviour Therapy*, **17**, 308–311.

Jacobson, E. (1929). *Progressive relaxation*. Chicago, Ill.: University of Chicago Press.

Jacobson, E. (1970). *Modern treatments of tense patients*. Springfield, Ill.: Thomas.

Jalfre, M., Monachaon, M., Polk, P. and Haefely, W. (1972). A possible role of GABA in the control of PGO wave activity. In W. P. Koella and P. Levin (eds). *Sleep: physiology, psychology, pharmacology, clinical implications*. Basel: S. Karger.

Johns, M. W. (1975). Factor analysis of subjectively reported sleep habits and the nature of insomnia. *Psychological Medicine*, **5**, 83–88.

Johns, M. W., Gay, M. P., Masterton, J. P. and Bruce, D. W. (1971). Relationship between sleep habits, adrenocortical activity and personality. *Psychosomatic Medicine*, **3**, 499–508.

Johnson, L. C. (1969). Psychological and physiological changes following total sleep deprivation. In A. Kales (ed.). *Sleep, physiology and pathology*. Philadelphia, Pa.: Lippincott.

Johnson, L. C. (1973). Are stages of sleep related to waking behaviours? *American Scientist*, **61**, 326–338.

Johnson, L. C., Church, M. W., Seales, D. M. and Rossiter, V. S. (1979). Auditory arousal thresholds of good sleepers and poor sleepers with and without flurazepam. *Sleep*, **1**, 259–270.

Johnson, L. C., Colquhoun, W. P., Tepas, D. I. and Colligan, M. J. (1981). Biological rhythms, sleep and shift work. In E. D. Weitzman (ed.). *Advances in sleep research* (Volume 7). New York: SP Medical and Scientific Books.

Jordan, J. B., Hauri, P. and Phelps, P. J. (1976). The sensorimotor rhythm (SMR) in insomnia. *Sleep Research*, **5**, 175.

Kahn, M., Baker, B. L. and Weiss, J. M. (1968). Treatment of insomnia by relaxation training. *Journal of Abnormal Psychology*, **73**, 556–558.

Kales, A., Allen, C., Scharf, M. B. and Kales, J. D. (1970). Hypnotic drugs and their effectiveness III: All night EEG studies of insomniac subjects. *Archives of General Psychiatry*, **23**, 226–232.

Kales, A., Bixler, E. O., Leo, I., Healey, S. and Slye, E. (1974a). Incidence of insomnia in the Los Angeles Metropolitan Area. *Sleep Research*, **4**, 139.

Kales, A., Bixler, E. O., Tan, T.-L., Scharf, M. B., and Kales, J. D. (1974b). Chronic hypnotic drug use: Ineffectiveness, drug withdrawal insomnia and dependence. *Journal of the American Medical Association*, **227**, 513–517.

Kales, A., Bixler, E. O., Vela-Bueno, A., Cadieux, R. J., Soldatos, C. R. and Kales, J. D. (1984). Biopsychobehavioural correlates of insomnia III: Polygraphic findings of sleep difficulty and their relationship to psychopathology. *International Journal of Neurosciences*, **23**, 43–56.

Kales, A., Caldwell, A. B., Preston, T. A., Healey, S. and Kales, J. D. (1976). Personality patterns in insomnia: Theoretical implications. *Archives of General Psychiatry*, **33**, 1128–1134.

Kales, A., Caldwell, A. B., Soldatos, C. R., Bixler, E. O. and Kales, J. D. (1983a). Biopsychobehavioural correlates of insomnia II: Pattern specificity and consistency with the MMPI. *Psychosomatic Medicine*, **45**, 341–356.

Kales, A. and Kales, J. D. (1984). *Evaluation and treatment of insomnia*. New York: Oxford University Press.

Kales, A., Kales, J. D., Bixler, E. O. and Scharf, M. B. (1975). Effectiveness of hypnotic drugs with prolonged use: Flurazepam and Pentobarbital. *Clinical Pharmacology and Therapeutics*, **18**, 356–363.

Kales, A., Scharf, M. B. and Kales, J. D. (1978). Rebound insomnia: A new clinical syndrome. *Science*, **201**, 1039–1041.

Kales, A., Soldatos, C. R., Bixler, E. O. and Kales, J. D. (1983b). Rebound insomnia and rebound anxiety: A review. *Pharmacology*, **26**, 121–137.

Kales, J. D. and Kales, A. (1987). Clinical selection of benzodiazepine hypnotics. *Psychiatric Medicine*, **4**, 229–241.

Kales, J. D., Kales, A., Bixler, E. O. and Soldatos, C. R. (1979). Resource for managing sleep disorders. *Journal of the American Medical Association*, **241**, 2413–2416.

Kales, J. D., Tan, T.-L., Swearingen, C. and Kales, A. (1971). Are over-the-counter sleep medications effective? All night EEG studies. *Current Therapeutic Research*, **13**, 143–151.

Kamgar-Parsi, B., Wehr, T. A. and Gillin, J. C. (1983). Successful treatment of human non-24-hour sleep-wake syndrome. *Sleep*, **6**, 257–264.

Kapuniai, L. E., Andrew, D. J., Crowell, D. H. and Pearce, J. W. (1988). Identifying sleep apnea from self-reports. *Sleep*, **11**, 430–436.

Karacan, I., Thornby, J. I., Anch, A. M., Booth, G. H., Williams, R. L. and Salis, P. G. (1976). Dose-related sleep disturbances induced by coffee and caffeine. *Clinical Pharmacology and Therapeutics*, **20**, 682–689.

Karacan, I., Williams, R. L., Finley, W. W. and Hursch, C. J. (1970). The effects of naps on nocturnal sleep: Influence on the need for Stage 1, REM and Stage 4 sleep. *Biological Psychiatry*, **2**, 391–399.

Karacan, I., Williams, R. L., Littell, R. C. and Salis, P. J. (1973). Insomniacs: Unpredictable and idiosyncratic sleepers. In W. P. Koella and P. Levin (eds). *Sleep*. Basel: S. Karger.

Karacan, I., Williams, R. L., Salis, P. J. and Hursch, C. J. (1971). New approaches to the evaluation and treatment of insomnia. *Psychosomatics*, **12**, 81–88.

Kazarian, S. S., Howe, M. G. and Csapo, K. G. (1979). Development of The Sleep Behaviour Self-Rating Scale. *Behaviour Therapy*, **10**, 412–417.

Kazdin, A. E. (1977). Assessing the clinical or applied importance of behaviour change through social validation. *Behavioural Medicine*, **1**, 427–452.

Kelley, J. E. and Lichstein, K. L. (1980). A sleep assessment device. *Behaviour Assessment*, **2**, 135–146.

Kellogg, R. and Baron, R. (1975). Attribution theory, insomnia and the reverse placebo effect. *Journal of Personality and Social Psychology*, **32**, 231–236.

Kent, G. and Gibbons, R. (1987). Self-efficacy and the control of anxious cognitions. *Journal of Behaviour Therapy and Experimental Psychiatry*, **18**, 33–40.

Killen, J. D. and Coates, T. J. (1979). The complaint of insomnia: What is it and how do we treat it? *Clinical Behaviour Therapy Review*, **1**, 1–15.

King, N.J. (1980). The therapeutic utility of abbreviated progressive relaxation: A critical review with implications for clinical practice. In M. Hersen, R. M. Eisler and P. M. Miller (eds). *Progress in behaviour modification* (Volume 6). New York: Academic Press.

Knab, B. and Engel, R. R. (1988). Perception of waking and sleeping: Possible implications for the evaluation of insomnia. *Sleep*, **11**, 265–272.

Kumar, A. and Vaidya, A. K. (1984). Anxiety as a personality dimension of short and long sleepers. *Journal of Clinical Psychology*, **40**, 197–198.

Kupfer, D. J., Wyatt, R. J. and Snyder, F. (1970). Comparison between electroencephalographic and nursing observations of sleep in psychiatric patients. *Journal of Nervous and Mental Disease*, **151**, 361–368.

Lacks, P. (1987). *Behavioural treatment for persistent insomnia*. New York: Pergamon Press.

Lacks, P., Bertelson, A. D., Gans, L. and Kunkel, J. (1983a). The effectiveness of three behavioural treatments for different degrees of sleep-onset insomnia. *Behaviour Therapy*, **14**, 593–605.

Lacks, P., Bertelson, A. D., Sugerman, J. and Kunkel, J. (1983b). The treatment of sleep-maintenance insomnia with stimulus control techniques. *Behaviour Research and Therapy*, **21**, 291–295.

Lacks, P. and Powlishta, T. A. (1989). Improvement following behavioural treatment for insomnia: Clinical significance, long-term maintenance and predictors of outcome. *Behaviour Therapy*, **20**, 117–134.

Lacks, P. and Rotert, M. (1986). Knowledge and practice of sleep hygiene techniques in insomniacs and good sleepers. *Behaviour Research and Therapy*, **24**, 365–368.

Lader, M. (1986). A practical guide to prescribing hypnotic benzodiazepines. *British Medical Journal*, 1048–1049.

Lader, M. and Lawson, C. (1987). Sleep studies and rebound insomnia: Methodological problems, laboratory findings and clinical implications. *Clinical Neuropharmacology*, **10**, 291–312.

Ladouceur, R. and Gros-Louis, Y. (1986). Paradoxical intention vs stimulus control in the treatment of severe insomnia. *Journal of Behaviour Therapy and Experimental Psychiatry*, **17**, 267–269.

Lang, P. J., Rice, D. G. and Sternbach, R. A. (1972). The psychophysiology of emotion. In W. S. Greenfield and R. A. Sternbach (eds). *Handbook of physiology*. New York: Holt, Rinehart and Winston.

Last, C. G., Barlow, D. H. and O'Brien, G. T. (1983). Comparison of two cognitive strategies in treatment of a patient with generalised anxiety disorder. *Psychological Reports*, **53**, 19–26.

Lawrence, P. S. and Tokarz, T. (1976). A comparison of relaxation training and stimulus control. Paper presented at Association for the Advancement of Behaviour Therapy, New York.

Leigh, T. J., Bird, H. A. Hindmarch, I., Constable, P. D. L. and Wright, V. (1988). Factor analysis of the St. Mary's Hospital Sleep Questionnaire. *Sleep*, **11**, 448–453.

Levey, A. B., Aldaz, J. A., Watts, F. N. and Coyle, K. (1991). Articulatory suppression and the treatment of insomnia. *Behaviour Research and Therapy*, **29**, 85–89.

Levin, D., Bertelson, A. D. and Lacks, P. (1984). MMPI differences among mild and severe insomniacs and good sleepers. *Journal of Personality Assessment*, **48**, 126–129.

Levy, M. and Zylber-Katz, E. (1983). Caffeine, metabolism and coffee-attributed sleep disturbances. *Clinical Pharmacology and Therapeutics*, **33**, 770–775.

Lichstein, K. L. (1980). Treatment of severe insomnia by manipulation of sleep schedule. Paper presented at meeting of the American Association for Behavior Therapy: New York.

Lichstein, K. L. (1984). Interventions and dependent measures tailored for insomnoid states in the elderly. In S. N. Haynes (Chair). *Sleep disorders in the elderly*. Philadelphia: AABT Symposium.

Lichstein, K. L. (1988). Sleep compression treatment of an insomnoid. *Behaviour Therapy*, **19**, 625–632.

Lichstein, K. L. and Fischer, S. M. (1985). Insomnia. In M. Hersen and A. S. Bellack (eds). *Handbook of clinical behaviour therapy with adults*. New York and London: Plenum Press.

Lichstein, K. L., Hoelscher, T. J., Eakin, T. L. and Nickel, R. (1983). Empirical sleep assessment in the home: A convenient inexpensive approach. *Journal of Behavioural Assessment*, **5**, 111–118.

Lichstein, K. L. and Kelley, J. E. (1979). Measuring sleep patterns in natural settings. *Behavioural Engineering*, **5**, 95–100.

Lichstein, K. L., Nickel, R., Hoelscher, T. J. and Kelley, J. E. (1982). Clinical validation of a sleep assessment device. *Behaviour Research and Therapy*, **20**, 292–298.

Lichstein, K. L. and Rosenthal, T. L. (1980). Insomniacs' perceptions of cognitive versus somatic determinance of sleep disturbance. *Journal of Abnormal Psychology*, **89**, 105–107.

Lick, J. R. and Heffler, D. (1977). Relaxation training and attention placebo in the treatment of severe insomnia. *Journal of Consulting and Clinical Psychology*, **45**, 153–161.

Liljenberg, B., Almqvist, M., Hetta, J., Roos, B.-E. and Agren, H. (1988). The prevalence of insomnia: The importance of operationally defined criteria. *Annals of Clinical Research*, **20**, 393–398.

Lindsay, W. R., Gamsu, C. V., McLaughlin, E., Hood, E. M. and Espie, C. A. (1987). A controlled trial of treatments for generalised anxiety. *British Journal of Clinical Psychology*, **26**, 3–15.

Loomis, A. I., Harvey, E. N. and Hobart, G. A. (1937). Cerebral states during sleep as studied by human brain potentials. *Journal of Experimental Psychology*, **21**, 127–144.

McGhie, A. and Russell, S. M. (1962). The subjective assessment of normal sleep. *Journal of Mental Science*, **108**, 642–654.

Mackintosh, N. J. (1977). Stimulus control: Attentional factors. In W. K. Honig and J. E. R. Staddon (eds). *Handbook of operant behaviour*. Englewood Cliffs, N.J.: Prentice-Hall.

Mahoney, C. (1974). *Cognition and behaviour modification*. Cambridge, Mass.: Ballinger.

Mancio, M. and Mariotti, M. (1985). Brain mechanisms of synchronous sleep. *Clinical Neuropharmacology*, **8** (Suppl. 1), 41–48.

Marchini, E. J., Coates, T. J., Magistad, J. and Waldum, S. J. (1983). What do insomniacs do, think and feel during the day? *Sleep*, **6**, 147–155.

Mavissakalian, M., Michelson, L., Greenwald, D., Kornblith, S. and Greenwald, M. (1983). Cognitive-behavioural treatment of agoraphobia: Paradoxical intention vs self-statement training. *Behaviour Research and Therapy*, **21**, 75–86.

Meichenbaum, D. H. (1977). *Cognitive-behaviour modification: An integrative approach*. New York: Plenum.

Mellinger, G. D., Balter, M. B. and Uhlenhuth, E. H. (1985). Insomnia and its treatment. *Archives of General Psychiatry*, **42**, 225–232.

Mendelson, W. B. (1987). Pharmacotherapy of insomnia. *Psychiatric Clinics of North America*, **10**, 555–563.

Mendelson, W. B., Garnett, D., Gillin, J. C. and Weingartner, H. (1984). The experience of insomnia and daytime and night time functioning. *Psychiatry Research*, **12**, 235–250.

Mendelson, W. B., Garnett, D. and Linnoila, M. (1984). Do insomniacs have impaired daytime functioning? *Biological Psychiatry*, **19**, 1261–1264.

Mendelson, W. B., Gillin, J. C. and Wyatt, J. R. (1977). *Human sleep and its disorders*. New York: Plenum Press.

Michelson, L. and Ascher, L. M. (1984). Paradoxical intention in the treatment of agoraphobia and other anxiety disorders. *Journal of Behaviour Therapy and Experimental Psychiatry*, **15**, 215–220.

Milan, M. A. and Kolko, D. J. (1984). Paradoxical intention in the treatment of obsessional flatulence ruminations. *Journal of Behaviour Therapy and Experimental Psychiatry*, **15**, 167–172.

Mitchell, K. R. (1979). Behavioural treatment of pre-sleep tension and intrusive cognitions in patients with severe pre-dormital insomnia. *Journal of Behavioural Medicine*, **2**, 57–69.

Mitchell, K. R., and White, R. G. (1977). Self-management of severe pre-dormital insomnia. *Journal of Behaviour Therapy and Experimental Psychiatry*, **8**, 57–63.

Monroe, L. J. (1967). Psychological and physiological differences between good and poor sleepers. *Journal of Abnormal Psychology*, **72**, 255–264.

Monroe, L. J. (1969). Transient changes in EEG sleep patterns of married good sleepers: The effects of altering sleeping arrangements. *Psychophysiology*, **6**, 330–337.

Monroe, L. J. and Marks, P. A. (1977). MMPI differences between adolescent poor and good sleepers. *Journal of Consulting and Clinical Psychology*, **45**, 151–152.

Montgomery, I., Perkin, G. and Wise, G. (1975). A review of behavioural treatments for insomnia. *Journal of Behaviour Therapy and Experimental Psychiatry*, **6**, 93–100.

Morgan, K., Dallosso, H., Ebrahim, S., Arie, T. and Fentem, P. H. (1988). Characteristics of subjective insomnia in the elderly living at home. *Age and Ageing*, **17**, 1–7.

Morin, C. M. and Azrin, N. H. (1987). Stimulus control and imagery training in treating sleep-maintenance insomnia. *Journal of Consulting and Clinical Psychology*, **55**, 260–262.

Morin, C. M. and Azrin, N. H. (1988). Behavioural and cognitive treatments of geriatric insomnia. *Journal of Consulting and Clinical Psychology*, **56**, 748–753.

Morin, C. M. and Gramling, S. E. (1989). Sleep patterns and ageing: A comparison of older adults with and without insomnia complaints. *Psychology and Aging*, **4**, 290–294.

Morin, C. M. and Kwentus, M. D. (1988). Area review: Sleep disorders—behavioural and pharmacological treatments for insomnia. *Annals of Behavioural Medicine*, **10**, 91–100.

Morin, C. M. and Schoen, L. S. (1986). Validation of an electromechanical device to measure sleep/wake parameters. Paper presented at the Annual Meeting of the Association for Advancement of Behaviour Therapy, Chicago, Ill.

Moruzzi, G. (1964). Reticular influences on the EEG. *Electroencephalography and Clinical Neurophysiology*, **16**, 2–17.

Moruzzi, G. and Magoun, H. W. (1949). Brainstem reticular formation and activation of the EEG. *Electroencephalography and Clinical Neurophysiology*, **1**, 455–473.

Nicassio, P. M. and Bootzin, R. R. (1974). A comparison of progressive relaxation and autogenic training as treatments for insomnia. *Journal of Abnormal Psychology*, **83**, 253–260.

Nicassio, P. M., Boylan, M. B. and McCabe, T. G. (1982). Progressive relaxation, EMG biofeedback and biofeedback placebo in the treatment of sleep-onset insomnia. *British Journal of Medical Psychology*, **55**, 159–166.

Nicassio, P. M., Mendlowitz, D. R., Fussell, J. J. and Petras, L. (1985). The phenomenology of the pre-sleep state: The development of the Pre-Sleep Arousal Scale. *Behaviour Research and Therapy*, **23**, 263–271.

Nicholson, A. N. (1980). Hypnotics: Rebound insomnia and residual sequelae. *British Journal of Clinical Pharmacology*, **9**, 223–225.

Nicholson, A. N. and Stone, B. M. (1979). L-tryptophan and sleep in healthy man. *Electroencephalography and Clinical Neurophysiology*, **47**, 539–545.

Norton, G. R. and De Luca, R. V. (1979). The use of stimulus control procedures to eliminate persistent awakenings. *Journal of Behaviour Therapy and Experimental Psychiatry*, **10**, 65–68.

Ogilvie, R. D. and Wilkinson, R. T. (1984). The detection of sleep-onset: Behavioral and physiological convergence. *Psychophysiology*, **21**, 510–520.

Ogilvie, R. D. and Wilkinson, R. T. (1988). Behavioral versus EEG-based monitoring of all-night sleep/wake patterns. *Sleep*, **11**, 139–155.

O'Hanlon, J. F. and Volkerts, E. R. (1986). Hypnotics and actual driving performance. *Acta Psychiatrica Scandinavica*, **74**, 95–104.

Oswald, I. (1968). Drugs and sleep. *Psychopharmacological Review*, **20**, 273–303.

Oswald, I. (1979). The why and how of hypnotic drugs. *British Medical Journal*, 1167–1168.

Oswald, I. (1980). Sleep as a restorative process: Human clues. *Progress in Brain Research*, **53**, 279–288.

Oswald, I. (1981). Assessment of insomnia. *British Medical Journal*, 874–875.

Oswald, I. (1982). The poor sleeper. *Psychiatry in Practice*, **1**, 8–13.

Oswald, I. French, C., Adam, K., and Gilham, J. (1982). Benzodiazepine hypnotics remain effective for 24 weeks. *British Medical Journal*, 860–863.

Oswald, I. and Priest, R. G. (1965). Five weeks to escape the sleeping-pill habit. *British Medical Journal*, 1093–1095.

Ott, B. D., Levine, B. A. and Ascher, L. M. (1983). Manipulating the explicit demand of paradoxical intention instructions. *Behavioural Psychotherapy*, **11**, 25–35.

Ott, B. D., Levine, B. A. and Farley, T. W. (1982). Reducing reactivity in sleep assessment. *Behavioural Engineering*, **7**, 93–100.

Paxton, J. T., Trinder, J. and Montgomery, I. (1983). Does aerobic fitness affect sleep. *Psychophysiology*, **20**, 320–324.

Pendleton, L. R. and Tasto, D. L. (1976). Effects of metronome-conditioned relaxation, metronome-induced relaxation and progressive muscle relaxation on insomnia. *Behaviour Research and Therapy*, **14**, 165–166.

Pokorny, A. D. (1978). Sleep disturbances, alcohol and alcoholism: A review. In R. L. Williams and I. Karacan (eds). *Sleep disorders: Diagnosis and treatment*. New York: Wiley.

Poulton, E. C., Edwards, R. S. and Colquhoun, W. P. (1974). The interaction of the loss of a night's sleep with mild heat: Task variables. *Ergonomics*, **17**, 59–73.

Power, K. G., Simpson, R. J., Swanson, V. and Wallace, L. A. (1990). Controlled comparison of pharmacological and psychological treatment of generalised anxiety disorder in primary care. *British Journal of General Practice*, **40**, 289–294.

Price, V. A., Coates, T. J., Thoresen, C. E. and Grinstead, O. (1978). The prevalence and correlates of poor sleep among adolescents. *American Journal of the Diseases of Children*, **132**, 583–586.

Puca, F., Bricola, A. and Turella, G. (1973). Effect of L-Dopa or Amantadine therapy on sleep spindles in Parkinsonism. *Electroencephalography and Clinical Neurophysiology*, **35**, 327–330.

Puder, R., Lacks, P., Bertelson, A. D. and Storandt, M. (1983). Short-term stimulus control treatment of insomnia in older adults. *Behaviour Therapy*, **14**, 424–429.

Rachman, S. and Hodgson, R. (1974). Synchrony and desynchrony in fear and avoidance. *Behaviour Research and Therapy*, **12**, 311–318.

Rechtschaffen, A. (1968). Polygraphic aspects of insomnia. In H. Gastaut, (ed.). *The abnormalities of sleep in man*. Bologna, Italy: Aul. Gaggi Editore.

Rechtschaffen, A. and Kales, A. (1968). *A manual of standardised terminology, techniques, and scoring system for sleep stages of human subjects*. USA: National Institute of Health.

Rechtschaffen, A. and Verdone, P. (1964). Amount of dreaming, effect of incentive, adaptation to laboratory and individual differences. *Perceptual and Motor Skills*, **19**, 947–958.

Regestein, Q. R. (1983). Relationship between interview findings and insomnia pattern in sleep clinic patients. *Sleep Research*, **12**, 248.

Regestein, Q. R. (1988). Polysomnography in the diagnosis of chronic insomnia. *American Journal of Psychiatry*, **145**, 1483.

Relinger, H. and Bornstein, P. H. (1979). Treatment of sleep-onset insomnia by paradoxical intention: A multiple baseline design. *Behaviour Modification*, **3**, 203–222.

Relinger, H., Bornstein, P. H. and Mungas, D. M. (1978). Treatment of insomnia by paradoxical instruction: A time series analysis. *Behaviour Therapy*, **9**, 955–959.

Reynolds, C. F. (1987). Sleep and affective disorders: A minireview. *Psychiatric Clinics of North America*, **10**, 583–591.

Reynolds, C. F., Kupfer, D. J., Taska, L. S., Koch, C. C., Sewitch, D. E. and Spiker, D. G. (1985). The sleep of healthy seniors: a revisit. *Sleep*, **8**, 20-29.

Ribordy, S. C. and Denney, D. R. (1977). The behavioural treatment of insomnia: An alternative to drug therapy. *Behaviour Research and Therapy*, **15**, 39–50.

Richardson, G., Carskadon, M., Flagg, W., Van den Hoed, J., Dement, W., and Mittler, M. (1978). Excessive daytime sleepiness in man: Multiple sleep latency measurement in narcoleptic and control subjects. *Electroencephalography and Clinical Neurophysiology*, **45**, 621–622.

Rimm, D. and Masters, J. (1979). *Behaviour therapy: Techniques and empirical findings*. New York: Academic Press.

Roehrs, T., Lineback, W., Zorick, F. and Roth, T. (1982). Relationship of psychopathology to insomnia in the elderly. *Journal of the American Geriatric Society*, **30**, 312–315.

Roehrs, T., Zorick, F., Sicklesteel, R., Wittig, R. and Roth, J. (1983). Excessive daytime sleepiness associated with insufficient sleep. *Sleep*, **6**, 319–325.

Rogers, K. L. (1987). Rational use of sedative/hypnotics. *Primary Care*, **14**, 785–801.

Roth, T., Kramer, M. and Lutz, T. (1976). The nature of insomnia: A descriptive summary of a sleep clinic population. *Comprehensive Psychiatry*, **17**, 217–220.

Rutenfranz, J., Colquhoun, W. P., Knouth, P. and Ghata, J. N. (1977). Biomedical and psychosocial aspects of shift work. *Scandinavian Journal of Work, Environment and Health*, **3**, 165–182.

Salzman, C. (1974). Chlordiazepoxide-induced hostility in a small group setting. *Archives of General Psychiatry*, **31**, 401.

Sanavio, E. (1988). Pre-sleep cognitive intrusions and treatment of onset-insomnia. *Behaviour Research and Therapy*, **26**, 451–459.

Sanavio, E., Vidotto, G., Bettinardi, O., Rolletto, T. and Zorzi, M. (1990). Behaviour therapy for DIMS: Comparison of three treatment procedures with follow-up. *Behavioural Psychotherapy*, **18**, 151–167.

Sanchez, R. and Bootzin, R. R. (1985). A comparison of white noise and music: Effects of predictable and unpredictable sounds on sleep. *Sleep Research*, **14**, 121.

Sassin, J. F. and Mitler, M. M. (1987). An historical perspective on sleep disorders medicine. *Psychiatric Clinics of North America*, **10**, 517–523.

Sassin, J. F., Parker, D. C., Mace, J. W., Gotlin, R. W., Johnson, L. C. and Rossman, L. G. (1969). Human growth hormone release: Relation to slow-wave sleep and sleep-waking cycles. *Science*, **165**, 513–515.

Schaefer, A., Brown, J., Watson, C. G., Piemel, D., De Motts, J., Howard, M. T., Petrik, N., Balleweg, B. J. and Anderson, D. (1983). Comparison of the validities of the Beck, Zung and MMPI Depression Scales. *Journal of Consulting and Clinical Psychology*, **53**, 415–418.

Schneider-Helmert, D. (1987). Twenty-four hour sleep-wake function and personality patterns in chronic insomniacs and healthy controls. *Sleep*, **10**, 452–462.

Schneider-Helmert, D. (1988). Why low-dose benzodiazepine-dependent insomniacs can't escape their sleeping pills. *Acta Psychiatrica Scandinavica*, **78**, 706–711.

Schoicket, S. L., Bertelson, A. D. and Lacks, P. (1988). Is sleep hygiene a sufficient treatment for sleep-maintenance insomnia? *Behaviour Therapy*, **19**, 183–190.

Schoonover, S. C. (1983). Depression. In E. L. Bassuk, S. C. Schoonover, and A. J. Gelenberg (eds). *The practitioner's guide to psychoactive drugs*. New York: Plenum Medical Book Co.

Schultz, J. H. and Luthe, W. (1959). *Autogenic training: A psychophysiologic approach in psychotherapy*. New York: Grune and Statton.

Scott, J. (1979). Why are we killing clinical medicine? *Medicine World News*, **20**, 6.

Seidel, W. F., Ball, S., Cohen, S. Patterson, N., Yost, O. and Dement, W. C. (1984). Daytime alertness in relation to mood, performance, and nocturnal sleep in chronic insomniacs and noncomplaining sleepers. *Sleep*, **7**, 230–238.

Seltzer, L. F. (1986). *Paradoxical strategies in psychotherapy: A comprehensive overview and guidebook*. New York: John Wiley and Sons.

Semple, C. G., Gray, C. E., Borland, V., Espie, C. A. and Beastall, G. H. (1988). Endocrine effects of examination stress. *Clinical Science*, **74**, 255–259.

Sewitch, D. E. (1984). The perceptual uncertainty of having slept: The inability to discriminate electroencephalographic sleep from wakefulness. *Psychophysiology*, **21**, 243–259.

Shealy, R. C. (1979). The effectiveness of various treatment techniques on different degrees and durations of sleep-onset insomnia. *Behaviour Research and Therapy*, **17**, 541–546.

Shealy, R. C., Lowe, J. D. and Ritzler, B. A. (1980). Sleep-onset insomnia: Personality characteristics and treatment outcome. *Journal of Consulting and Clinical Psychology*, **48**, 659–661.

Shepherd, M., Cooper, B., Brown, A. C. and Katton, G. (1966). *Psychiatric illness in general practice*. London: Oxford University Press.

Shute, G. E., Fitzgerald, S. G. and Haynes, S. N. (1986). The relationship between internal attentional control and sleep-onset latency in elderly adults. *Journal of Gerontology*, **41**, 770–773.

Slama, K. M. (1975) Unpublished Master's Thesis, University of Iowa, USA.

Slama, K. M. (1979). Discrepancy between self-report and EEG indications of sleep in good and poor sleepers. Paper presented at meeting of the Western Psychological Association, USA.

Soldatos, C. R., Kales, J. D., Scharf, M. B., Bixler, E. O. and Kales A. (1980). Cigarette smoking associated with sleep difficulty. *Science*, **207**, 551–553.

Solyom, L., Garza-Perez, J., Ledwidge, B. C. and Solyom, L. C. (1972). Paradoxical intention in the treatment of obsessive thoughts: A pilot study. *Comprehensive Psychiatry*, **13**, 291–297.

Spiegel, R. (1981). Sleep and sleeplessness in advanced age. In E. D. Weitzman (ed.). *Advances in sleep research* (Volume 5). New York: SP Medical and Scientific Books.

Spielberger, C. D., Gorsuch, R. L. and Lushene, R. E. (1970). *Manual for the State-Trait Anxiety Inventory*. Palo Alto Calif.: Counselling Psychologist Press Inc.

Spielman, A. J., Caruso, L. S. and Glovinsky, P. B. (1987). A behavioural perspective on insomnia treatment. *Psychiatric Clinics of North America*, **10**, 541–553.

Spielman, A. J., Saskin, P. and Thorpy, M. J. (1983). Sleep restriction: A new treatment of insomnia. *Sleep Research*, **12**, 286.

Spielman, A. J., Saskin, P. and Thorpy, M. J. (1987). Treatment of chronic insomnia by restriction of time in bed. *Sleep*, **10**, 45–56.

Steinmark, S. W. and Borkovec, T. D. (1974). Active and placebo treatment effects on moderate insomnia under counterdemand and positive demand instructions. *Journal of Abnormal Psychology*, **83**, 157–163.

Stekel, W. (1920). *Die impotenz des mannes*. Vienna: Urban and Schwarzenberg.

Stepanski, E., Zorick, F., Roehrs, T., Young, D. and Roth, T. (1988). Daytime alertness in patients with chronic insomnia compared with asymptomatic control subjects. *Sleep*, **11**, 54–60.

Sterman, M. B., Howe, R. C. and MacDonald, L. R. (1970). Facilitation of spindle-burst sleep by conditioning of electroencephalographic activity while awake. *Science*, **167**, 1146–1148.

Storms, M. and Nisbett, R. (1970). Insomnia and the attribution process. *Journal of Personality and Social Psychology*, **16**, 319–328.

Stoyva, J. and Budzynski, T. (1972). Biofeedback training in the self-induction of sleep. Progress report to the San Diego State College Foundation.

Strong, S. R. (1984). Experimental studies in explicitly paradoxical interventions: Results and implications. *Journal of Behaviour Therapy and Experimental Psychiatry*, **15**, 189–194.

Sugarman, J. L., Stern, J. A. and Walsh, J. K. (1985). Daytime alertness in subjective and objective insomnia: Some preliminary findings. *Biological Psychiatry*, **20**, 741–750.

Taub, J. M. and Berger, R. J. (1973). Performance and mood following variations in the length and timing of sleep. *Psychophysiology*, **10**, 559–570.

Taub, J. M. and Berger, R. J. (1976). The effects of changing the phase and duration of sleep. *Journal of Experimental Psychology (Human Perception)*, **2**, 30–41.

Taub, J. M. and Hawkins, D. R. (1979). Aspects of personality associated with irregular sleep habits in young adults. *Journal of Clinical Psychology*, **35**, 296–304.

Taylor, J. A. (1953). A personality scale of manifest anxiety. *Journal of Abnormal Psychology*, **48**, 285–290.

Terrace, H. S. (1966). Stimulus control. In W. K. Honig (ed.). *Operant behaviour: Areas of research and application*. Englewood Cliffs, N.J.: Prentice-Hall.

Thoresen, C. E., Coates, T.J., Kirmil-Gray, K. and Rosekind, M. R. (1981). Behavioural self-management in treating sleep-maintenance insomnia. *Journal of Behavioural Medicine*, **4**, 41–52.

Tokarz, T. and Lawrence, P. (1974). An analysis of temporal and stimulus control factors in the treatment of insomnia. Paper presented at meeting of the Association for the Advancement of Behavior Therapy, Chicago.

Toler, H. C. (1978). The treatment of insomnia with relaxation and stimulus control instructions among incarcerated males. *Criminal Justice and Behaviour*, **5**, 117–130.

Torsvall, L. (1983). Sleep after exercise: A review. *Journal of Sports Medicine and Physical Fitness*, **21**, 218–225.

Traub, A. C., Jencks, B. and Bliss, E. L. (1973). Effects of relaxation training on chronic insomnia. *Sleep Research*, **3**, 164.

Trinder, J. (1988). Subjective insomnia without objective findings: A pseudodiagnostic classification? *Psychological Bulletin*, **103**, 87–94.

Tune, G. S. (1969). Sleep and wakefulness in 509 normal human adults. *British Journal of Medical Psychology*, **42**, 75–80.

Turner, R. M. and Ascher, L. M. (1979a). A controlled comparison of progressive relaxation, stimulus control and paradoxical intention therapies for insomnia. *Journal of Consulting and Clinical Psychology*, **47**, 500–508.

Turner, R. M. and Ascher, L. M. (1979b). A within-subject analysis of stimulus control therapy with severe sleep-onset insomnia. *Behaviour Research and Therapy*, **17**, 107–112.

Turner, R. M. and Di Tomasso, R. A. (1980). The behavioural treatment of insomnia: A review and methodological analysis of the evidence. *International Journal of Mental Health*, **9**, 129–148.

Turner, R. M., Di Tomasso, R. A. and Giles, T. (1983). Failures in the treatment of insomnia: A plea for differential diagnosis. In E. B. Foa and P. M. G. Emmelkamp (eds). *Failures in behaviour therapy*. New York: Wiley.

Vander Plate, C. and Eno, E. N. (1983). Electromyograph biofeedback and sleep-onset insomnia: Comparison of treatment and placebo. *Behavioural Engineering*, **8**, 146–153.

Van Egeren, L., Haynes, S. N., Franzen, M. and Hamilton, J. (1983). Presleep cognitions and attributions in sleep-onset insomnia. *Journal of Behavioural Medicine*, **6**, 217–232.

Van Oot, P. H., Lane, T. W. and Borkovec, T. D. (1982). Sleep disturbances. In P. Sutker and H. Adams (eds). *Handbook of psychopathology*. New York: Plenum Press.

Walsh, J. K., Sugarman, J. L. and Chambers, G. W. (1986). Evaluation of insomnia. *American Family Physician*, **33**, 185–194.

Webb, W. B. (1975). *Sleep: The gentle tyrant*. Englewood Cliffs, N.J.: Spectrum.

Webb, W. B. (1982). Sleep in older persons: Sleep structures of 50 to 60 year old men and women. *Journal of Gerontology*, **37**, 581–586.

Webb, W. B. and Agnew, H. W. (1974). The effects of a chronic limitation of sleep length. *Psychophysiology*, **11**, 265–274.

Webb, W. B. and Agnew, H. W. (1978). Effects of rapidly rotating shifts on sleep pattern and sleep structure. *Aviation, Space and Environmental Medicine*, **49**, 384–389.

Webb, W. B. and Campbell, S. S. (1980). Awakenings and return to sleep in an older population. *Sleep*, **3**, 41–46.

Webb, W.B. and Schneider-Helmert, D. (1984). A categorical approach to changes in latency, awakening, and sleep length in older subjects. *Journal of Nervous and Mental Disease*, **172**, 291–295.

Webster, J. B., Kripke, D. F., Messin, S., Mullaney, D. J. and Wyborney, G. (1982). An activity-based sleep monitor system for ambulatory use. *Sleep*, **5**, 389–399.

Weil, G. and Goldfried, M. (1973). Treatment of insomnia in an 11 year old child through self-relaxation. *Behaviour Therapy*, **4**, 282–284.

Weissbluth, M. (1982). Modification of sleep schedule with reduction of night wakening: A case report. *Sleep*, **5**, 262–266.

West, S., Safranek, R., Kamens, L., Dickson, S. and Haynes, S. N. (1977). Laboratory analysis of sleep-onset insomnia: Implications for behavioural intervention. Paper presented at meeting of the Association for Advancement of Behavior Therapy, Atlanta, USA.

Wheatley, D. (1986). Insomnia in general practice: The role of temazepam and a comparison with zopiclone. *Acta Psychiatrica Scandinavica*, **74**, 142–148.

Williams, H. L. and Lubin, A. (1967). Speeded addition and sleep loss. *Journal of Experimental Psychology*, **73**, 313–317.

Williams, R. L., Karacan, I. and Hursch, C. (1974). *Electroencephalography (EEG) of human sleep: Clinical applications*. New York: Wiley.

Wolpe, J. (1958). *Psychotherapy by reciprocal inhibition*. Stanford, Calif.: Stanford University Press.

Woolfolk, R. L. (1975). Psychophysiological correlates of meditation. *Archives of General Psychiatry*, **32**, 1326–1333.

Woolfolk, R. L., Carr-Kaffashan, L., McNulty, T. F. and Lehrer, P. M. (1976). Meditation training as a treatment for insomnia. *Behaviour Therapy*, **7**, 359–365.

Woolfolk, R. L. and McNulty, T. F. (1983) Relaxation treatment for insomnia: A component analysis. *Journal of Consulting and Clinical Psychology*, **51**, 495–503.

Zigmond, A. S. and Snaith, R. P. (1983). The Hospital Anxiety and Depression Scale. *Acta Psychiatrica Scandinavica*, **67**, 361–370.

Zodun, H. I., Gruszkos, J. R. and Strong, S. R. (1983). Attribution and the double bind in paradoxical interventions. Unpublished manuscript, Department of Psychology, Virginia Commonwealth University, USA.

Zung, W. W. K. (1965). A self-rating depression scale. *Archives of General Psychiatry*, **12**, 63–70.

Zung, W. W. K. (1971). A rating instrument for anxiety disorders. *Psychosomatics*, **12**, 371–379.

Zwart, C. A. and Lisman, S. A. (1979). Analysis of stimulus control treatment of sleep-onset insomnia. *Journal of Consulting and Clinical Psychology*, **47**, 113–119.

Author Index

Subject Index